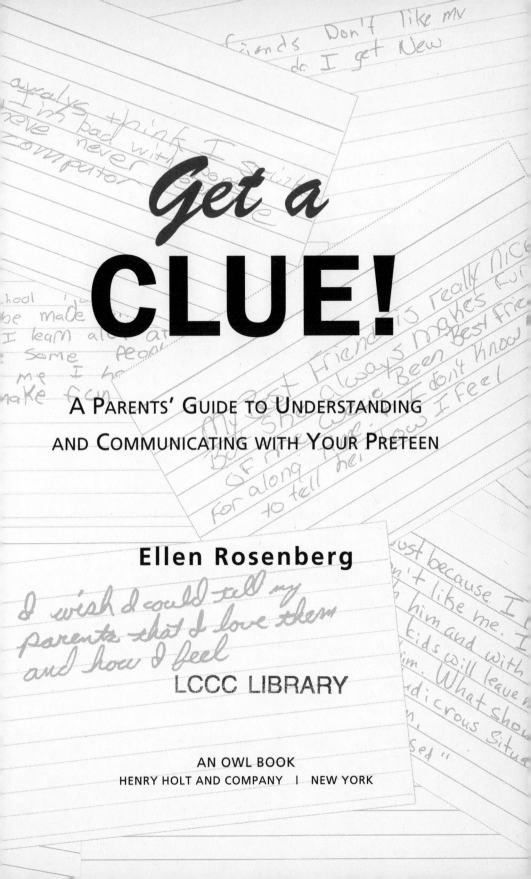

Get a CLUE!

A PARENTS' GUIDE TO UNDERSTANDING
AND COMMUNICATING WITH YOUR PRETEEN

Ellen Rosenberg

AN OWL BOOK
HENRY HOLT AND COMPANY | NEW YORK

Henry Holt and Company, LLC
Publishers since 1866
115 West 18th Street
New York, New York 10011

Henry Holt ® is a registered trademark of
Henry Holt and Company, LLC.

Published in Canada by Fitzhenry & Whiteside Ltd.
195 Allstate Parkway, Markham, Ontario L3R 4T8.

Library of Congress Cataloging-in-Publication Data
Rosenberg, Ellen.
    Get a clue! : a parents' guide to understanding and communicating with your
preteen / Ellen Rosenberg.—1st ed.
        p.   cm.
    ISBN 0-8050-5895-8 (pbk. : alk. paper)
    1. Preteens—United States—Psychology.   2. Preteens—United
States—Family relationships.   3. Parenting—United States.
I. Title.
HQ777.15.R67   1999   99-20602
649'.124—dc21   CIP

Henry Holt books are available for special promotions and
premiums. For details contact: Director, Special Markets.

First Edition 1999

Designed by Kelly S. Too

Printed in the United States of America

1   3   5   7   9   10   8   6   4   2

To my parents

In loving memory of my father, Samuel Greenfield,
And for my mother, Shirley Greenfield,
for all the life lessons you taught me by your example,
for always making the time to listen,
for loving me unconditionally and making family so important,
a part of you will always remain a precious part of me.

To all parents

May you and your child be blessed with the ability to grow
closer through your understanding of one another,
stronger in the bond of love between you,
and may you share a lifetime of treasured moments,
one day at a time.

Whenever I try to talk with my parents they always make a joke of it & never take it seriously. What should I do?

My parents tell me on Saturday mornings why don't you go to the mall with your friends. But I don't have any. What should I tell them? I don't want them to be disapointed.

How do you tell your PARENTS someTHING EVEN if they say you can tell them anything if you know you'll get in trouble

I'm in 8th grade and I'm 13, sometimes it's kind of hard to tell my parents whats going on in my personal life because, they would probaly say "You're too young what can I possibly do".

Contents

Girlfriend Can Influence How Kids Value Themselves ·
When Parents Don't Approve of Their Child's Boyfriend or
Girlfriend · If Your Child Wants a Girlfriend or Boyfriend
(How to Help) · Helping Kids Let Someone Know They're
Interested · Helping Kids Deal with Their Decision to Ask
Someone Out · Helping Your Child Deal with Other "Going
Out" Issues · A Note About Breakups · Reputations ·
Parties

8: PEER PRESSURE, CHOICES, AND RISKS
(Alcohol and Other Drugs, Sex, Smoking,
or Anything Else)   175
When to Start Preparing Kids to Handle Peer Pressure ·
Beyond the Facts, Beyond Our "Don'ts" · Communication
Skills · Social Skills · Decision-Making Skills · Helping
Kids Understand What Ownership Means · Helping Kids
Believe the Risks Are Real · Risk Reduction—Our Own
Expectations Need to Be Reality Based · When Kids Make
Mistakes · "I'd Never Do That" · Our Approachability · If
Kids Are Worried About a Friend · When Kids Worry
About a Parent · Helping Your Child Become More Safety-
Minded · When Do You Start Talking About All of This?

9: FAMILY RELATIONSHIPS   211
Relationships Between Brothers and Sisters · When Older
Siblings Move Out · When Kids Share a Room · Blended
Families, Blended Feelings · Family Hurts, Family
Stresses, Family Issues · Another Kind of Family Stress,
Different Hurts—When Parents Separate or Get a Divorce ·
Grandparents and Other Relatives · Family Meetings Can
Help

10: SCHOOL   255
Past Influences on Your Child's Feelings About School
Today · Teachers · Different Classes, Different Feelings ·
Grades · Redefining Success · Pressure to Achieve, Pres-
sure to Earn "Good" Grades · When Kids Must Repeat
a Grade · When Kids "Skip" a Grade · Homework ·

Motivation · Taking Tests · When Kids Want to Cheat Off Your Child's Homework or Tests · Locker-Room Feelings · When Kids Move to a New School · Some Final Thoughts (Before the Bell Rings!)

When a Loved One Is Seriously Ill · If Your Child Is the One Who Is Ill · Realistic Hope · Teaching Kids to Make the Most of the Time They Have with Older Relatives · When Death Is Sudden · Helping Your Child Deal with Death · Finality of Death · Dealing with Grief · Ceremonies, Services, Funerals · Death Can Be a Blessing · If a Pet Dies · Suicide

Acknowledgments

So many people made *Get a Clue!* possible. A special thank-you to the following:

Roger Rosenberg, my husband: for all your encouragement, support, understanding, for never losing your sense of humor through another deadline, for never refusing to listen to another paragraph, and especially for your love.

George Greenfield, my agent: *Get a Clue!* is a reality because of your creative efforts. Thank you for sharing yet another of my dreams and making it your own.

Wendy Sherman: Thank you for believing in me and working so hard to make *Get a Clue!* happen. It was so special to have the chance to work with you.

Amelia Sheldon, my editor: for the wonderful experience of working with you so closely. Thanks for being so accessible, for your laserlike ability to zero in on what's most important, for your warmth and friendship.

To all the children, parents, teachers, and staff who have participated in my programs: Thank you for trusting me, for sharing so deeply. All that you taught me has significantly enriched my ability to write this book.

To my dear friends and family members who read and offered invaluable comments on various parts of my manuscript: Linda Longua, Andy Rosenberg, Hillary Rosenberg, Bea Rowe, Mary Jane Goff, Jane Gould, and Shirley Greenfield.

To all those at Henry Holt and Company, LLC: Thank you for believing in me and working so hard to make *Get a Clue!* a reality.

HOW SHOULD I APPROACH MY FATHER ABOUT HIS FATHER'S DEATH? I NEVER KNEW MY GRAND FATHER AT ALL.

I am really close to my mom and my parents are divorced and I would like to spend more time with my dad, but I'm so afraid of hurting my mom even though she has told me it was ok. What should I do?

My mom works, sometimes I feel like she cares more about her work than me. I know its not true but it feels that way. How can I tell her this without her or I getting mad.

How do you deal with the feeling that no matter how good you do it's not good enough for your parents?

Preface

In the early 1970s, while I was teaching a course in health and human sexuality at the college level, I began to be concerned about how students arrived in my classrooms each semester. Too many seemed to lack self-confidence. Too many expressed how lonely or disconnected they felt on campus, and admitted that it was uncomfortable to go up to someone even to say "Hi." There were students who didn't get along with their parents as well as they wished they could, those who couldn't communicate effectively with their boyfriend or girlfriend, those who told me they didn't believe they could be successful, and countless others who wanted guidance in dealing with other important "life" issues.

I thought to myself, If this is how students arrive at college, we can't be giving kids what they need. And so, in 1976, I called an elementary-school principal in my hometown to propose an idea for a student assembly program that I hoped would be able to make a difference. She responded positively. We set up a program for students and two parent-education presentations—one prior to meeting with the students, and one afterward. The student assembly was scheduled for boys and girls in the fifth and sixth grades.

In my health and sexuality classes, I had always given my students a chance to air concerns by writing them down on index cards and submitting them. No one needed to know who wrote which "sharing" card, and they could feel comfortable addressing their most relevant personal life issues.

I used the same anonymous sharing method at that first assembly program when I spoke with younger children. What came out on those cards was staggering to me:

- "People always tease me about my skin color on the bus. What can I do?"
- "My parents are divorced, and I never see my father."
- "I don't have any friends. Please help."
- "I always sit alone at lunch."
- "I don't know if my friends are really my friends."
- "I wish I could talk about personal stuff with my mother. What should I do?"
- "My friend is nice to me when we're alone but acts like I'm not there when we're with other people."

I had never thought about the fact that kids might not know how to make a friend or deal with their friendships once they developed. I was truly surprised to find that so many kids didn't seem to know how to express what they felt.

I had collected hundreds of cards from the fifth and sixth graders at that first program, and by the time the bell rang to end the assembly, there were still so many that I didn't have the chance to discuss. I was astounded by the extent of the students' needs. I wondered, "Who is talking with kids about this everyday kind of stuff?" It occurred to me that, perhaps, no one was. It then struck me that this "regular" everyday stuff is actually what matters the most. Everything that the kids said they wanted and needed to know related to how they valued themselves, how they treated each other, how vulnerable they were to risk taking, how they felt about family life, and whether they felt confident in school. I wanted to do more to help children cope with these day-to-day challenges.

At that first program, I had also invited parents to write anonymous concerns. Their cards brought out the reverse side of the issues their kids were raising. For example, they wrote:

- "How can I get my child to open up and talk?"
- "How can I get my child more verbal and comfortable talking about [sex, drugs, etc.] with me?"
- "How can my child deal with peer pressure?"
- "My son is very shy. How do you help your child learn to make friends?"
- "As a single parent, what would be the best way to introduce your child to your date without the child feeling threatened by a new relationship and/or friend?"

Questions and issues written by parents further confirmed the need to talk about the feelings, issues, and experiences that were part of daily life.

I also started speaking with teachers at my staff development programs and was further intrigued by what they wrote on their cards:

- "How do I deal with a loner in my classroom?"
- "The cruelty among my students is terrible."
- "I have a student whose parents are making her feel very pressured about her grades. How can I handle this?"

Another view of the same issues that children and parents raised was there in the teachers' cards. What became clear to me is that everything was connected. If kids were uncomfortable with friends, that could affect their ability to concentrate in the classroom. If kids were saying they wanted to be closer to their parents, it was no wonder that parents were writing that they didn't know how to approach their children.

Common sense? Absolutely, once you think about it. The problem is, common sense is not so common. As I presented more programs, I consistently found that parents, teachers, and administrators were "overwhelmed" by what kids wrote on the sharing cards I collected and addressed. They often told me they had "no idea" that kids were dealing with all of these things. I didn't either, until I started listening to so many children's fears, concerns, and questions. That's why I refer to all that I've learned as "uncommon sense." I've learned that what we need to teach our children is what too many people mistakenly believe they already know.

The more schools I visited, the more cards I collected, the more fueled I was by the needs I was documenting. I continued to be amazed by what kids were telling me, things that they said they had never told anyone else. They trusted me with all kinds of issues: what they wished they could tell their best friend, what they couldn't let their parents know, what they had a hard time dealing with in school, why their grandparent visits were so difficult. The more they shared, the more I listened. The more I learned what children didn't know how to handle, and how much they kept hidden, the more passionate was my desire to make a difference by helping students, parents, and teachers open and develop lines of communication. I started out presenting local programs and then gradually began to travel with my presentations. With parents and staff, as well as students, I continued to collect those cards. I learned that no matter where I was, small town or large city, the feelings, issues, pressures, confusions, and yearnings were all the same.

Since the needs I was documenting were universal, and there never seemed to be enough time to read and respond to all the cards at my assembly programs, I decided that perhaps writing a book was the only way to reach more children and families. That would give me the chance to respond to all that kids told me they wanted and needed to know—without a bell ringing to end what they wished me to share. That's how and why I wrote my first book, *Growing Up Feeling Good*, which is especially for kids. And now, it means so much to have the opportunity to write *Get a Clue!* for parents and other adults who work with children and want to better understand and know how to communicate more effectively with them. My hope is that it, too, will help make a difference.

Since I started my programs in 1976, I've listened and responded to more than a million students, staff, and parents at the elementary-school through college levels in forty-six states. As I continue to travel to schools around the country, I find that too many questions remain unanswered—at home, school, anywhere. And too many kids still keep their feelings hidden. There are hidden feelings trapped inside even the kids who are considered most popular, best athlete, best looking, and most talented. There is no rule, no absolute guarantee that smiles on the outside aren't covering up tears or confusions within. Surely this has been proven time and again when "bright," "popular," "wonderful," "happy" children have committed suicide for reasons that their shocked families have never been able to figure out.

Even if there are no serious confusions that demand immediate attention, everyday life is filled with experiences that trigger feelings and responses that can be significant. Naturally, some days will go smoother than others. But throughout the growing-up years, friends may change and bodies are sure to develop, with no promise of how or when. Your kids will be exposed to new experiences, faced with pressures to handle, decisions to make, expectations to meet, and increasing responsibilities. Along with each experience, there will be feelings that they may or may not express.

What I have learned from young people themselves is that even when they want to respond—to parents, teachers, friends, or anyone else—they may not know how and therefore just keep quiet. Many kids are too uncomfortable, too scared, too embarrassed, and simply don't know what words to say. The result has been, and continues to be, that too many important feelings and concerns remain hidden— even when parents and children are close. Silent feelings live on in the hearts and minds of every child. It's just a matter of how many, which ones, and how the silence is taking its toll.

A NOTE ABOUT THE "SHARING CARDS" IN THIS BOOK

The copies of cards incorporated throughout this book in original children's handwriting, as well as those that are typeset in a different script and set apart from the text, are all actual cards that were written anonymously at my programs. All of these questions and issues were written by eight- to fourteen-year-old children at the elementary and middle-school levels, except where indicated otherwise.

It is my hope that the insights that can be gained from what kids have shared on these cards—along with the information, perspectives, and suggested ways to approach your child—will help to enrich your relationship and enhance your understanding of what your child may be feeling and needing, but not be able to tell you.

Get a
CLUE!

My friends Don't like my
parents! How do I get New
Parents!

my parents and I aren't to close
the y both work and often leave before
I get up in the moring and get home
afer I go to bed. when I see them
it's a treat, How can I get close to them?

What do you do
when you want to
talk to your parents
but when you get a
chance you dont
ever get the nerve to.

My father died lastyear and my mom
has been having a hard time & now she has
to work and she doesn't have as much
time to spend with me anymore but
I don't know what to tell her because
this is a hard time in her life, but I
Need her attention.

1

HOW YOU AND YOUR CHILD
RELATE TO EACH OTHER

There are many parents who would never imagine that their child doesn't have the nerve to talk with them. When I first created my school programs more than twenty years ago, I was amazed at how many thousands of children told me they felt this way and hadn't let their parents know.

If your child had the chance to write his or her feelings anonymously about how you relate to each other, what do you think he or she would express? How close do you think your child feels to you? How close do you feel to your child?

Maybe you've never had the closeness with your own parent that you'd like to have with your child. Maybe you find it difficult to talk about your own feelings. Maybe it's even hard for you to say, "I love you." Over the years I have met so many parents and children who told me they couldn't. Even with the best parent/child relationships, everything is always changing. Nothing can be taken for granted. Figure that anything you share in a positive, loving manner will have a ripple effect. Being close with your child can be a life-changing, fulfilling, enriching lifetime endeavor. I can't think of a more important role as a parent.

I don't know your child. (Maybe you feel like you don't know your child, either!) However, I believe it's possible for parents to get

closer to their children. The ability to work at developing a closer
relationship with our children is a process that parents and children
can work at and grow with over time. No matter how difficult things
might seem, keep in mind that most children wish they could be
closer with their parents. Even when things go horribly wrong, those
can be the most important growth experiences. So don't be too hard
on yourself. Go slowly, and take things one step at a time. Think of
this process as an adventure. Anything you do to try to improve your
relationship with your child is wonderful. Your efforts to communicate more openly and become closer can have lifetime benefits for
your child as well as for yourself.

Whether we have one child or ten, we can only attempt to
embrace, love, and appreciate each child to the best of our ability.
The interaction with each child is going to be different. And certainly, each of our children will have his or her own perception of
who we are and how we respond to them.

We need to understand our children's challenges and fears in
order to become even closer, but we must also take stock of ourselves. Among the many key factors we need to examine are the
way we respond to our children, the manner in which we communicate, and how clear we are about what we can and cannot control in
their lives.

As you examine your own style of relating to your child, please
keep in mind, the purpose here is not to fuel frustration about not
having addressed these issues years ago so you could have a more
open relationship today. Perhaps that's the point: It *is* today. The fact
is, we can't go backward. We can't change what happened five minutes ago with our kids, much less five years ago. What you are doing
today is what's important.

We can only do our best with our children. Especially if you're
reading this book right now, I have to believe that your heart is in
the right place. You deserve to trust and value that your intentions
are pure.

In the relationship between parent and child, as in any relationship, responsibility applies to both parties. Especially when children
are teens and preteens, I believe that no matter how they feel about
relating to us, as parents there is still much we can and must do in
their regard. Our example and our guidance can be significant in

making a difference in how they feel about themselves, how they relate to others, and how prepared they are to face the issues and experiences that are part of growing up today.

With that in mind, let's go forward. It is my hope that the insights and approaches that I have included in this chapter will help you enrich and broaden the way you and your child are able to relate to each other.

WHAT ARE THE DYNAMICS BETWEEN YOU AND YOUR CHILD?

I want my mother to be closer to me. I wish I could talk to her about my problems.

Before reading further, you might find it helpful to put down this book, grab a notebook, and seriously consider noting your thoughts on the following:

HOW WOULD YOU DESCRIBE THE NATURE OF YOUR INTERACTION WITH YOUR CHILD?

- Strained? Easy? Rocky? Argumentative? Do you feel a sense of warmth between you?
- Are you able to talk together?
- When you start discussing something, do you end up yelling? (Always? Sometimes? Never?)
- Do you feel a sense of connection with your child?
- Can you be honest with each other, even about difficult issues?
- How do you respond if you disagree with your child? How does your child respond if he or she disagrees with you?
- What does it feel like when you talk with each other?
- Do you get the sense that your child feels you listen attentively when he or she is speaking to you? (Always? Sometimes? Never?)
- If you're reading or watching television, how do you respond if your child wishes to have your attention?
- Do you often make a joke of what your child tells you? Do you think your child believes you take him or her seriously?

- Are there any topics that are difficult for you to discuss with your child?
  - Sex
  - Boyfriends/girlfriends
  - Development/maturation
  - Illness/death
  - Achievement in school
  - Family stress
  - Others?
- Are there any topics that you think your child finds difficult to talk about with you?
- How do you respond when your child disappoints you? Goes against your word? Gets into trouble?
- What, if anything, about yourself have you consciously held back from your child?
- How much alone time do you spend with your child?
- What changes do you wish could take place in the dynamics of your interaction with your child

My purpose for presenting you with these questions is strictly for self-examination, not to have you check how many yes or no answers you had so you could determine what "how you and your child relate" category you might fit into. The point of this examination is to further help you understand as much as you can about what factors are influencing the way you relate to your child and how your child relates to you.

If you haven't recently asked your child how he or she feels about the way you talk with and understand one another, perhaps this is an ideal time to do so. Even if your feelings are positive and you have no reason to question that your child feels the same way, it's still a good idea to do a double-check. If you confirm that you're right about things being positive, at the very least it can be a wonderful opportunity to let your child know how much you appreciate that this is so.

Why do my parents hate me?

If you don't feel as positive as you want to about your relationship with your child, consider the specific factors that might cause you to feel this way. To clarify your thoughts, it often helps to write these issues down. Think through these observations. No matter how bad things may seem, and no matter how hard it might be to imagine how you will ever have a close relationship with your child, it's certainly worth every effort to work at it.

THE FIRST STEP TO GETTING CLOSER WITH YOUR CHILD

Before even attempting to address any of the specific issues that you identify as concerns, the first step you can take is simply to let your child know you'd like to get closer.

All you actually need to say for starters is:

"I've been thinking, and it would really mean a lot to me, if we could improve our relationship. I would love for us to be closer."

You can say this in a written note or aloud. Either way, it's a beginning. This is all about opening the lines of communication. It may not be easy to do and can be very awkward when you initiate the effort, especially if the lines have been clogged for years. That's okay. Remember, you can't go backward. At this point, what's most important to get across to your child in the most simple terms is that you love him or her very much, and that how you relate to each other is something you're hoping can be worked at together in order to become closer and feel better about your relationship.

WHEN IT'S TIME TO TALK

When you feel you're ready to address some of the specific issues of concern that you think are affecting how you and your child relate to each other, it's important to figure out a time to talk that can be open ended. This is not a conversation to be rushed.

Since it's possible your child may think that something must be wrong if you wish to actually set aside time to speak with him or her, you might find your child will respond positively to an approach such as, "I'd love to speak with you about something I've been thinking about. Good things. Nothing is wrong."

Then you can figure out together when it will be possible to spend some alone time with each other. You might combine your talk with an activity you enjoy, such as taking a walk or going for pizza. If you have a car and are planning to drive somewhere with your child for any length of time, that's often an excellent setting for a personal, private conversation. If things are going well on your way home, you can always continue your talk by deciding to miss your street . . . and keep talking.

PLANNING YOUR APPROACH:
TURNING FEELINGS INTO WORDS

How you approach your child can make all the difference in how your child hears you and whether or not he or she will even choose to listen. A key concern to keep in mind is not to put your child on the defensive, although some children may hear it that way. Rather, this is an attempt to reach a better understanding, a chance to bring to the surface what may be getting in the way of your ability to be closer with each other. There need not be any magic in figuring out what you can say to begin your conversation. Simply identify what you think might be affecting how your child relates to you, and start by addressing that.

What follows are some examples that can help you turn what you or your child might be feeling into words.

Whenever I try to talk with my parents, they always make a joke of it and never take it seriously. What should I do?

If this card could have been written by your child, you might start by saying:

"I've been thinking, and I realize that a lot of times when you tell me things, I make a joke out of it. I guess maybe that might make you think that I'm not taking you seriously. I really do take you seriously, though. I want you to know that. So if I ever made you feel this way, I'm really sorry."

If you know that things haven't been smooth between you, that's exactly how you can start:

"I know that things haven't been so easy between us. That hasn't felt good to me, and I can't imagine that it feels good to you. I was hoping that we could talk about this. I'd love for us to be closer."

I feel I can't go to my dad because he's always yelling at me.

If you realize how often you end up yelling at your child, you can say just that:

"I've been thinking about how often we end up yelling. That doesn't ever feel good to me, and I can't imagine that it feels good to you. I'm hoping we can work at talking with each other more. . . . I'd like to try."

Sometimes what causes children to hold back from a parent is not what that parent says or does but rather what's going on in the parent's or the family's life.

So if you haven't spent much time together, whether due to a hectic schedule or any other reason, you can let your child know you are aware of this. If your situation has been strained and you know you've been pressured, you can acknowledge that to your child. Doing so will potentially open the door for discussing important feelings that your son or daughter might not be comfortable enough to share otherwise. What you say can also help prevent your child from taking your strained manner personally.

If you have been dealing with painful or stressful circumstances, another effective way to begin your conversation is to acknowledge that you're aware of this. Here again, your starting words can identify what you think your child may not have been able to tell you. For example, you could say:

"I know we've been having a real hard time since Daddy passed away. I've been working so much and I haven't had as much time to spend with you. I guess since it's been so hard for me, I've just not paid attention to how hard it must be for you, too. I'm so sorry. . . ."

My dad comes home from a long day's work, changes, watches the news, eats dinner, and watches sports or goes

to a friend's house, then goes to bed. I do great in school and sports, and my social status is Ace! But I'd give it all up to do something with my dad. Unconsciously I try to get attention but nothing works. I even GOT SUSPENDED!

Whatever you feel is or could be having an impact on the way you and your child interact with each other, you can let your child know that you know. This may not immediately improve the dynamics between you, but at least your child will know that you care about what is going on between you. That itself can be a starting point for relating to each other in a more positive way.

BREAKING THROUGH COMMUNICATION BARRIERS
(If You Feel Like You're Talking to a "Brick Wall")

If you're saying to yourself, "A conversation with my child? You must be kidding! You don't know my child!" That's true, I don't. But I do know that most children would rather feel more positive than negative about how they relate to their parents.

Where does it leave you if you find your child is speechless after you take the initiative to talk about this? Here are some responses you might consider if that is how he or she responds:

"I really am serious about wanting to know how you feel about this. I know some kids don't feel very good about relating to their parents and it's too hard for them to let their parents know why. So I meant it when I asked you if you think I'm doing anything or saying anything that is making you uncomfortable, or making it hard for you to feel good about how we relate together. Maybe you could at least think about this for a while and we can talk later. . . .

"Sometimes writing your thoughts and feelings down when no one else is around can make it easier to share things that are difficult. If you want to write something to me, I'll read it when I'm by myself and then we can talk together afterward. I really love you and care about what you feel. Would you at least think about it?"

IF YOUR CHILD ACTUALLY ANSWERS

My friends don't like my parents! How do I get new parents!

If you are planning to ask your child hard questions, you need to be ready for the answers.

If your child responds with something like, "You know, since you asked, it really bothers me when you . . . ," a response from you like "That's ridiculous! I don't do that!" will probably not be as positive as:

> "Thank you for telling me that. I never meant to come across that way. But if that's the way you hear me, I need to know it."

You can add:

> "I'll try to keep that in mind. But if you find that you're feeling that way again, maybe we could have a special signal. Then you could let me know right away."

Also keep in mind that the way your child sees you is all in his or her perception. Even if you believe that your child's concern is not valid, the important thing to understand is that's how your child views or responds to you. That's the reality you need to face.

My family is very rich. I hate being rich. My parents ignore me. They feel that they can buy my love. They fill my day up with activities. What can I do to help them notice me?

HOW TO BECOME EVEN MORE APPROACHABLE

How do you tell your parents something even if they say you can tell them anything, even if you know you'll get in trouble?

I don't believe it's enough for us to say to our children, "I'm here for you. I hope you'll trust that you can come to me about anything. I'll be there to help you in any way I can, no matter what." There's no question that this is great for children to hear. But too many children won't take their parents up on the invitation, even when they wish to.

The many and varied reasons why children don't approach their parents include that they:

- are too scared
- are afraid they'll be grounded until they're at least forty-two years old

- are afraid they won't be taken seriously
- are too embarrassed
- think their parents won't understand
- think their parents are too old-fashioned
- believe their parents will think they're too young to know
- feel it's too hard to say what they want and need to say
- don't know how to say what they want and need to say
- are afraid their parents won't keep what they say private
- are afraid that if they let their parents know how worried they are about friends who are doing something dangerous, parents will believe they're a poor influence and won't want them spending time together anymore

The list could go on and on.

Which of these and what other reasons might apply to your child? A key part of increasing your approachability is to identify what feelings might prevent your child from approaching you. This process can also be very beneficial to teachers, coaches, and other adults who work closely with children.

I suggest that beyond saying "I'm here for you," we also say:

"Even as I say that, I worry. I worry that maybe you'll be afraid. Maybe you'll think if you let me know that you're worried about what your friends are doing, I'll say you can't hang out with them. Maybe you're afraid I'll never trust you again. . . ."

I have a friend and she doesn't do the right things, and she wants me to do those things. What should I do?

Add to your conversation any reason that could potentially prevent your child from coming to you.

The next step in this process is to reinforce what I suggested in the sample dialogue included in the section "Breaking Through Communication Barriers" (the fact that our children don't need to wait until they're comfortable to be able to talk openly with us).

I'm in eighth grade and I'm thirteen. Sometimes it's kind of hard to tell my parents what's going on in my personal life

**because they would probably say, "You're too young." What
can I possibly do?**

For example:

"If you're not comfortable coming to me, that's okay. Lots of kids think
they have to wait until they're comfortable to say what they really want
to say. The problem is, they wait and wait and then find that they're still
not comfortable. So they end up keeping their feelings silent.

"If you're scared or not comfortable, that's okay. It's just not okay to
let being scared or uncomfortable stop you from saying what you need
to say anyway."

Then, to be even more specific with your skill building, you can
provide your children with the actual words to help them express
what might otherwise be too hard for them to say. Refer back to the
"Turning Feeling Into Words" section of this chapter to review some
specific examples of how you can teach your children this skill.

It can help to let your child know you realize that even if he or she
knows how to figure out what words can be said, that doesn't make it
easy to say them.

Here are some more examples of how you can teach your child to
begin a conversation, no matter what he or she is feeling:

- If embarrassed, your child can begin with:
  "This is embarrassing for me to say . . ."
- If it's hard, your child can begin with:
  "This is hard for me to say . . ."
- If your child is scared, he or she can begin with:
  "I'm really scared to say this to you, but . . ."
- If your child feels funny saying something, he or she can start with:
  "I feel kind of funny saying this to you . . ."
- If your child is afraid to hurt your feelings, he or she can start with:
  "I've been trying to think of a way to tell you this without hurting
  your feelings. I don't want to hurt you, but I need you to know . . ."

Kids don't even have to know what they want to say to their parents. They just need to know that they want or need to talk. You can

reassure your child if you suspect that this might be the issue he or she is struggling with as well. For example:

- If your child thinks something might be wrong and doesn't have any idea what it could be, you can suggest that he or she can start with:
  "I don't even know what to say to you. But I get the feeling that something is not right. . . . Can you help me?"

This is so basic. By teaching our children this skill, we can help them communicate even the most difficult thoughts and feelings. Giving our children the tools to be more open with us—the skill of turning feelings into words—can help them be more honest now and in the future with other family members, friends, boyfriends, girlfriends, teachers, and anyone else in their lives.

My parents are jerks. I said I wanted to die and got in trouble.

Over the years, what I repeatedly said to my own children was:

"Worse than what you think would be the worst possible thing you'd want to share with me . . . would be if you felt you couldn't."

The meaning of those words cannot be taken for granted. As adults, my children continue to share their thoughts and feelings openly with my husband and me. They have both confirmed that when times were especially difficult, it made such a difference that we had encouraged their honesty and had reinforced our commitment to be there for them, no matter what.

My mom works. Sometimes I feel like she cares more about her work than me. I know it's not true, but it feels that way. How can I tell her this without her or I getting mad?

Many parents have said to me that there are things their kids share that they aren't sure they want to hear. It might help to remind our children that while we really do mean what we say about wanting to be there for them, we're human. And, depending on what they tell us, they may find that we'll be in shock, cry hysterically, go into a panic, or lose control for a few moments. Some things may be very hard to hear, and if a child shares them, we may initially be very upset. We may need a little time to process what they're telling us and let it sink in. The important thing we need to reinforce with our children here is that no matter what our initial response is, they must trust that we will absolutely be there for them—no matter what. And then we need to follow through on that significant promise.

Hopefully, our children will believe us. That is their part in this relationship of trust. Our child's trust to share with us and our promise to support them no matter what is a fundamental part of the foundation on which our relationship with our children is based. We can choose our words carefully, but we can't hear them or act upon them *for* our children. Beyond all our efforts to let our children know that we will be there for them, it is up to them alone to take us up on what we offer.

SHARING YOURSELF WITH YOUR CHILD

Perhaps one of our greatest gifts to our children is to simply be who we are, to be human. We can only do what we can to live each day and relate to our children to the best of our ability. We can acknowledge when we've been insensitive, admit when we've made a mistake, and show our children that we can benefit and even become stronger from every experience. We can help our children learn that sometimes what may seem like the most awful mistakes can teach us the most powerful lessons.

We can and must teach our children that sometimes life is up and sometimes it's down. That's real life. And as my mother always taught me, we can help our children accept that things happen for reasons. You can help your children understand that they can view even the most difficult experience as one of life's gifts, as a chance to learn invaluable lessons.

Many parents think they're doing their children a favor by protecting them from difficult emotions and painful experiences. They are afraid to break down in front of their children, reluctant to cry or even share their sadness. This kind of protection prevents a child from experiencing life fully. It's easy to deal with the easy stuff. But life is not always easy. Whether times are joyful or difficult, sad or seemingly cruel, it's all part of what our kids need to be exposed to in order to be able to face and deal with all kinds of life experiences. Besides, it's the rare child who would be oblivious to tough circumstances even if parents don't explicitly share the details of what's happening. In the end, if you attempt to protect your children from painful times, that can add stress to your life and theirs.

Several years ago, a thirteen-year-old girl shared her fears and sadness with me regarding her mother's illness. She told me:

> "In all the years my mother was in and out of the hospital, only once did I ever see her cry. And I was so relieved because most of the time, I just go into my room and cry in my pillow. I'm so afraid to upset her."

Consider what areas of your life you might be holding back from your child. What feelings, frustrations, disappointments, pressures, heartache have you found difficult to share? What have you wanted to share but didn't? What were you unsure your child could handle?

What immediately comes up for me is my own experience facing a hysterectomy when I was thirty-five years old. This was very traumatic for me. I was scared, emotional, and really didn't feel well much of the time. It took me several weeks after learning that I needed this surgery to sit down with my husband and two children in our living room and talk about it. Until then, it had been too hard for me to let our children know.

At that point, my son was ten and my daughter eight. I shared with them that I needed to go to the hospital to have an operation and that I was very scared. I said that I trusted my doctor and knew that I was in good hands. But still I was scared.

Sharing my feelings seemed to give my children permission to let me know how they really felt as well. It helped to explain to them that sometimes, even the people who are closest to you may not realize how badly you hurt inside. So I told them if they were very sad and needed extra hugs, they could just put their arms around me or their dad and say, "I'm very sad" or "Mommy, I wish you didn't have to go into the hospital. That makes me scared."

Then I picked what I thought was the right moment to say to my children, "Lots of kids worry that if their parent has to have an operation in the hospital, they'll never come home again." I definitely was on target. My children seemed to be relieved when I explained that those feelings are very natural, even for grown-ups. It also helped to talk further with them about what the operation meant, how much I trusted my doctor, and to suggest that we all continue to have faith and say our prayers.

We don't have the power to take away our children's natural fears. However, the way we personally approach the situations we must help them face can do a lot to take the edge off their fears. We can often ease much of their pressure by assuring them they are not alone in experiencing their fears.

I am really worried about my dad. He has a heart problem. He almost passed out once and it really scared me. My dad tells me not to worry but I do. How can I help my problem?

You can safely figure that if a situation is stressful for you, your child may not be bold enough to ask what's going on. It can be a relief to them if you bring up the troubling topic. If children sense something is wrong, they often think they are to blame or that the worst will come to pass. In some ways, imaginary fears and worries can be worse than real ones. Children will have greater security if parents talk openly with them, share what is age-appropriate, and can trust that parents will keep them informed if there are any changes. If the situation is not as serious as your child thought it might be, he or she would probably be relieved to know. Basically, by communicating openly, that will help you and your child to face fears and gain strength from working through the issues together.

If we tried to protect our kids from all the tough realities of what can happen in our lives, we would be doing more harm than good. We need to share honestly, offer support, and teach our kids how to cope by our example. They can gain immeasurably by learning the philosophy of "when a door closes, a window opens," along with the fact that we cannot plan for or anticipate every life event that will come our way. What we can teach them as well is that we are adaptable and resourceful, and we can choose not to give up. By example, we can show them that we don't have to handle difficult times by ourselves. It's positive to depend on family and friends and seek professional help when needed. In addition, many people find tremendous strength and faith through prayer.

Aside from letting children know about plans for going into the hospital and needing to have surgery, parents have also talked with me about how hard it is to share feelings related to

- becoming unemployed
- plans to move
- plans to separate or divorce
- the news when close family members are diagnosed with a serious illness
- the fact that a loved one has passed away

What you tell your child when you're dealing with tough family situations is your personal judgment call, based on your sense of what is age-appropriate and able to be understood by your child. Trust your instincts and share as much as you can.

Ask your child to make a personal "tough issues" list as well. The discussions that can stem from this self and joint examination of both your and your child's thoughts and feelings can further enhance the understanding between you.

A NOTE ABOUT LEAVING NOTES

No matter how much your child prefers to seek out friends to deal with life issues, you don't need permission from your child to leave a note. Notes can often provide greater freedom to think through and say what we feel is important to share, without the emotional interference that can take place in discussions.

Even if your son or daughter doesn't acknowledge that your concerns are valid, if you're still worried, you can write what you feel would be relevant, and what you want to make sure your child understands. On paper, you can still talk about feelings, offer explanations, discuss approaches, raise cautions, examine choices, and reinforce that you're there if your child feels like talking.

Here are some suggestions for beginning or ending your notes:

- "Just in case you're dealing with this . . ."
- "I had a feeling it's possible you're dealing with something like this. I thought it might be helpful to think about . . ."
- "Please know I'm not looking to invade your privacy. I know and am glad you have good friends. But just in case this would be helpful to you, I thought I'd write this down and you could read it on your own time. I don't expect you to talk about this with me unless you choose to . . . so know that I'm not waiting for your reply."

MAKING THE MOST OF THE TIME YOU HAVE WITH YOUR CHILDREN

When I finally finished writing the first edition of my book *Growing Up Feeling Good*, my daughter, then eight years old, taught me a lesson that at the time felt like an emotional slap in the face. I will never forget what she said and will thank her for the rest of my life for what she taught me.

The conversation went like this:

My daughter: "Mom, I'm so glad you finally finished your book. Now you can finally be with me!"

Me: "But I have been with you. I've taken car pool, we've gone shopping together, we've played games together. I've been with you!"

My daughter: "No, you weren't. You always looked at your watch. . . ."

She was so right. I was only with her physically, not emotionally. The truth is that I wasn't present. My mind was always on my next chapter.

I thought for a few moments and then told her that she was absolutely right, that I did look at my watch, and that although I genuinely wanted to be with her all of those times, I was preoccupied. I admitted that I didn't think there were words that would be powerful enough to take away the hurt and frustration she must have felt. I told her how very sad and sorry I was, and apologized as we cried together and held each other. And I acknowledged that while I knew that we couldn't relive those moments with each other, I had just learned some very important life lessons from what she was brave enough to share with me. I told her that I felt proud of her and would always value the fact that she could be honest with me, even if what needed to be said might hurt.

Privately, I needed to work at forgiving myself and making peace with how awful I felt just imagining what she, as an eight-year-old, had experienced because I couldn't or didn't separate myself from my writing deadline in order to truly be with her. It took a while before I was finally able to let go of what I knew intellectually I could not change and accept the reality that was. I couldn't recapture those moments with her. It might make you smile to know that these lessons really did translate into much more positive and quality inter-action with her and my son after that conversation. Being "present" is something I consciously work at—and will continue to do so. As much as we hope to teach our children "life lessons," we have much to gain from what *they can teach us*.

Rather than beat our heads against the wall or drown ourselves with guilt about the time we are not able to be with our kids, we're best off appreciating and making the most of the time we do have with them. I've learned that the key is to be able to be with your child when you're with your child. It's as simple and as complicated as that.

Even if the time you have with your child is limited, being "pres-ent" can make all the difference. We need to pay attention when our kids are speaking with us and focus only on them. During those times, we need to stay off the phone, not watch TV, or be concen-trating on work or what will be made for dinner that night. And if, for any reason, we are emotionally preoccupied at that time, it can help to let children know that we realize this is true. That way, at least there's no pretending to be with them when we're really not.

KEEPING THINGS IN PERSPECTIVE

I can't promise that if you say to your child, "I would love for us to relate better," you and your child will automatically be able to do so. I can only promise that if you don't let your child know you wish to relate better, he or she might not know you feel this way. It would be unfortunate to miss the opportunity to improve your relationship simply by assuming your child knows how you feel.

Remember that this is all a process. You can't rush it. You can control only your own part of how you and your child relate. It can help to keep the "one day at a time" concept in mind if you get impatient. We'd all need a crystal ball to be able to determine how things will turn out with regard to our ability to relate to our children, weeks, months, or even years from now. However, if relating better to your child is important to you, just keep working at it. Your ongoing conscious effort may make more of a difference to your child than you might think.

As your child grows older, there will probably be other variables that will affect how you relate to each other. These can include family needs, family changes, your own schedule, and your child's schedule (rehearsals, practices, etc.). Plus, as kids develop, they often share more with their friends than they do with their parents. We need to put that into perspective and not take it personally if their increasing preference is to be with friends rather than with parents or other family members. This change is a natural part of a child's development. The main concern is this: If our children want to approach us, can they? Will they? And, whether or not our children take the first step in approaching us, will we know how and when it would be important to approach them? We must do all we can as parents to keep the communication open between ourselves and our children. I hope the information in this chapter will help you do that. Now let's move on to specific issues your child may be struggling with and how you can help.

Why are parents always on your case and always want to know everything about you?

It is my hope that the remaining chapters will help you become more sensitive to and better anticipate your child's feelings and needs. This, hopefully, will help to enhance your relationship and improve the communication between you and your child as he or she matures and faces life's challenges.

Sometimes I feel like A Toy
thrown up in the closet.

I feel like everybody is better
than I am. And I find myself doing
stupid stuff just to be as good as
they are.

People awalys think I stink
cause I'm bad with sports
but they've never seen me
on a computor

People take ADVANTAGE
of me asking for money
& snacks or favors
Because they know I
Won't turn them down
Because at least I'll
know they'll Be Nice to
Me for awhile

2

HELPING KIDS VALUE THEMSELVES

I have found that very few students of any age actually understand that they're valuable, important, and special . . . simply because they are. Most kids don't know that there is nothing extra that they have to do to be valuable, that their worth is not and need not ever be tied to anything or anyone outside of who they already are.

I've also learned that there is no age cutoff for a child's need to understand this. Countless parents over the years have asked me how they can help their children value themselves when their own sense of personal worth is so low. I know only too well that depending on the day, depending on the circumstances and expectations, it can be very difficult to remain clear about the fact that we're each unique, and that we're all equal as human beings. We need not and ought not compare ourselves to anyone. We don't need anyone else's approval or validation to be valuable.

I wish that all we would need to tell our children is "You're so special!" for them to be able to believe it too. I wish it were that simple. There's no question that all children need to hear this. Certainly, not enough do. However, those words don't seem to be enough. The reality is that it's easier for adults to say this than it is for kids to believe.

I wish someone would like me. (Boy) It would really make me feel good that someone thinks I am special. Deep down I know I could be special if someone just gave me a chance.

If we wish to make a more significant impact on how our children value themselves, we need to take a different approach. To help children feel more positive, we need to help them identify why they feel negative. We need to help our children to identify the negative elements that are affecting their definition of themselves. Once identified in concrete terms, negative judgments are often easier to eliminate, easier to let go.

There is this person who always has to try to be better than me and smarter than me. What do I do? Do I try to ignore her? Or should I just let her make me feel stupid and worthless?

If we can help children understand how they are measuring themselves, and how much power they might be giving to others by allowing them to define who they are, then we have a chance to help them make their own internal changes in how they perceive their worth. I don't suggest that this is an easy process. As far as I know, there are no quick fixes for being able to truly value oneself. However, no matter how long any given child has been viewing him- or herself in a negative way, I believe that it's never too late to make positive changes. This chapter is dedicated to examining the factors that commonly influence how kids value themselves and how we can help them take control of their self-portrait and make it as strong and positive as possible, regardless of what other people may think.

I'm weight challenged. Everyone makes fun of me because of my weight.

HOW KIDS OFTEN MEASURE THEIR VALUE

Looking back on my own growing-up years, it didn't seem to matter that I had been voted most popular and best athlete in my senior class in high school. It didn't matter that I was on sports teams, had a leading role in our senior play, had a really cute boyfriend, was an officer in several organizations, including National Honor Society, was the oldest of four, and was unquestionably adored by my family. Most of my closest friends, including my boyfriend, were ranked from valedictorian to number twenty-five in our graduating class. I wasn't (not even close!). That made me feel that I wasn't as smart or as good as they were.

I am very smart and a musical talent but I hate myself. Why is this? I do have a lot of friends. I have a very, very comfortable life but, still, I really hate myself.

Today, with all the emphasis on strengthening self-image and self-esteem, with all the efforts to try to help kids get past differences and realize that each person is equal and special, not much has changed. Kids still compare themselves to others. Kids still judge themselves by anything and everything. Our children usually feel more or less valuable depending on how they feel they measure up—to others or to their own high standards and expectations for themselves.

Why do you have to prove yourself to another person? Why do you have to be perfect to fit in a group?

Kids' definitions of being valuable are often tied into what they have been able to accomplish. Many kids fail to understand that the accomplishments, while great to strive for, are gravy. Accomplishments are those extra kinds of things that add dimensions to inner satisfaction. Kids deserve to feel good about what they are able to do, but they don't deserve to feel less worthy if they don't do, don't win, aren't picked, etc. So, again, they need to be helped to realize that there is a distinction between feeling good about what they're able to accomplish and allowing whether or not they accomplish something to define their worth.

Recently, I spoke with third-, fourth-, and fifth-grade students at a local elementary school. One of the boys in the fifth grade raised his hand and said, "What if you think you're nothing?" I tried to help him and the rest of his class understand that no one is "nothing," that each person counts, each is important. I asked him to think about what might have happened in his life, what someone might have said, or if there was something he thought he should have been able to accomplish, to cause him to think that he's "nothing." I also suggested that it might be helpful to him to try to remember when he started thinking this way. How long had he had this question about himself? In essence, I wanted him to try to figure out what triggered those thoughts.

Unfortunately, my presentation ended a few minutes later because it was lunchtime. Although the teachers planned to follow up this discussion in their classrooms, I wish I could have gotten the chance to ask this boy privately if he had any thoughts about why he felt the way he did. It breaks my heart to know how many children of all ages are walking around with the kinds of feelings that this boy expressed.

NEGATIVE JUDGING—IT'S ALL IN YOUR CHILD'S PERCEPTION

What kids need is the ability to enact a paradigm shift in terms of how they view themselves. Part of our challenge in helping them alter their thinking process is to, first, be aware of what negative judgments our children are actually making. Then we need to clearly get the message across that those judgments are just that, judgments. They're outside measures of worth. Kids need to know that how they see themselves is a choice. No one can make this choice for them, unless they allow that to happen. We must tell our children that while others may offer up visions of who they are and may provide negative ones, these don't have to be the images our children choose to accept.

Nobody in my family is close to me. I feel unwanted. What should I do?

Negative messages have to start somewhere. The reality is that even one statement, one word, one look can be powerful enough to impact your child for a lifetime. You can do much by helping your child identify the source of negativity, if there is one in his or her life, and addressing that specifically.

Do you know what it's like to be alone at lunch? And when anytime you walk by somebody who doesn't like you and they make funny sounds and call you names, and you didn't do nothing to them? They just do that because they hate you. Help me (please). Signed: No Friends.

If your child seems to be struggling with self-esteem, and does not choose to be open or simply is not able to identify his or her concerns, try your best to determine what negative messages might be influencing him or her. Scrutinize all situations, experiences, pressures, and relationships that your child is involved in on a daily basis. You can also speak with your child's teacher(s) to get feedback about how things are going in the classroom.

At my school assembly programs, the chance to share anonymously on index cards makes it easier and more comfortable for kids to express feelings and concerns that they might otherwise keep silent. While it would probably be difficult for your child to share as anonymously at home, you might still find that he or she will feel more comfortable and will actually share more openly by writing concerns on an index card or in a journal used specifically for sharing difficult or private thoughts with you. Your son or daughter can then let you privately read what was written so you can discuss this together.

WAYS TO HELP

Let's look at a wide range of negative judgments that kids often make about themselves. For each issue, I've offered some perspectives and suggestions as to what you might say to help your child turn negatives into positives if he or she has similar concerns.

My hair is long and disgusting, I have thick glasses and braces, and everyone makes fun of me for it! I have few friends!

Some parents may be inclined to respond to this girl's thoughts by saying:

"Don't be ridiculous! Your hair is great. And you look really good in your glasses. . . . Don't listen to what other kids say!"

According to Scott, age ten, many kids would respond to a parent who says, "Oh, you have great hair. I don't think it's that bad . . ." by thinking, "Yeah, you're my parent. You're supposed to say that!" It can help to anticipate that kids may think this is so . . . and actually say those exact words to our kids:

> "You're probably thinking, 'Yeah right . . . I'm your parent, I'm supposed to say these kinds of things.' But I didn't have to say it. I really mean it."

A better first response would be to validate this child's concern. A comment such as

> "It must be really hard to deal with all of those things!" can then be followed with something like,
> "But it doesn't seem to me that everything has to stay that way. I'll bet there are some things we can figure out together that can make you feel better . . . at least about some of the things you're saying."

SOME PERSPECTIVES AND IDEAS FOR TAKING POSITIVE ACTION

Explain that some things are within your child's control and some things are not. Children don't always know the difference. It can help to put this down in writing with your child. Set up two columns, one for "can control" and the other for "cannot control." Then start with the first concern, which according to this card is "My hair is long and disgusting." Actually write down the words "long and disgusting hair" in the "can control" column. You might just find that this will cause your child to start smiling, and the process of diminishing his or her pain or frustrations will have started.

Together with your child, continue to take each of his or her concerns and write them in whichever column seems most appropriate. This exercise alone can lead to meaningful discussion about such concepts as needing to accept what cannot be changed. Once the list is completed, you and your son or daughter can consider what can or cannot be done about each area of concern.

Let's continue a bit further with some ways that the "long and disgusting hair" issue can be addressed. Before saying, "Great news! This is an easy thing to change . . ." it would be good to ask if your child truly thinks his or her hair is long and disgusting or just saying that because kids have made fun of it.

If you determine that your child really thinks his or her hair is disgusting, you can suggest that this may be the perfect time to change hairstyles. Long hair can be shaped, curled, straightened, or cut shorter. There is lots of room for creativity. The hair does not have to remain "long and disgusting" if that's how a child feels it is. If your son or daughter is open to change, make an appointment with a barber or hairdresser as soon as possible. He or she will probably feel very good about the fact that you're taking this concern seriously and are acting so quickly upon what you've discussed could make a difference.

If the decision is to go with a new hairstyle, it would also be important to talk with your child about how kids might respond. Your child needs to be prepared for the possibility of more teasing, regardless of how good he or she feels about his or her new look. It can help to reinforce that this new look is not something that is anyone else's business. They may make it their business, but it's not. You can also help prepare your child to go off to school armed with responses such as, "Well, I really don't care what you think about my hair. It's my hair, not yours." Or, "I don't tell you how to wear your hair, and I'm not interested in what you think of mine."

> Sometimes people judge me by the clothes I wear, by the way my hair is styled, and generally the way I look. I just want to be a normal person. What do I do? I am losing friends real fast. Help!

It can also be of tremendous help to remind children that it's common for others to tease about a variety of different things related to outside appearance, such as glasses, braces, hairstyle, size, shape, looks, or clothes, and that this teasing might represent a negative influence on how they view themselves. But they don't have to allow themselves to feel negative. You can explain that even though each person will grow and age and change, what never has to change is the inner beauty that is inside all of us. No matter what anyone looks like on the outside, that inner beauty can remain and continue to glow no matter what.

Each other issue can be discussed, one by one. For example, in this same card, the next concern is about thick glasses. Depending on the prescription, you and your child may discuss the possibility of new glasses or, perhaps, even contacts.

Next, braces. Kids are often teased about braces. It may help to remind your child that it's a luxury to have the chance to straighten teeth that are not quite lined up as they're supposed to be. If other kids make fun, your child can simply turn to them and make the widest possible "braces smile" possible, then turn and walk away. Most kids who tease are looking for a reaction. If they don't get it, there's a better chance that they'll stop.

The last issue on this card has to do with having "few friends." The perspective here is that what is most important about friendship is not the number of friends, but who friends are, how your child feels about them, and how they feel about your child. Many kids are very concerned about being part of a crowd. Let your child know that two people can be a crowd. If he or she actually does have a few friends, that's wonderful.

If your son or daughter would like to make more friends, you can talk together about the "Rosenberg plan of action" on dealing with friendship, which I discuss in chapter 6.

I feel so left out. Nobody likes me and I'm always used.

Let's take a look at this card and address everything that was shared. Isolate the issues and then discuss each one separately. For example, if this were your child's card, you could open with the concern that he or she feels left out. After validating that this is not a happy or easy feeling for anyone to have, you can turn your focus toward specific ways your child can deal with feeling left out.

As I just mentioned, the steps offered in chapter 6 will help you help your child learn what can be done to start a friendship. If children understand that they have the ability to make the first move and learn how they can make the first move, there is a greater chance they won't be sitting around feeling left out, waiting for someone to come up to them.

With regard to the issue "I'm always used," the truth is that this child, once again, has a choice. Any child who is aware he or she is being used is allowing that to happen. Children need to be reminded that they're worth more than that. Help them see that they are wise to recognize what is going on and that now they can take the next step of deciding whether to tolerate such behavior, address it, or simply distance themselves from the source of it.

This is also a good opportunity to raise the point that if someone likes your child only for what he or she can get, as opposed to who your child is, that's not a very good friendship. This is an ideal time to talk about qualities of a true friend so your child can know the difference between that and a less sincere connection with someone.

One of my friends thinks that no one likes her and she's ugly! But she's really pretty! I don't know how I could encourage her. I really wish she would feel better about herself!!

Kids often define themselves in terms of their perception of how other people view them. I'll never forget the time I was approached by a fifth-grade student after one of my assembly programs. She privately told me that a lot of kids called her ugly, and she wanted to know if I thought she was ugly. I responded with something like, "Do you mean if I say you're not ugly, then you'll believe you're not? I only wish I had the power to help you see how beautiful you really are." Tears welled up in her eyes when I said that to her. Although I never saw that student again, I know that after talking together further, and sending her off with a hug, I felt I had left her a bit more reassured, with something concrete to think about. I asked her to consider why she viewed herself that way—and emphasized that someone else's words don't have a right to take away from her beauty, both inside and out.

What we need to teach our children is that just because someone says, "You're ugly" (or "a loser," "nerd," "wimp," or anything else) doesn't mean it's true. It would certainly be sad if we had to depend on other people to decide if we are beautiful or valuable. Does that mean if someone likes us, that person will say we're beautiful, and if they don't, we're doomed to be ugly? Present this line of thinking to your child and talk about how it may be faulty. Discuss alternative sources and opinions your child might have heard on the subject he or she has raised. Point out that some influences are positive and some are negative, and that this will usually be the case. Then ask your child what he or she thinks.

By reducing these issues to the bare-bones basics, we can help kids better understand how much power they may be giving to other people with regard to their self-image and sense of self-worth. Figure that what often seems like the most obvious observation or perception regarding your child's concerns is exactly what you need to voice.

How children see their situation, how they interpret their parents and family's response to them, can be a very big factor in how they view themselves. What they perceive is what we need to know. If we can see through their eyes, we will have a much greater ability to help.

> My parents had a child before me and he's smart, and whenever I do something wrong they say, "Well your brother never did that." I told them that it hurts me but sometimes they still do it. It makes me so upset. Even when my grandpa calls, he always asks about him, and not me. What should I do?

> How do you deal with the feeling that no matter how good you do, it's not good enough for your parents?

Based on how you know you treat your child and what is going on in your child's life, consider the following:

- What feelings might he or she be having but not expressing?
- Could there be any question that he or she feels loved by you and/or other family members?
- Do you think it's possible that your child might feel as if he or she doesn't live up to your expectations?
- Are you often critical of your child?
- Do you think your child would think you view him or her positively or negatively?
- How much undivided attention do you give your child?
- Do you make comparisons with your child and other siblings? Do you hear others comparing your children?
- Can you identify any situation, any experience that could

have caused your son or daughter to perceive that he or she is not as wanted or not as important as his or her siblings (or anyone else)?

· How do relatives treat your child?

Also consider the talents, strengths, personalities and accomplishments of siblings, cousins, or close friends. Even if you know you haven't compared these with those of your child, it's possible that your son or daughter thinks you and/or other family members do. You can follow this same line of thinking with an issue you believe might be concerning your child. The more aware you are of what your child might be feeling and possibly not telling, the more on target you will be when you talk with your child.

I feel pressured about my grades because my brother is always getting 100s, and although my mother doesn't say anything, I know she's comparing me and I HATE THAT.

At one of my presentations, a woman in the audience stood up and shared with everyone that it wasn't until after her mother's recent death that her brother told her that all those years he thought their mother favored her. Although I couldn't know exactly, the woman appeared to be in her seventies, or at least sixties. Think of it. For sixty years, her brother believed his mother favored his sister over him. I can't even imagine what kind of influence that had on how he valued himself as well as the relationship he had with his sister. These are the kind of perceptions that are often silenced for entire lifetimes. Since children and adults often keep difficult thoughts and feelings hidden, it's even more critical to remain as aware as possible of the verbal and nonverbal messages your child might be receiving from you and others.

If you think there is even the slightest chance that your son or daughter could feel he or she doesn't measure up, or might have any other potentially negative feeling about him or herself, it is important to address this.

At the very least, you might consider starting with:

"I've been thinking. And I realize I probably don't let you know enough how very important you are to me. I love you very much."

Just saying these words or trying any of the other approaches I've suggested cannot guarantee that your child will embrace them, hang on to them, or even believe you really mean them. However, kids can usually sense when we mean what we say. If you're just saying the words I or anyone else has suggested to try to help your child feel better, but those words are not truly coming from within you, what you say will probably not have the kind of impact that you might hope it would. On the other hand, if you speak from your heart and base your conversation in your own core beliefs, what you say will most likely have a greater effect on your child and how he or she responds to you. Therefore, know that the approaches and ideas for dialogue that I've shared in this chapter and throughout the book are simply examples, guidelines, for you to consider, and if they don't sound like you, I encourage you to rephrase them in your own voice.

> **My teacher always yells at me and I hate it. And I hate myself. And I'm a very bad student—the worst in the grade—and I study but it does not help. What should I do? Nobody ever listens to me. I hate it and myself.**
>
> **I feel so bad because just about everybody in my grade has a chest but me. What should I do? I want them so bad.**

Since space prevents me from addressing all the possible things that could be troubling your child, the samples given in this chapter are meant to help you better anticipate what your child might be feeling and why, even if he or she does not tell you. The approaches I've suggested can be applied to most any subject or area of concern. Simply substitute any other issue that might relate to your son or daughter and:

- validate your child's feelings
- pick apart and focus on each of the issues your child shares or that you suspect are concerning him or her
- help your child understand what he or she can and cannot control
- share insights that will help your child put negative judging from others and him-/herself in better perspective

- talk with your child about what he or she can say or do to go forward feeling more positive

ANOTHER APPROACH

Sometimes an excellent way to offer perspectives about what you think your child might be dealing with but not sharing is to talk about that very same issue in the form of a story from your own childhood. That way, the focus will be on you rather than on your son or daughter. This path is usually much less threatening to a child who may be very nervous or uncomfortable with a troubling topic.

You'll then have the opportunity to share how you felt (identifying what you think your child feels), how your friends might have reacted, how you handled those feelings, how you dealt with the situation, and what the experience taught you. You can talk about how you might handle the situation differently now in comparison with how you did then, if you feel that would be the case, and tell your child why. You'll be providing your child perspectives and ideas for going forward in a more positive way without actually letting on that this is what your intention is.

Some kids will figure that out, some won't. Depending on the response you get, you can choose to leave the story in the context of your own childhood or you can decide to say something like, "I've been thinking that what happened to me is very similar to what you seem to be going through." Whether or not your child admits this is true, you will have provided some helpful insights that will, hopefully, broaden the context in which your child can think of his or her situation. Your openness may make a dent in any negative feelings your child might have.

REALISTIC PRAISE, REALISTIC EXPECTATIONS

Unrealistic praise can cause children to think they're on a pedestal that, in reality, has a shaky foundation. Such praise can nurture a false sense of confidence that can ultimately lead to disappointment and hurt. Children need and deserve to have truthful feedback from you, even if it might be hard for them to hear it. That can help them be realistic in their appreciation and acceptance of themselves.

If you or others make expectations that are unrealistic for your children, they may grow into old age thinking that they never quite measured up. There needs to be a balance to what we say to our children. We need to keep in mind that there's a fine line between positive encouragement and negative pressure. That line can be at differing points for each child, even in the same family. Beyond trusting your own gut sense as to where that line falls, you can also gain insight from others who have close contact with your child, such as teachers, coaches, and Scout leaders.

My parents think that just because I'm smart I can't do anything wrong or get any Bs or Cs in school.

Even if praise is realistic, I worry about kids who feel good about themselves only because of the praise or because they actually lived up to their parents' expectations. Our messages need to reinforce that while praise is nice to receive, that's not what makes a kid special. With or without praise, whether or not expectations are met, every child is valuable and special.

WHEN KIDS THINK THEY NEED TO BE "PERFECT"

Sometimes our children have unrealistic expectations of themselves that, as parents, we don't push or reinforce. Some kids are harder on themselves than anyone else is. These are often high achievers, excellent athletes, kids who are popular (and may think the only way to remain popular is to make the team, make the catch, make the honor roll). They expect themselves to always be "the best," at least their own definition of best. Whether it be in the area of sports, academics, or anything else, these children seem to expect themselves to always perform at the highest level, and they're usually not very forgiving of themselves when they fall short. A self-imposed pressure such as this can make it hard for any child to fully appreciate and value themselves.

If you believe your child is in this category, you might try saying something like:

"I wish I could figure out what I can say to help you be kinder to yourself. It seems that you think you have to do everything perfectly. I see you putting yourself under such pressure and that has to be so hard. I get the feeling that you're not very forgiving. I wish you would ease up on yourself."

Or you might say:

"It's very painful to me to see how hard you're being on yourself. That can't feel very good."

Then you can take the discussion from there, based on your son or daughter's response.

Part of the reason why kids who are perfectionists get so upset when they fall short is that they're scared that people will then see them as less than who they would like to be. Here again, it is vital to teach children that their value, their importance, is not tied into their sports ability or their grades or anything else. It would probably help the children in your life to hear you say that whether they make the baseball team or don't, whether they make the honor roll or not, they are still the same person. They are still valuable and they will always have that unique value whether they accomplish everything they set out to do or not.

Even if children want to be less hard on themselves, change usually involves a process. We need to help them understand that because their instinct to judge themselves harshly has become such a natural part of their response pattern, they may still find that their immediate reaction in any situation they perceive as less than perfect is to get down on themselves. While it may be natural for them to immediately respond with the same feelings of disappointment to anything they view as less than their best, what can begin to change— and what needs to begin to change—is what they do with those feelings. That is within their control. Children can choose to let the disappointment fester and intensify or talk with themselves, saying something like, "Hey, wait a minute. Don't do this to yourself. You know you tried your best. Give yourself a break. Lighten up. . . . It's okay." If you can give them this positive suggestion on what they can say to themselves in times of pressure, you will have given your children a very helpful tool.

As kids consciously work at easing up on themselves, the length of time between their initial negative reaction and their ability to put it in healthier perspective will be less and less. The hope is that eventually they will be able to eliminate their unrealistic expectations and not experience as much pressure in the first place.

Kids who don't feel they're perfect can be pressured to feel they have to be perfect in response to expectations they perceive family and other people have for them. Simply telling a child that you know the pressure he or she feels can also help ease the sense of expectation he or she feels from others.

"JUST BE YOURSELF"

Sometimes I forget who I am because I'm too busy acting for my friends.

We need to teach our children that "being yourself" means they don't have to pretend to be who they're not. "Being yourself" involves being true to their own personal beliefs, values, and boundaries. It means behaving in ways that are consistent with their own beliefs and feelings rather than in ways that are not reflective of who they know they are, just to fit in.

Sometimes children might need help identifying what their core beliefs and values are. Parents can discuss this with their children, creating a chance for them to explore their personal thoughts and feelings about what is right and wrong, what they feel is important in relating to others, and what behavioral boundaries they feel are appropriate to establish in order to be consistent with their beliefs. Parents might find it will help clarify how children define what "being yourself" might mean by asking them to consider such questions as:

- How would you characterize your personality?
- What are your most important qualities? (Are you honest? A loyal friend? A caring and responsible family member?)
- What are your strengths? Your weaknesses?
- What are your boundaries? Identify what you feel are important rights and wrongs.
- Do you stand up for what you feel is safe and right,

regardless of what friends might be doing? Or do your go along with the crowd?

· How do you interact with others? How do you respond to differences of any kind?

· Do you ever change what you want to say because you worry how friends will respond? (Under what circumstances?)

· Do you keep your feelings hidden from friends or family members? (What kinds of feelings are hard to express?)

· Do you ever behave in ways that you know are not you just to get other kids to accept you? (In what ways have you changed your behavior?)

You and your child can add to the list of considerations. Your child may wish to answer the questions for him- or herself in a journal rather than discussing responses with you. In either case, the self-examination can add a dimension to what your child understands about being true to who he or she is.

How can you tell a friend to be her own person and not follow everyone else? To let her have her own personality.

When people are being themselves, they can relax. They can "chill," as my kids would say. They don't have to act. They can just be. They need not worry about judgments on the part of anyone around them, trusting that they're fine just the way they are. With these ideas, you can help your child understand how "being yourself" feels, even if they might not understand the exact conditions that led them to hide behind a false image.

If people don't like your child for who he or she is, then it's probably not worth it to spend the time and energy to try to convince them otherwise. If kids change to get people to like them, and people start liking them for who they pretend to be, what good would that be? Whom would they be liking? How long would this child have to keep pretending to be someone else? That would be an unfortunate basis for a friendship (not to mention emotionally exhausting). Children need to be taught that true friends accept you for who you are and love you because of who you are. They don't want you to change. That wouldn't be "you." It can help to talk through all of this if you sense your child might be struggling with friends who want him or her to change.

FINDING SPECIAL INTERESTS AND STRENGTHS

Each child has his or her own special talents, strengths, and interests. Many have no idea what these areas are. Maybe they never had the opportunity to explore the range of options that could actually be available to them. Especially with children who seem to have difficulty valuing themselves, it may make a significant difference in their self-confidence if they could find one talent they can call their very own.

Sarah, now in her sixties, shared:

"We have four children. Our oldest son is third youngest, and he had competition within the household with two older sisters who were athletically inclined and a younger brother. He was in between. His younger brother was the baby in the house and was given a lot of attention by everyone. So in order to give him an identity of his own, we first built a shop for him and got him tools. He liked to do things with his hands. So his father taught him how to do carpentry. We got a jigsaw and different other tools. He liked to use the workbench.

"But he also was interested in music. He had a very good ear for music. We wouldn't give him piano lessons because his older two sisters played the piano. So we got him a guitar, and he loved it. That was the thing he adored.

"We were very mindful of the different needs of our children. Our son wasn't as social or athletic as his sisters, so he needed something for himself. The guitar made a big difference in how confident he was and how good he felt about himself. It's a parent's observation of what the tendencies and talents of their children are. Parents need to help a child find an area in which no other child in the family can excel. Nobody else in our family took the guitar, and our son got his recognition . . . which he needed."

Sarah's experience with her son and his guitar clearly demonstrates the need for children to find some area of concentration or expression that is their own. There are so many fields of interest to consider. Soccer, fishing, gymnastics, dance, computers, horseback riding, tennis, singing, musical instruments, swimming—the possibilities are vast. Consider individual and team sports, and special areas of study that would suit and appeal to each of your children. Think of your own environment and consider what programs are offered in your community. There are often free classes and lessons that are available through community and recreation centers. If one area of consideration doesn't work out, encourage your son or daughter to try another. This effort can prove to be life-changing for your child.

Keep in mind that this is not about finding a sport or talent in which kids are better than anyone else. Rather, the idea is helping children find something that they can develop for themselves, something that they can grow with and love to do, something that gives their confidence a boost, something they can call their own that makes their heart smile.

PARENTS AS ROLE MODELS

Everything we say and everything we do, verbally and nonverbally, can potentially contribute to or chip away at our kids' sense of self-worth. We're teaching all the time, by our example. We're role-modeling all the time, positively and negatively. Daily, we're contributing to our children's sense of who they are and how they might relate to each other.

How we communicate with each other, how we openly express our feelings, how we handle disagreements, how we respond to disappointments, how we deal with stress and difficult life experiences, whether we can hold on to our sense of humor and laugh at ourselves, how we deal with mistakes, how we respond to people who are rude, whether we stand up for ourselves, whether we behave consistently with our beliefs, how we take criticism, how respectful we are to others, and how we deal with differences. All of these can contribute to how our children handle these very same things.

The list of everyday relationships and experiences we handle in front of our children can go on and on. Everyone's list will be slightly different. You may find it enlightening to make your own. It's hard to be sensitive to every single message we send and all we might be teaching our children consciously and unconsciously. As you examine your own day-to-day life experiences and the way you handle them, think about how your children might have been and continue to be influenced by your example.

If you identify any negative areas of influence, consider ways in which you can make positive changes. For example, if you realize you've been holding back your feelings, you might start sharing more. Or you might even choose to discuss what you realized with your child, starting with, "I realize that there are many times I don't share what I really feel . . ."

As I've said before, please keep in mind (as I remind myself to do) that if we know our heart has been in the right place, we must forgive ourselves for any negative influence we might have had up to this point in our lack of communication or how we think our actions might be influencing our children. We can't know until we know. Once we "know," we can then live and express ourselves in a more sensitive manner. That itself represents an important lesson about the ability to learn from everything and make positive changes. That's a great lesson to share with your children.

SEEKING OUTSIDE HELP

If you sense is that your child does not value him- or herself, and nothing you say or do seems to be able to make a dent in those negative feelings, it's important to seek outside help.

If you haven't already done so, check with your son's or daughter's teacher(s) to determine whether behavior and performance at school is consistent with what you're concerned about at home. Speak with your school counselor. You might find it helpful to initially meet with the counselor alone to discuss how best to proceed with arrangements to help your child. Most communities have school guidance counselors as well as school psychologists and social workers. Counseling is offered by schools at no charge. If the school counseling staff feels the issues that need to be addressed are beyond their domain, they ought to let you know.

Anticipate that it's possible that children might think they must be "crazy" or "nuts" to need counseling. It can help to tell them that going for help is a gift, a chance to learn more about themselves and figure out how to deal with tough feelings. Explain that counseling is an opportunity to speak with someone who is professionally trained to listen, a chance to learn tools and perspectives so they can feel more positive about themselves. Kids often don't appreciate that it takes courage and strength to go for help. Discuss both of these important perceptions associated with counseling when you talk with your child about why you'd like to have him or her go and what positive outcomes you think the counseling experience might help to bring about.

Kids also worry that if they do go to the school counselor, someone might see them. Well, that's possible. That's why it can help to teach all children that if they do notice that someone is going for counseling help, a great attitude would be "good for them! That's a really brave thing to do." Then they must know to respect that person's privacy. Children can share this perspective if others tease them about getting help.

Remember, if your son or daughter ends up needing professional counseling, it does not mean that you have in some way failed as a parent. Many parents blame themselves for not being able to make their kids feel important and happy. We don't have that power. We can't feel valuable for our children. We can only do our best to help them see their true worth as an individual. The rest is up to them. Our "best" involves knowing when we have exhausted our own efforts to help, and at that point going forward and seeking help from a trained school counselor, psychologist, or school social worker. Doing so is a gift that children may or may not appreciate at the time. In later years, they're likely to look back and understand that you cared enough to step in and push them toward help.

If I don't have hair, under my arms can I still use deodorant?

Every time I try to talk with my dad about sex he falls asleep

I am on a diet i've been on it for awhile and everybody calls me fatboy and things like that.

What if your parents keep saying something like boy you need a bra, & you want one but you can not say you want it. But if you get one your friends will make fun of you. what do you do?

3

PHYSICAL GROWTH AND
SEXUAL DEVELOPMENT

The place: my college class in family life and human sexuality
The unit: male anatomy and physiology
What I said to my students: "One testicle is slightly lower than the other.
   That's fine. That's natural. They're supposed to be that way."
The response from a male student in the back of the classroom:
   "Whew! All of these years I thought I had arthritis or something. No
   one ever told me . . ."

If you're smiling, think about the fact that this student had to have
been at least eighteen or nineteen years old. And he was absolutely
serious.

That exchange occurred more than twenty-five years ago. The
more I documented the misconceptions and lack of information
among my college students, the more strongly I believed that if this
is how they arrived at college, we couldn't be giving children what
they needed to know in elementary school, middle school, or high
school. That's what motivated me to start programs for younger
children.

As I presented program after program and collected more questions and issues from children of all ages, including my college students, I further confirmed that we can't take anything for granted.

We can't assume kids "should just know" what may seem like the most obvious things when it comes to their own bodies.

I remember thinking to myself, "Who thinks of these things?" The more I listened, I continued to learn—kids do!

I am scared to have a period.

With that in mind, this chapter is dedicated to sharing what I've learned we need to make sure to explain to our children in order to address their common questions and ease their fears about their bodies and puberty. I'll also identify specific "not so typical" information that would be important to include in your discussions with your son or daughter, approaches that can help ease discomfort, and ideas about how to defuse emotionally charged issues.

Is sex important?

Why do people make fun of other people's gay parent?

WHEN TO START, HOW MUCH DO YOU TELL?

Since it's hard to predict when any given child is going to start puberty, a good guideline is to be aware that girls can start to develop as early as second or third grade and boys just slightly later, around the age of nine or ten.

You may be thinking that they're just little kids at that point, how could they need to learn this information that early? That's true, they are little kids. But I personally know girls who started wearing a bra by the end of second grade and those who started their period in the third grade. There are boys who have talked with me about developing pubic hair as early as third or fourth grade and those who have shared that they already had started to ejaculate at age eleven. That's the earlier end of development, but it is still possible for your child to experience the big changes that come with puberty at this younger age. The best thing you can do is help your child understand the changes he or she will face with straightforward information about their body.

Should you be worried if you haven't started to develop at the age of fourteen?

Kids who develop earlier than most of their peers need to know that what's taking place is normal. And kids who are among the last of their peers to develop need to understand that's okay, too. Whether kids develop earlier than, later than, or somewhere in the middle of when most of their peers are developing, they all deserve to be able to trust that this is just fine. Each child will grow according to his or her own time schedule, or, as I like to put it with kids, the child's own "growth clock."

They call me shrimp.

When will I know when puberty has struck?

As long as you're sensitive in your presentation, and share information in an age-appropriate way, you won't harm your child by letting him or her know what's ahead. Children will take in what they're capable of and file the rest away. The bottom line is that they need to know this information sooner rather than later. If we wait for kids to ask, we may never have this talk. So it's up to parents to take the first step.

There are very simple, cartoon-type books out for younger children that present physical changes in an easy-to-understand, often humorous way. Check these out in your libraries and bookstores and share them with your child, answering the other questions or issues that naturally arise.

Sometimes adults are more emotionally charged about these topics than their kids are. My son was seven the first time he asked about how babies are made. I purchased a wonderful book with that exact title, thrilled that it presented information in very simple terms along with pictures showing how conception took place. The book explained what happens with flowers, then dogs, cats, and eventually, humans. I remember that the butterflies in my stomach were out in force as I anticipated with great emotion the moment when we would actually get to the page dealing with human reproduction. Our son would finally "know"! When we finished the book, he looked up rather calmly, and his very first comment was "Too bad they didn't include giraffes." Remembering that comment still makes me smile.

I've learned that kids can often handle more than adults think they can. Even if it seems your child is very immature, physically and/or emotionally, it is still essential to explain the changes that will eventually take place during puberty—prior to when they start happening. Specifically, that means you should be sharing information on this subject with your child when he or she is eight, nine, or certainly by ten years old.

How do you know your child is undergoing puberty and its changes? Changes in height are hard to miss. So is hair on the upper lip. Unless your daughter wears three sweatshirts at all times, it's likely that she will not be able to hide her breast development. However, if kids start growing pubic hair or experience a discharge, we may not know it unless they tell us. That's part of the problem. Because the topic areas related to development are usually so sensitive and awkward, even when kids talk with their parents about "everything," they may not talk about their body and development.

So if you're waiting for your son or daughter to approach you with questions or a status update about any physical changes, you may be waiting for years or forever. That's why, even if kids don't ask, it's up to us as parents to know what they need to know and when. Unless you initiate "the talk" about puberty, you may miss the opportunity to help offset your child's anxiety and concerns that can result from not understanding what is taking place at the moment those changes start.

How do you know when you had an ejaculation?

If the fluid from your vagina starts to come out a lot, does that mean something is wrong?

"THE TALK": OPENING LINES OF COMMUNICATION

The first time I approached my daughter to talk with her about all of "those things," she said flat out that it was all too gross and disgusting and she just didn't want to talk about it. I think she was nine at the time.

My first thought was "How ironic. Here I am helping other people's kids deal with all of this information and my own daughter is too uncomfortable and grossed out to want to talk with me about it." I knew it would do no good to try to force the conversation at that point. She had clearly put up a block, and I had to respect that. I also knew her response had very little to do with me (parents can't take this personally) and much more to do with her own feelings of discomfort. I knew that she simply and purely was still only a nine-year-old who just didn't feel ready to deal with all those grown-up changes that had not shown even a tiny hint of beginning.

Our pediatrician had pronounced my daughter as being a "late bloomer" physically. And she was. Many of her classmates and friends were not. Some of them literally towered over her, and a few were already beginning to look more womanly. My daughter still very much looked like a little girl. However, just as with the growth process itself, children can only be where they are with regard to their readiness to approach this information. I was challenged because even though my daughter didn't want to hear it, I knew it was important for her to learn. She needed to know about what was going on then, and what she could anticipate would happen when puberty began. She needed to be able to understand that although her friends were developing and she was not, that was okay, her time would come.

While I had to be respectful of where she was at emotionally and physically, I attempted to be creative and tried different ways to explain to my daughter the changes she would experience. I left notes on her pillow telling little bits of information along with lots of feelings, stating that I wasn't expecting her to answer me, I just thought she might like to know about whatever it was. I told her funny old stories about my first bra, how the tissues that one of my classmates stuffed into her bra flew out onto the gym floor when she jumped up to hit a volleyball in our gym class, how my mother cried when I first got my period. I casually brought things up when the moment seemed right, such as when we were driving somewhere alone together or when I was making dinner and she kept me company in the kitchen.

Little by little, my daughter's comfort level seemed to build, and I found we were able to talk about more of the things that were initially too sensitive for her. This was a real conscious process for me of identifying out loud for her what I sensed she might have been feeling and sharing information a few smidgens at a time in order to slowly build a foundation of knowledge that would help her understand what I anticipated she wanted and needed to know.

All children are going to have their own point of readiness when it comes to listening to this information about their bodies. That may or may not coincide with when we believe they need to receive this information. How we approach our children can help to make a difference in their receptivity. Here are a few ideas that can help you get started if you haven't already done so:

If you think your son or daughter may instantly turn deep shades of purple at the mere mention of puberty, "private parts," etc., you might start with:

> "I know we haven't really talked about things like all the changes that will happen to your body as you're getting older. . . ."

Pause to check if your child is starting to look like an eggplant and then keep going. Identify what it seems he or she is feeling—for example:

> "From the look on your face, I get the feeling that this topic is a little hard [or a little funny, or a little embarrassing] to talk about. That's okay. Lots of kids feel that way. So do lots of parents! It's kind of funny for me, too. But it would be so great if we could talk about this together. There's lots I want to make sure you understand so you can feel really good about all your changes."

I want to know about breasts but it's hard to hear about them.

I know everything already!!

If your son or daughter tells you, "That's okay. You don't have to tell me, I know that stuff already!" you can say:

> "That's so great! It's really important for you to know it. But I'll feel much better (and so much more responsible as a parent!) if we could

still talk about it, anyway. Or, if you don't feel like talking, you don't have to say anything. You could just listen. That way you could check and be sure that you really do understand everything you believe you understand. And I'll get the chance to share what I'd love to share with you. If I leave out something, or say something that doesn't seem right, you could teach me, too!"

Are you thinking, "That sounds nice, but what if my child won't buy into this?" Sure, it's possible that kids still won't want to talk about it. If this is your child's response, you might as well not push further, at least not at that moment. You can say, "Maybe another time would be better"—then think about a creative "plan B," as I did with my own daughter.

This is less a matter of needing to talk about the information and more a matter of making sure your son or daughter gets the information. So books and personal notes can work just fine until you eventually get a personal conversation going. You might also try sharing what you wish by recording it into an audiocassette tape so your child can listen to you privately.

Another way to begin dialogue is sharing what happened when your mom or dad talked with you for the first time:

"It makes me laugh to think of the first time my mom or dad talked with me about these kinds of things. I remember feeling so embarrassed. I thought everything was so GROSS! I didn't want to hear it, but I really wanted to know about it."

You can then go on to say:

"It would really mean a lot to me if we could talk together. . . .

"Even though it was so hard to talk about this with my parents, it made me feel so much better that I could go to them with anything I wanted to ask. It would be great if you could feel the same way with me."

Or even:

"My parents never talked about this stuff with me. That's why I hope we can talk together."

No matter what approach you take, it would help if you don't make "the talk" seem like "THE TALK." Approach your child more casually. Don't make it seem so planned, even if it is. Remember, concepts can be built gradually. You needn't rush to teach your child everything at one sitting. You wouldn't be able to, anyway.

The first conversation has a great deal to do with setting a tone for future sharing, beyond any information that you hope to impart. It's essential to communicate that your door is open for conversation about all the things that are usually so hard to talk about. If you set a caring, safe, welcoming tone that incorporates both silly and serious elements, you'll be doing much to break through any barriers and encourage ongoing interaction.

One more thought: Many people, adults and children alike, think that they have to wait until they feel comfortable to talk about sensitive things. We need to let our kids know that it's normal to feel uncomfortable about these topics. It's even okay to feel uncomfortable. It's just not okay to let being uncomfortable cause kids to withdraw and remain silent about what they want and need to know.

What if you're too shy to talk to anyone about anything?

This is where the "turning feelings into words" concept (see chapter 1, p. 8) can be so helpful. Aside from telling our kids they don't have to wait until they feel more comfortable to talk with us, we need to explain how. Any kid (or parent) who feels uncomfortable can simply begin by saying, "It's really hard" or "I feel really uncomfortable talking about this . . ." and then take it from there.

MOM OR DAD, OR BOTH?

After one of my school programs, a student followed me into the hallway and asked, "How can I help my friend? She only lives with her father. How can she talk with him about bras and periods and all those girl kind of things?"

I realized she may have been talking about herself. Regardless, I was glad I had the opportunity to say that she could let her friend know that even though fathers don't wear bras, they know about them! And although dads don't get periods, they know about them too. And, more than anything else, I told her that I'd bet it would really mean so much to her friend's dad if she could trust that he would be there for her to talk with about those things and deal with anything else that mattered to her.

What happens if only my dad is home when I get my period?

So many kids seem to think that girls should only talk with moms and boys with dads. They need to know that there is no such rule, and that it can be so enriching for both moms and dads to interact with sons as well as daughters on all subjects, including these sensitive ones. Even if kids are reminded that they can talk with parents of either sex, that's not enough to guarantee they'll act upon it. It may still be hard for boys to talk with their moms about such things as ejaculations or for girls to imagine they could ask their dad to buy sanitary pads. It's difficult enough for many kids to approach a parent of the same sex on these issues. But your child should know that he or she has the option of approaching either parent.

When my breasts develop, how do I ask my mom for a bra?

Whether you are a single parent or there are two parents (or guardians) in your home, beyond staying mindful of the possibility that your "other sex" children might feel uncomfortable approaching you about sensitive issues, it can help to acknowledge to them that you're aware of this. The same applies for those who are of the same sex. Doing so may not completely eliminate discomfort but can help take the edge off. Sometimes being playful can reduce the uneasiness even further.

Here are some sample opening line ideas that can help "break the ice."

Dads to daughters:

"Some girls probably think they can't talk with their dads about bras and periods and those kinds of things. I hope you know you can talk with me about anything. Even if you feel kind of funny, I'll bet the more we talk with each other, the easier it will be."

"Even though men don't get periods, I want you to know I know about them. So, if you ever need me to go to the store to get you sanitary pads, that's no problem!"

Moms to sons:

"There are probably lots of boys who think that they can't talk with their moms about wet dreams or getting pubic hair or anything else like that. I just want you to know that it would be so special to me if we could talk together about anything important to you, even these things."

Moms to daughters:

"I know how hard it was to ask my mom to go bra shopping! So if you ever think you're ready to go, even just to see what it feels like to try one on, I'm there with you. Just say the word."

Dads to sons:

"I remember wondering if I should even tell my parents when I had my first wet dream."

It's also important to reinforce that moms and dads can talk with sons and daughters about both male and female development. Boys and girls need to know about their own bodies, but they also need to learn about each other's. That can help to eliminate (or at least reduce) teasing and increase understanding and respect.

WHAT KIDS FEEL BUT MAY NOT TELL YOU ABOUT THEIR DEVELOPMENT

I spoke with Clare, mother of three, who told me that when her daughter was in the sixth grade, her breasts were already fairly well developed. Clare wanted her daughter to wear a bra, but she refused. Throughout that school year, Clare periodically tried to encourage her daughter to go bra shopping with her. The answer remained a staunch "no." Clare said it wasn't until she went shopping with her daughter for summer camp clothes that she asked to get a bra. She wanted to have one in case the other girls in her camp cabin were wearing one. That summer, Clare's daughter asked her to send three more bras. There lies the power of needing to fit in with peers! If your child resists your encouragement to accept and respond to personal needs related to his or her development, just be patient while periodically voicing your support.

Summer camp, sleepovers ("overnights"), and changing in the locker room are all settings that many kids view with dread while others strut around as if they're Kings of the Forest. Depending on whether they're more or less developed than their peers, and how they perceive they fit in, children may be more or less comfortable about their own body image, live in fear of being teased, or continually worry how their stage of development might affect friendships and boyfriend or girlfriend relationships. The more aware you are of where your son or daughter seems to fit in with peers developmentally, the more sensitive you can be to what he or she might be feeling and not telling about body changes and body image.

I'm taller than most of my friends. It makes me feel like I don't fit in because they are so tiny. What should I do?

For each of the following areas of maturation, I've listed feelings and concerns that kids have told me they found difficult to tell their parents (or anyone). I've also included some perspectives that you might find helpful to share if you sense your son or daughter has similar feelings to the ones that are listed.

Some of the things I've included may seem obvious. Again, that's the whole point. It's the "obvious" that is exactly what we must make sure our kids know.

BREAST DEVELOPMENT

Your daughter may not let you know:

- her breasts hurt
  She needs to know this is normal.

Is it normal for your breasts to hurt?

- she wants to go shopping for a bra
  Keep your antennae tuned for questions such as, "Do you think this shirt looks right on me?" That might mean "I think I'm ready for a bra."
- she's worried that she's going to grow lopsided because one breast seems to be peeking out earlier than the other
  Reinforce that this is possible and normal. If obvious at all, it will probably be to those girls who are so anxious to develop breasts and are even setting an alarm clock in the middle of the night to check if they've started to grow yet. No kidding. I've had grown women confirm to me that no one ever told them breasts could grow at a slightly different rate and they were unnecessarily upset and worried because they didn't know that the other breast would catch up and develop right along with the one that showed itself first.
- her concern if one nipple looks different from the other, or if both appear different from those of friends
- her friends are developing and she's upset because she's not
  She may worry how her lack of development might affect her socially; that includes the worry that maybe boys won't be as interested. It would help to reinforce that if someone likes your daughter only for what she looks like or some aspect of her development, instead of who she is, that's not a good relationship to have.
- the reason she keeps her jacket on in school is to hide what chest she has or doesn't have

Your son may not tell you:

- he's worried that the swelling in the area of his chest makes him feel embarrassed
  All boys and girls need to understand that this swelling is common . . . and doesn't mean that a boy is more like a girl! It would help if all parents would reinforce the importance of being respectful and sensitive about differences.

I am a boy and I have a bigger chest than most girls. I am embarrassed in the locker room.

HAVING A DISCHARGE

Your daughter may not tell you:

- that she's having a discharge

  Unless you explain this is normal, she might worry that something is wrong.
- if her discharge changes significantly in amounts, changes color, or starts to itch

  Let her know she needs to tell you if any of this takes place.
- since she has a discharge, she thinks her period might start any day

  This doesn't mean her period is about to start tomorrow at 2 o'clock! It's more a statement that her hormones are actively working and puberty is in progress.

I have my discharge, I think. Does that mean I'll have my period soon?

- it bothers her to feel damp

  You can mention the idea of using a panty liner.

CIRCUMCISION

Your son may not let you know:

- he's worried that his penis won't grow normally if he's not circumcised

  Reinforce that circumcised or not, his penis will grow as it is supposed to grow, and work or function as it's supposed to.

- he's uncomfortable, embarrassed, or confused if his penis appears to be different from that of other boys

Should you be embarrassed if you're uncircumcised?

PENIS SIZE

Your son may not talk about:

- how devastated he is that his penis is smaller than those of his friends (changing in the locker room, at sleepovers, or summer camp, etc.)

  You need to reinforce that since not everyone grows at the same rate, each boy's penis will grow at the time and in the way that's right for his body. No matter whether a boy's penis is a little larger or a little smaller, they all "work" the same.

How big should a penis be?

Boys may wonder about the size of their penis, and think it relates to their "manliness" or sexual proficiency.

Help them to understand that they will be manly because of who they are, not their penis size, how built up their muscles are, how much hair they have on their chest, how deep their voice, or anything else.

TESTICLES

Your son may not ask you:

- if it's normal that one testicle is slightly lower than the other
  It's perfectly normal.
- if there is any concern about the size of his testicles

EJACULATION AND "WET DREAMS"

Your son may not let you know:

- that he has had an ejaculation

  (He himself may not know what this is unless he was taught what it is.)
- he's worried that ejaculation will hurt, be scary, that it will happen in class

  Reinforce that ejaculation will not take a boy by surprise when he is awake—he will feel it; the passing out of semen is a good feeling and won't hurt.

When boys have an ejaculation and semen, does it hurt?

- he's worried he'll wake up in a pool of fluid from his "wet dream"

  No, he won't have to swim to the side of his bed! You can measure 1–2 teaspoons of water from your sink and explain that that's approximately how much semen will flow out during a single ejaculation. It's a very tiny amount.
- he's confused about when his ejaculations will happen

  There is no schedule, no materials needed as with a girl's period. Once he starts ejaculating, it simply means his body has reached the point of development where he's now able to experience this.
- he's embarrassed about the idea that there might be a "spot" on his sheets—and that his mom (or dad) might see it

  Reinforce that your son doesn't have to worry about hiding the fact that he had an ejaculation in his sleep. You might say that he's welcome to change his own sheets if he wishes. If not, you'll just know that he's normal. And that's great.

What if the sperm drowns?

I had an ejaculation on Sunday. What will happen next? Am I a man or not?

PERIODS

Your daughter may not let you know:

· that she got her first period

For many girls, this news is hard to share.

· how scared she is to get her period

I don't like blood at all. I'm scared if I get my period that I'm going to panic if no one's around. From, Scared.

· that she'd like to have a supply of sanitary pads just in case her period starts
Before your daughter's first period, especially if she has already shown signs of development, it can bring her extra peace of mind if you purchase a small supply of sanitary pads for her. Besides having them available for her in your home, these can be put other places, such as the glove compartment of your car, brought along on vacations, etc., just in case. Since this is very hard for girls to ask for, it can make things much easier if you're the one to make this suggestion. Or just buy them and let your daughter know you thought it would be a good idea to have them around . . . just in case.
· about confusion related to when and how to change pads, whether to play sports, what to do about swimming, bathing, or showering

If you don't have a period, should you still change your sanitary pad every two or three hours?

Ask your daughter to think of any situation she might find herself in—in class, at a party, at the movies, taking a test, playing soccer, at a park, etc.—so that you can brainstorm together ways she can be creative and take care of her needs. Remind her that if she goes to the bathroom and finds that her period has started, she can put some toilet tissues into her underpants and be okay until she gets a pad. If need be, she can keep changing the tissues. She can also use folded paper napkins or paper towels.

What happens if you get your period in an elevator?

Pubic Hair

I'm in eighth grade and I don't have pubic hair? What do I do? Please help.

Your son or daughter may not let you know:

- he or she is worried that it will grow too long

    No, kids will not trip over their pubic hair. Let them know they won't need a pubic haircut. Their bodies will know just how much is right to grow.
- he or she is embarrassed about having more or less pubic hair than friends

    Reinforce that, as with other changes, each kid will grow hair when his or her own body is ready. It's all up to those hormones. So everyone's body will be at a different stage of growing. Kids can't yank pubic hair out if it hasn't yet started to grow, and they can't stick it back in once it has started. So, basically, they got what they got.

Other Body Hair

Your daughter may not let you know:

- how disturbed she is about the hair on her legs

    There are girls who tell me they wear stockings under their shorts in gym class because they don't want anyone to see how hairy their legs are.
- how much she wants to shave

    I realize that this decision can be influenced by culture. For those whose background dictates not shaving under arms, that's not as likely to be an issue. For girls whose mom or female guardian does shave, shaving legs or shaving under arms can be emotional if a girl is told she is not allowed to shave and secretly wants to do so very badly. I'm not suggesting that you automatically give in, but it would be important to know that girls can have very strong feelings about this. So listen carefully, even between the lines. It may not be worth torturing your daughter with restrictions about shaving that truly have a deep impact on how she feels.

VOICE CHANGE

Your son may not tell you:

- how much he hates being mistaken for his sister or mother when answering the telephone.

 Remind your friends and family to ask rather than assume they know who has answered.

UNCOMMON KNOWLEDGE
THAT KIDS MAY NOT THINK TO ASK

- Girls need to be taught to wipe themselves from the front to the back.

 Since the first opening (urethra) and middle opening (opening of the vagina) are sensitive and prone to infections, it's a healthier practice not to wipe from rear opening (anus) from which bowel movements pass.
- Both boys' and girls' sexual organs are also referred to as genitals
- There is no bone in the human male penis.

What does erection mean?

Kids often use the slang expression "boner" to refer to an erection. The reason why the penis becomes harder, longer, and slightly wider is that an extra blood supply is signaled to fill into the spongy tissues inside the penis. The blood vessels then constrict for a few moments, causing the penis to remain in the harder and longer state. After a short while, the penis becomes soft and non-erect again as the blood leaves the tissues of the penis.

 Boys also might not realize that it's normal to have erections at different times throughout the day and night. They might even find they wake up with an erection. When a boy has an erection, it's often much more obvious to him than it is to anyone else (unless he's wearing a skintight bathing suit at the time!).

When you get a boner, how does it get hard when you have no bones in your penis?

What if the girl's eggs run out?

· The entire outside area between a girl's legs is referred to as the vulva (make sure to tell your kids that's not to be confused with the car, the Volvo)
· Teach girls the name and location of the clitoris (where the top folds of the inner lips come together), and the fact that there are three openings between a girl's legs

Doesn't a tampon block the urine from coming out?

· A tampon will not prevent a girl or woman from urinating
· Hair around the nipples is normal for women
  Girls need to know that if they find a few hairs around their nipples, that doesn't mean something is wrong or that a "boy thing" is happening to their body. (Don't yank the hairs, just be kind to them, and know they're normal.) I've had college students in my classes who admitted that they were very upset about these hairs because they never knew they were normal while they were growing up.
· Hormones do have an influence on the emotions, and emotions and other factors (i.e., stress, extreme exercise) can have an influence on the workings of the hormones. PMS is real for many girls and women.

My sister has her period and she usually gets cranky. Is that normal? Or is she just cranky?

This is by no means an all-inclusive list of all the feelings or questions that are possible for children to have regarding their body's development. Nor did I attempt to address every aspect of the changes kids will experience while going through puberty. This is only a guideline, a way of thinking, and confirmation that there are likely to be many questions that our kids are trying to handle on their own. No matter what they choose to share with us, there's likely to be more they keep to themselves. That's where our sensitivity needs to kick in even further. We, as parents, have to be aware, open, and share information our children might be concerned or worried about.

If, in your proactive approach to addressing these kinds of issues, you identify a concern that actually is not applicable to your son or daughter, there's no harm done. You'll probably end up having an interesting discussion, anyway. The more you talk together, the more open you'll be able to become with each other on these and other issues.

Please note: I did not go into extensive factual detail about each of the developmental changes, as that information is easy to find in a variety of books for kids, including my own *Growing Up Feeling Good*. These are wonderful for kids to read by themselves, share with friends, and share with parents. You can read them yourself to learn as much as you can about what your child needs to know and how that information is best presented. Your local or school library and bookstores will have a variety of resources on these topics as well. My main goal here is to discuss how you might help yourself and your child discuss these issues that are often sensitive and hard to talk about, and to help you be more aware of what your child might be feeling but not telling you.

BE VERY SPECIFIC

Do you only wear a pad when having a period, or just all the time like every day for the rest of your life, changing it every day?

I cannot emphasize enough the need to be specific with regard to the information you share with your child. So if you're explaining ejaculation, make sure you clearly let your child know that urine and semen don't ever mix, even though they pass through the same passageway. Make sure that you say "days and nights" rather than simply saying periods last three to seven days or so. Be sure to mention that when bleeding does occur for a girl's period, that's blood that the body does not need. We even need to be sure to say that the sticky side of the pad goes on the underpants and the soft side faces upward between a girl's legs! Some kids actually don't understand this.

I've said a few times already that I believe the advice, information, negativity, or wisdom in one word or one sentence can last a lifetime. Aside from the need to be specific, because we cannot assume kids know even what may seem to be obvious, it's also important to be as clear as possible because we cannot control how kids will interpret what we say.

We can control only what we say to our children; we cannot control how they hear us. That's why it's so important to be as explicit as we can be. That will leave less room for an incorrect or harmful interpretation. Your openness to questions and your patience in taking time to discuss your child's concerns are, therefore, also very important in diminishing any misunderstandings your child might have.

How many times does a woman have to have sex to have babies?

WHAT YOU CAN SAY IF YOU DON'T KNOW WHAT TO SAY
(Defusing emotionally charged questions and issues)

In light of the overexposure to sexually related material that kids have on talk shows, in movies, on cable TV, and certainly, in the news media, you'd be wise to anticipate that at some point you're going to have to call upon every creative cell in your body to respond to an emotionally charged question or issue raised by your child. Not to worry.

Does it hurt to have sex?

Is having sex a great moment?

I've come to believe that the ability to defuse rather than fuel any emotionally charged issue is an art form. We can do this even if we don't think we're very artsy. While we cannot control what our children choose to ask or say to us, we can control how we respond.

One of the key factors is not to even let on that you feel whatever was said is emotionally charged. Statements such as "You're too young to know that" or "I can't believe that came out of your mouth!" or "I don't ever want to hear you say that again!" would not be helpful in the defusing process. Better to keep your cool. If need be, double-check that you clearly heard whatever was said. You may even wish to start by asking where the question came from, where your son or daughter got the idea to ask you what they did. Then direct your response to whatever offshoot or aspect of the issue you feel would be most appropriate to concentrate on. Defusing the emotional climate involves taking charge of where the conversation goes next. How you transition is where the art comes in.

It will be up to you to decide how much depth to go into, what's appropriate to say, what is better left unsaid. For example, I was giving a presentation related to puberty to fifth-grade boys and girls in an assembly setting. From the back of the room, one of the boys yelled out, "What's 69?" I didn't skip a beat, didn't raise my eyebrows, and simply answered, "Oh, that just refers to the position two people are in. One faces one direction, the other person faces in the other direction. Like a six and a nine." I didn't refer to "sexual position," I just answered from the standpoint of position and went on to say, "Are there any other questions?" I answered quickly, was matter-of-fact and truthful enough without going into what I felt was inappropriate further detail, and didn't make a big deal of it. No one even paused to giggle. I wasn't thrown off balance, and my sense of calm seemed to relax the room filled with children. We went on to the next question. It seems that's all they needed.

What is masturbation?

There's no telling what kids will ask us. One of the many other questions that kids have asked me that would be considered to be in the "emotionally charged" category is "How do gay people have sex?" It might be helpful for you to think about how you would respond if your son or daughter came to you with that question. If you've already dealt with this, how did you feel about the way your conversation went?

Here are some thoughts that I have found useful when addressing such questions that you might find helpful. Of course, it's your own personal judgment call as to how you may wish to focus your answer. Remember, your child has raised a question you might not have expected, but you can maintain a degree of control in how the conversation progresses. While some parents may be inclined to say, "How could you ask that!", it would be better to just deal with whatever aspect of the question you feel comfortable zeroing in on. With this question, you've got a great deal of flexibility in choosing a focus that seems right for you and your child.

For example, you might start by asking what "gay" means to your child. Or you could respond with: "How two people share themselves with each other is very personal between those two people." You don't even have to get into the idea of a couple being homosexual or heterosexual. You can also broaden your answer to deal with peer pressure, sexual pressure, and the point that no one should force themselves sexually on someone else, no one should take advantage of someone else, and that there needs to be respect in all relationships between people. You can take this opportunity to include your feelings about abstinence, as well. You could also turn the focus to the unfortunate existence of gay bashing and other kinds of violent hate crimes. You could discuss the need for people to value human life and respect all kinds of differences, even if those differences might be totally against your own beliefs. You can cover all that material in response to just one question. When a challenging question arises, look for the offshoots. You can take the conversation anywhere that seems appropriate and worthwhile to you.

If a child asks a question that seems too advanced, or that would warrant more expansive knowledge to be able to understand your answer, you might say, "That's such a good question. But I think my answer would make much more sense if I first talked with you about. . . ."

Why do people have orgasms?

Here again, the point is although you can't control what your child might ask, you can control how you choose to answer. If your son or daughter wants more information after you go back to basics, you can make another judgment call as to how far you wish to take your additional explanations.

I'm not suggesting that you respond to anything and everything your child raises, even if you feel he or she really is too young to receive an answer. However, there's a difference between saying, "You're too young to know that!" and "Wow. That's a real grown-up question. I think my answer would be easier to understand if I help you learn some other things first." Then you can follow through on whatever information you feel your child can handle. Afterward, you can add something like, "When you get a little older, we can talk about this even more."

What may seem emotionally charged to a parent may be very innocent on the part of the child who asked the question. A key factor here is to realize that once something is said, it's out. To say to a child, "You shouldn't have said that" or "You shouldn't be talking about those things," when he or she already has, is not going to help your child. If it's out, whatever your son or daughter said needs to be dealt with in an informative discussion rather than a slamming judgment. The latter will most likely make your child think twice before raising his or her questions and concerns with you in the future.

IF YOU'RE AT A COMPLETE LOSS FOR WORDS

If you can't think of anything to say on the spot when your child asks a question, that's okay. You can buy some thinking time by saying something like:

> "Interesting question! I want to give you an answer that will help you understand this issue. But honestly, you caught me by surprise with that one. And I need a little time to think of what would be the best way to answer you. Let's plan to talk a little later."

Or you could say:

> "I'm not really sure of the answer. Let me check into it and we can talk a little later."

Then you have choices. Speak with your spouse or significant other. Call your closest friend and ask, "How would you handle this?"

or "What would you say?" Go to the library and get a resource that you can read together with your child. There's really no one way to handle any question that comes up. We need to just trust that we can take each situation for what it is and try to make the best of it.

It's okay to say, "I don't know." That doesn't make you inadequate. Aside from helping your son or daughter with the particular issue that was raised after you've obtained the correct information, you'll also be reinforcing a very positive message about how smart it is to admit if you don't know an answer. Even parents don't know everything, but there is a way to find out answers. You and your child can even research subjects together. In this way, you will help your child become more resourceful when faced with finding out what he or she doesn't know.

NEGATIVE SELF-IMAGE, EATING DISORDERS

Why do you have to be skinny and pretty to be in the group?

Extensive literature is readily available (from pediatricians and other doctors, counselors, school health offices, libraries, bookstores, and national organizations related to eating disorders) for understanding the facts and treatment approaches for anorexia nervosa, bulimia, compulsive overeating, and other eating disorders. Therefore, I have chosen to focus here mainly on feelings related to these disorders that kids often find hard to express.

It is my hope that the insights provided in this section will help you be that much more sensitive to what your own child might be feeling and experiencing—and how you can help.

I wish I was anorexic.

What might seem like an innocent enough remark can turn into a nightmare for some kids. "Your legs look a little heavy in those shorts" could be an offhand remark you've made and forgotten. But your daughter might carry that with her along with the comments of others and build a serious worry about her weight. It's important to try to make your comments to children constructive.

Certainly, I agree that it is important for us as parents to be honest and sensitive about how we express ourselves. If we have a serious concern about a son or daughter who appears to be overweight or noticeably too thin (to us), my feeling is it would be unfortunate if we didn't at least share our concern.

If we say:

"I hope you don't mind my saying this. But I'm really getting concerned about how thin you're getting. I know a lot of kids are very worried about how they look and what they weigh. I just want to make sure you're okay."

that might be heard differently than "You're too thin!"

If your child has reached the point where he or she is faced with losing weight (or gaining weight), you might find this additional approach helpful. I said the very same thing to my own daughter at several points throughout her years of growing up:

"I don't know what to say except today is a new day. You can't go backward. But you can make a new start. If you're not comfortable with your weight, you can decide to do something about it. You can change the choices you're making and do some different things for yourself that would help you begin to feel better. Why don't we plan a menu together?"

Then it's a matter of examining together what action your child would like to take or what he or she would like to do differently. Together you can, for example, plan a menu for the week ahead: Go shopping for food and snacks that would be great to have in your home. Have your child make snack packages for school or after school. If your child is going to be around other kids who are eating things like chips and cake and pizza, he or she needs to have fruit and healthful-type mixes. You can also help your child incorporate exercise into his or her schedule if it isn't already there. That, combined with watching what he or she eats, can begin to make a difference. You can also encourage your child to drink a lot of water, and bring water bottles to have throughout the day. It might also help to seek advice from your family doctor or a nutritionist if you aren't sure how to help your child make positive changes.

We need to hear what our kids are saying. We need to consciously encourage them to express their feelings and teach them how to turn difficult feelings into words. We need to work at our approachability and be even more sensitive in how we choose the words we share with them.

Our kids need to be told how important it is to talk with someone if they're scared or even raise the question if something might be growing into a serious concern for them. They need to know that they can come to us. But if they don't choose to or cannot for some reason, they also need to know that there are other adults who can offer support to help them deal with whatever it is they must face.

All of my friends are as skinny as twigs. I'm overweight and a lot of people do not like me because of that. I've tried to improve my outside by getting expensive clothes, combing my hair, and everything. Nothing works. Nobody except my best friend can see past my weight. What should I do?

It can be a helpless feeling to know that we cannot "fix it" and solve all the problems for our kids. However, we can offer to listen, ask how we can help, and keep reinforcing the value of getting proper help when it's needed. Although we cannot face for our children what they can only make peace with for themselves, we can more actively stay on top of what might represent even the slightest change in their patterns of behavior. We owe it to our children to speak up about any concern we have for them regarding their comfort level with even a small issue or their feeling of powerlessness over a larger one. Our kids may or may not admit to us what's really going on. If we're not sure what to say or do, just speaking up, airing our concern and our desire to work on a solution together, can make a significant difference to our children and their future happiness. We owe them this support and should do whatever it takes to summon the courage to voice our feelings to them (aloud or in writing). While we may not know the answer to the struggles our children face, and even though we must acknowledge that the battles they may face are not ours to fight, I do know our silence won't help and our support can't hurt.

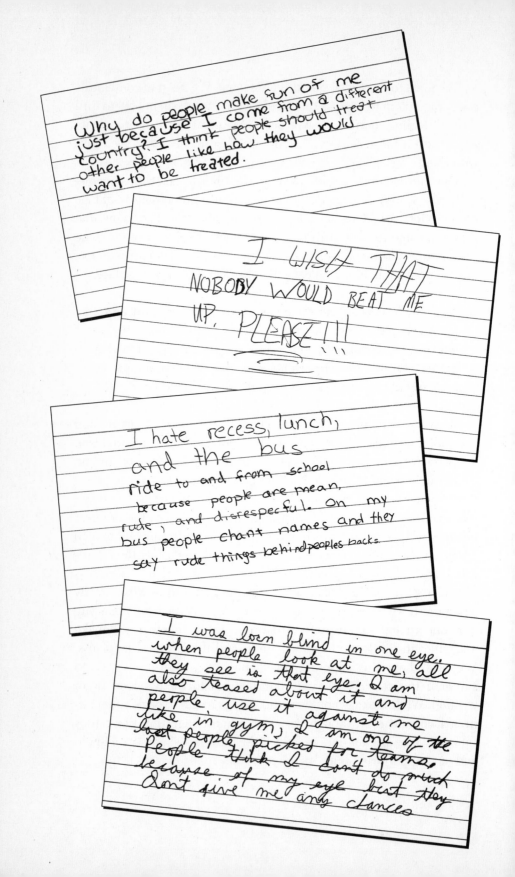

Why do people make fun of me just because I come from a different country? I think people should treat other people like how they would want to be treated.

I WISH THAT NOBODY WOULD BEAT ME UP, PLEASE!!!

I hate recess, lunch, and the bus ride to and from school because people are mean, rude, and disrespecful. On my bus people chant names and they say rude things behind peoples backs.

I was born blind in one eye. when people look at me, all they see is that eye. I am also teased about it and people use it against me like in gym, I am one of the last people picked for teams. People think I cant do much because of my eye but they dont give me any chances

4

ENCOURAGING RESPECT
FOR DIFFERENCES

For too many kids, being "different" means being taunted, teased, left out, gawked at, shunned, or beaten up. While I realize this is nothing new, it's definitely not okay. Based on what kids continue to share with me at my programs, the extent of disrespect, cruelty, and violence seems to be getting worse for our children instead of better.

This chapter will focus on how differences in others can affect the way kids relate to and treat each other. It will include perspectives and approaches that you can share with your own children to help enhance their sensitivity toward others and provide the tools to help break through barriers of discomfort that can be related to differences—their own or those of others. It will also offer you the opportunity to think about your own influence, what messages you might be giving to your kids about relating to others who are different from you in any way.

> I am involved in an interracial relationship and I want my parents to know but I'm afraid of what they'll say. How do I tell them this without hurting them because my parents are prejudiced?

I feel that one person is making my life hard. This person teases me about what I believe.

The anonymously written student questions and issues from my programs that I include throughout this chapter are testimony to how broad the spectrum of judging differences can be among our kids—and how heartless the comments can be.

Why do people insult or make fun of crippled people?

THE POWER OF PREJUDGMENTS

In the worst-case scenario, prejudgments can engender blind hatred and lead to unthinkable violence. With all the national and individual school efforts to help people of all ages deal with diversity, one would think and certainly hope that respect for differences would be much more widespread. That would be wonderful, but it's just not the way things really are.

While the word "violent" may be too dramatic to characterize most of the day-to-day behavior that goes on in the lunchroom, halls, at recess, in classrooms, or on the bus, children continue to tell me that teasing and other kinds of denigration that usually involves judgments related to differences still causes them a lot of hurt and anguish.

I am overweight. Everybody makes fun of me. I can't help I'm overweight. I think I'm a nice person. If people could give me a chance, they could see that too. Why don't they give me a chance?

There are kids who decide that they can't relate to someone because of their different appearance with respect to height, weight, clothes, perceived attractiveness, skin color, disability, or nationality. Sometimes children set others apart because of grades, if someone is in special classes, religion, where someone lives, how much money their family has, sports ability, gender, sexual orientation, and many other issues. Many children are ostracized or isolated before anyone even knows their name or anything at all about them as individuals.

I feel torn apart when I get teased. I wish people won't look at the clothes you wear, how much money you have, and where you shop to be able to talk to you or be good friends with you.

Many kids seem to view these differences as reason enough to justify being cruel.

I'm gay and people don't respect me for what I am. Who can I talk to about this?

We can teach our kids that they have a choice as to whether or not they wish to relate to someone, and a choice to make in their decision about how they treat other people. No matter how much a person's background might differ from our own, no matter how much the particular difference might be opposed to our own personal religious or other beliefs, we can still encourage our children to respect and value every human life.

We can also teach our children that if they don't like someone, they can leave that person alone and still respect that person's right to feel positive about him- or herself. We can help strengthen the skills for our children to be able to negotiate conflicts, work things out, learn they can agree to disagree and make compromises. They need to know that no one has a right to be demeaning, to tear someone down, to push someone around, to attack and violate another human being, physically, emotionally, sexually, or in any other way. Maybe through our children there can be hope for peace in our world, regardless of the many differences among the people who inhabit it.

While it's important to be mindful of what lessons to teach your son or daughter, it's crucial for you to know that you are already teaching powerful lessons every day by the example you set. If you make denigrating remarks, if you don't live in a manner that demonstrates what it means to respect and value all people, then any words you say to your children about kindness and respect might not be very meaningful, and may not even be heard.

During recess boys never pass to the girls. It is not fair. We are just as good as them. They are being so sexist.

I have a problem with a boy who always makes fun of my religion.

MORE WAYS TO HELP YOUR CHILD UNDERSTAND DIFFERENCES

Many kids don't know to appreciate the fact that while there could be a whole room of people with many kinds of "outside packaging," all of those people have different "inside packaging," as well. So, in addition to differences in looks, shapes, and sizes, each person has his or her own beliefs, own feelings and needs, own lessons that parents and family members have taught. Even kids in the same family who share the same family events will have their own personal feelings about what they experienced. No two people are exactly alike. Even identical twins have their own personalities. We're all different, all unique, all equal, and all valuable.

Why can't people like you for who you are instead of what you look like?

To pick this issue apart and illuminate it further, you can share the following possibility with your children:

Even if two kids were both born in the same town, both brought up with Catholic beliefs, both attended the same schools, were in the same classes, were on the same soccer team, both sang in the church choir, and their parents were friends, that doesn't mean that they would want to be friends. With all that they have in common, they may be very different from each other. Their personalities may just not connect. They might not even like each other.

Aside from reinforcing the idea of how different each person is, the lesson from this example can be broadened to include the idea that any dislike between these two children doesn't mean they need to or have a right to brutalize each other. No one has a right to be cruel to another person. They can still peacefully coexist at the same school, be in the same classes, be respectful in each other's company when they happen to be singing or playing soccer, and otherwise go their own way and have little or nothing to do with each other.

Sometimes hearing the same message said in a different way can help kids understand it better. So you have a few approaches to add to what you already might be sharing with your child. Choose whatever examples you think would be most relevant to your son or daughter in order to get the point across to respect all people

HELPING KIDS GET PAST DIFFERENCES

Many of the differences children are teased for come under the category of what I refer to as "outer packaging." Over the years, I have found that students respond positively to the perspective that there is a distinction between someone's outside appearance and who he or she is on the "inside." They seem to find it easy to grasp the idea that they don't become friends with a wheelchair or someone's clothes, but rather the person in that wheelchair or inside those clothes. You can use this concept to help your son or daughter understand this distinction with any other aspect of outer appearance that might be judged, such as, "You don't become friends with skin, you become friends with the person inside that skin, whether it's black, white, yellow, or green with polka dots." You can also apply this to other areas, and include words like these: "You don't become friends with grades or money. You become friends with a person who may or may not have those things."

Depending on the age of your child, you might want to take this even further. For example, you can add:

"You don't share secrets with a sweater! You share secrets with the person wearing that sweater. Whether the sweater is ragged and has holes in it, or is brand new . . . has nothing to do with whether that person will keep your secret. That has to do with who your friend is and how they relate to you."

The message to reinforce continually is "Be careful how you judge. What is most important about someone is something you can't see until you get to know them, until you spend some time together." I literally have gotten down on my hands and knees in front of large audiences of kids to reinforce the idea that they don't become friends with height, that someone's height is not who that person is. I ask kids questions such as, "Do you think I would be a different person if

I was this tall [on my hands and knees] or this tall [stepping up on a chair]? Would I be a different mom to my own kids, a different friend to my friends just because I was taller or shorter? Heavier or skinnier? Or if I was wearing sweatpants instead of what I'm wearing?"

I wish people would understand that if a person is very short, it doesn't make them any different from other kids.

Knowing beliefs or what someone looks like still doesn't tell you who that person is or who they could be to you in your life. The visual reinforcement can make this idea even easier for them to grasp.

You can help broaden your child's understanding with more specific examples. For instance:

Just knowing about someone's religious beliefs, where that person was born, or the color of a person's skin still doesn't tell kids if that person would be a good friend for them to have, a good parent, a good teacher, a good electrician, a good athlete, or anything else. Just knowing if someone is white, Asian, Italian, Jewish, Baptist, Native American, or Latino still doesn't tell kids if the person would be there for them if they were sad, has a great sense of humor, loves to collect stamps, prefers cats to dogs, likes mustard on turkey sandwiches, or is a vegetarian.

People make fun of me because I'm Irish and I wish people would give me a new chance. I am always misjudged.

There are kids and adults who would never dream of characterizing themselves as being prejudiced. They don't walk around consciously thinking, "I don't want that person as a friend"; it's not even a consideration. The stereotypes that kids learn to associate with those who are different can potentially be distancing as well as damaging without their even being aware of it.

I am judged by the color of my skin. People call me a Gandhi.

The earlier we teach this to our kids, the better. They need to be encouraged to give each other more of a chance. Even if their instinct is to judge initially, what they do with those judgments can begin to change.

ANOTHER KIND OF DIFFERENCE

I am gay.

The child who wrote the above card was in the seventh grade at the time. It may very well be that he is gay. It is also possible that he only thinks he is because of his perceptions of what being gay means—or because of his perception of how it seems other kids are defining him, especially if they're actually calling him "gay."

Because there is still a great deal of ignorance, stereotyping, discomfort, and fear related to homosexuality, this continues to be a difficult topic for people to discuss openly. And because this is such a sensitive topic area, children or adolescents are likely to keep any confusion silent.

How do I handle my gay tendencies?

The possibility or reality that a child is gay, lesbian, or bisexual can evoke many feelings that can be tough to handle, for parents as well as kids. Even if you feel that homosexuality is against your beliefs, it's still important to make sure your son or daughter knows that your door for communication is open. It would help for you to initiate a discussion to offset any confusion that your child might be experiencing, as well as create the opportunity to address homophobia. A child will probably be reluctant to bring the subject up, especially if he or she could have written one of these cards.

I am gay. How do I tell my parents?

I am kind of interested in people of the same sex. What should I do about this? I'm scared it will get out in a small school like this.

Depending on what your sense is about what your child might be dealing with personally, you can choose to focus on the possibility that your child might feel such confusion or simply broaden the concern for understanding and respecting others who are homosexual. Unfortunately, as with other areas of concern, the media are an excellent source for reinforcing and talking further with our children about the need to embrace and honor the idea that each human being is valuable, regardless of differences. Just recently, the death of a college student was in the news. He was beaten, tied up, and left to die, an assault reportedly related to the fact that he was gay.

I interviewed one woman, now in her forties, who told me she tried to commit suicide when she was a teenager because she was so confused about her preference to relate to other women. At that point, she said she had not spoken with anyone about her feelings. I interviewed a thirteen-year-old girl who talked extensively with me about how hard it was to listen to her friends make fun of "people who are gay," and how even though she laughed along with them, she was feeling so pained, thinking, "They're talking about my mother!" She said she kept the fact that her mother is a lesbian secret from all of her friends except one. I recently talked with a young man who told me his male partner came out to his family just a few years ago. They didn't accept his homosexuality. He said that when his partner's father was terminally ill in the hospital, his partner flew out to try to make peace with him, and even then, his father wouldn't recognize him as a member of the family because he is gay.

Since there's no way to predict that a child will be gay, lesbian, or bisexual, it is even more important to create the chance to help kids understand all the kinds of information about feelings related to homosexuality that might otherwise breed confusion or fear. The need to bring up the subject is not only to help your child make early peace with any potentially confusing feelings related to his or her sexual orientation but also to add an important dimension of understanding and respect for others.

IT'S NATURAL, EVEN OKAY, TO FEEL UNCOMFORTABLE

It's normal for adults as well as kids to feel uncomfortable with those who are of a different background or are different in any other way. Feelings of discomfort aren't a testimony to the need to avoid relating to someone. All being uncomfortable means is that you're uncomfortable. That's okay. It's not okay to let being uncomfortable prevent our kids (or us) from crossing lines of differences, anyway.

How do you talk to a colored person when you don't know their name and you don't want to hurt their feelings? P.S. I have nothing against colored people.

We can suggest to our kids that they take a chance. We can even suggest to our kids that they can say to someone, "Hi. I'm Sam. I'm sorry, but I don't know your name. . . ." Or "I'm a little uncomfortable because I never spoke before with a person who was in a wheelchair." Or "If I seem a little uncomfortable, I just want you to know I've never been with someone from your background before. It's really good to meet you. I hope we can become friends." Little by little, our kids can find out that they can increase their comfort level if they reach out and give someone a chance. The building of trust and comfort takes time.

As our children get older and move on to high school or college, the cafeterias are usually clearly sectioned off by groupings. No matter what the complexion of their school population, they'll probably still find kids hanging out together with others who are like them. African-American students will likely be sitting with other African-American students. Hispanic students with other Hispanic students. Asian students with other Asian students. International students with international students. Football players with other football players. Drama kids with other kids who are involved with drama. Those in Greek organizations with fellow Greeks. And so forth. It takes courage to cross the invisible cafeteria lines, courage and a conscious decision to cross similar lines that exist in clubs and organizations in which the majority of people are of one background or another. This, too, is a choice our kids can make. We can help them understand this effort that is often involved with reaching out to new and different people. We can also share with them the rewards that choosing a variety of friends will bring. They don't have to remain bound by the boundaries that seem to exist naturally. They can choose to broaden their world and hopefully have the opportunity to enrich the world of others, one person at a time.

PERSONAL CONTROL, OWNERSHIP, RESPECTFUL CHOICES

We need to help our kids understand that no matter what they feel (or what they believe they feel) about another person, they still have a choice as to how they wish to act upon those feelings. They can choose to be respectful, choose to be kind, choose to leave that person alone. We can and must teach kids that they are capable of taking personal control over what they allow themselves to do in another person's regard. No matter what anyone else is doing, each child needs to (and can) dictate his or her own behavior. Relaying this message is very different from telling kids how to feel. The message here is even if they believe they hate someone's guts, it's what children do about those feelings that matters. We need to impress upon them that this is what they can control. Even with hatred, there can be peace and respect. It's a choice.

PARENTAL ROLE MODELING

Perhaps this is a good time to take stock of what messages you might be giving your son or daughter about relating to those who might be different from you in any way. Lessons about relating to others start when our children are infants. Whether we cross the street to avoid a group of people who are of another race, or to avoid someone who is missing a leg, whether we go out of our way to speak with someone who moves around in a wheelchair; or whether we make disrespectful or degrading references about people who are homosexual or about those who have different religious backgrounds, children of all ages pick up on the messages we send in this regard. As I've said before, our messages can be a very powerful influence. Even one remark, one look, can have an impact on our children for a lifetime.

> My dad is prejudiced against blacks and Mexicans. He won't even let me talk to them, but I would like to. What should I do?

While some parents are more accepting, I've spoken with students who have shared with me that although they were best of friends with children of a different race, they could not be invited to their home (not even their birthday party), and in many cases could not invite them home.

I recently heard a wonderful story that lends insight to a child's perspective on this issue. It happened at my friend's grandson's birthday party. When he turned five a few years ago, his parents arranged for him to invite a few friends from school to celebrate with him by having lunch together at one of those special kids'-type lunch places near their home. When the birthday lunch day arrived, Jimmy told his mother that he was so happy that his friend Brian was going to be there. Then he proceeded to describe Brian so his mother would know who he was when he walked in. He told his mother Brian was a little bigger than he was and had black curly hair. When Brian walked in, he certainly had lots of black curly hair and he also had black skin. Her grandson had never mentioned that his friend, Brian, is African-American. That wasn't his focus. Her grandson saw him as his friend, not as his "black friend." We have much to learn from young children. They are usually able to see people purely for the beauty of who they are.

You might find it helpful to answer the following for yourself:

- Do you think your son or daughter would say you are accepting, non-accepting, comfortable or not so comfortable with people who are different? Do you consider yourself more or less comfortable or accepting?
- Is your family background different from that of most families in your community? How has that been received, how does that make you feel? If this is so, what do you think has been the impact on your son or daughter?
- Do you have close personal friends of a different background?
- Have you ever told your kids that they could not associate with or invite someone to your home because of their differences?
- Has your son or daughter ever been the brunt of teasing or fighting because of differences?

Your answers can help you be much more aware of what your own feelings are and what you have been teaching your children about relating to others who are different in any way. If any of your answers are troubling to you, remember that while you can't go backward, you can learn from everything. You, as well as your children, have the capacity to go forward with greater sensitivity and greater respect for others—if you choose to do so.

> **Why do people treat me like nothing? Just because someone's different doesn't make him stupid, dumb, or just disliked all the time.**

You are in a marvelous position to help influence the way your son or daughter respects and relates to other people. If you identified any negatives in your own manner of relating, you can talk with your child, acknowledge what you wish to put in different perspective, and all of you can decide to work at going forward in a more positive, open way.

CREATING TEACHABLE MOMENTS

Why is the world full of violence?

The news reports on television and radio, and in newspapers, about riots, hate crimes, and other kinds of violence are very prevalent. There always seems to be something in the news that is related to how people deal with their differences in a violent, negative way. Discussion of these incidents provides an ideal chance to reinforce with your child how destructive such violence can be. It's also an ideal time to teach your son or daughter that just because one or even a group of people of a certain background act in a hateful manner, it doesn't mean that is a reflection of their entire race, nationality, or whatever else is applicable.

There are also news articles and publicity about wonderful things like Special Olympics or acts of heroism in which someone of one background saved a person of another background. Even if the issue of background is not the main focus of a particular report, that's a wonderful thing for you to center in on when you talk with your child about it. Kids can gain from being reminded that we are all in this world together and that we need to be there for each other.

Use any opportunity that comes up to reinforce the way we can get past differences. When my kids were younger, one day I took them to play on the playground at a park near our home. There was a man in a motorized wheelchair who was there by himself. He was watching the children play. I took my kids by the hand and walked them over to him. When I approached him, I said, "That's an amazing wheelchair!", teaching my kids this was not something I intended to ignore.

In response to my comment, the man proceeded to tell us all about how he travels in this chair. He described his day trips and other special excursions. My kids and I talked afterward about the feelings they had as they first approached him and how much more comfortable they were after we spoke with him for a while. They realized he was just a "regular person" who happened to need a wheelchair to help him move about.

You can find other teachable moments around holiday time. No matter what your own religious beliefs, it can be positive to talk with your child about the belief systems of others and how others celebrate and observe their holidays. You can offer your child the opportunity to invite a friend or friend's family who is of a differing background to join your family in your holiday celebration. When and if you go shopping with your child, you can talk about kids who may not have the financial ability to shop at certain stores or who may need to rely on hand-me-downs and donations from other sources.

> **People make fun of me because I have big teeth. I wish people would stop calling me names because I have big teeth. I feel very sad when they call me names. I wish I could just be perfect.**

If you're taking your child to the dentist or orthodontist, you can talk about how some kids aren't able to have their teeth straightened, as this is very costly. Find any and every way you can think of to nurture sensitivity for differences and teach your child that clothes or other possessions are just that. They're not who a person is, they don't define a person, they aren't a measure of who can be a good friend.

Books about people of differing backgrounds can be taken out of the library and shared with your child. There are also books for young children that help them understand that, regardless of our differences, we are very much the same in many ways.

There are so many areas of differences. These deserve to be appreciated, understood, and respected. To do so, you can go to art displays, such as Egyptian or African exhibits. You can make special efforts to order handiwork created by people who have disabilities. You can also take your son or daughter to visit a nursing home or volunteer with you at a soup kitchen. You can go on AIDS marches and watch and discuss movies, such as *Philadelphia*, with your kids. Our active teaching and nurturing can help foster these feelings. Our differences deserve to be celebrated rather than feared. Differences can be so enriching if we can teach our children that it's possible to share each other's worlds.

The more you expose to your child with the idea of trying to help broaden his or her world, the more of a chance your child will be open to, gain from, and be more respectful of differences in others.

IF YOUR CHILD SAYS, "WHAT CAN I DO? I'M ONLY ONE PERSON . . ."

Children often feel helpless in the face of all the violence and disrespect there is in the world. Their tendency is to think, "What could one person, one child do?" They need to know they can do a lot more than they might think.

While children cannot control an entire nation, a state, a city, or even a school, they can control themselves. That can count for a lot. Ask your son or daughter to consider what significant change could take place if each child made the decision to respect, honor, and appreciate that each person is a valuable human being. Together with your child, you can think of specific situations in which he or she would have the chance to make a difference. For example, if when sitting at a lunch table, somebody makes a mean remark to another person, your child has the power to choose how to respond. To the person who said the remark, he or she can say something like, "I don't think that was a good thing to say," or "Come on, leave them alone." To the person or group targeted by the remark, your child can say, "Don't pay any attention to him [or her]." (Ideas about what your child can say if he or she is the one being picked on are shared in the next chapter, on teasing.)

Your child's decision not to go along with the cruelty is a statement of strength and courage, of caring about others. It's one that actually might serve as a terrific role model for others who were too scared to stand up for what they secretly believed. Your child might find that next time there will be more kids who won't go along with the abuse. Each child can contribute toward making a difference on a one-to-one basis. Each child who stops or stands up to cruelty contributes another stone in building the path toward peace.

I Be myself, still nobody likes me, in my class.

I wish people wouldn't look at me as a Bullie. I wish people wouldn't be scared of me too.

My Best Friend is really nice But She always makes fun of me. Weve Been Best friends for along time. + I don't know how to tell her how I feel

Sometimes kids call me a dork and stooped, because I were glasses. I feel that my heart is broken.

5

DEALING WITH TEASING

Teasing can make a kid's life miserable. Some kids are the brunt of it every single day. Even for those who are targeted only once in a while, teasing can be powerful enough to cause kids to doubt themselves, not to want to come to school, feel worthless, and wonder why they were ever born. That's not fair or acceptable.

As I said in chapter 4 with regard to disrespect for differences in others, this is nothing new. Unfortunately, we all know kids tease. Teasing has been going on ever since I can remember. It certainly took place when I was growing up. You probably have your own stories.

But the issue is that it's today. Teasing is still here, and our kids need help. The cruelty that I'm documenting now is even more extensive than it was more than twenty years ago, when I started my programs.

I feel awful sometimes about myself when people make fun of me. Why do people have to make fun of other people? I have a hip disease and people call me a faker. I don't really feel very special.

I've been in schools where whole months have been designated with themes such as "kindness month" or "make a new friend" month or "be nice to people who are different" month. Many teachers across the country have told me how their classes have created "class rules" together to deal with stopping put-downs and getting everyone to behave in a nicer manner to each other. The push for greater kindness (even "random acts") is something that is much more conscious, much more public than it probably ever was. Still, there are kids who are hurting terribly from being teased.

Considering all the creative efforts to stop the denigration from taking place, I have been able to figure out only one thing that has a chance to actually work. I believe the real solution boils down to helping kids take personal control in how they respond to what they cannot control—meaning, how they can respond if others choose to tease. We need to help them realize that they can still hold on to who they are, no matter what anyone says or does. No one's words or looks or behavior toward our children can take away from who they are and how they value themselves, unless they allow that to happen. I'm not suggesting that this perspective is easy to embrace. That kind of thinking takes great strength and trust in the fact that no matter what, "I'm still okay."

I often say to audiences of kids that I wish I had a magic wand. I wish I had the power to make everyone be kinder to each other. I wish someone did. But I know that no one can have the power to control anyone else but themselves. That power has to come from a decision made within each person. We need to remind our children that they have this power within them. They just need to call upon it.

This chapter is dedicated to helping you help your children understand why others (or they themselves) might tease and be more aware of how they can effectively respond if they get teased. To me, the anonymously written sharings I've included here are gut-wrenching. It is my hope that they will be a compelling testimony to the need for all of us to reach out more actively to the children in our lives in order to raise awareness, encourage respect, and build greater sensitivity for others, regardless of differences.

WHY KIDS MIGHT TEASE

It can help for you to talk together about why kids might tease, especially if your son or daughter is getting teased. If you provide your children with a greater understanding of the reasons for teasing, they may well be able to put any harsh words that come their way into better perspective. If your child is one who teases, looking at and talking about why he or she does that can also be beneficial. My hope is that by identifying the real underlying reason for teasing, he or she will decide to leave others alone and be able to face whatever personal issues your child is struggling with in a private, more positive way.

> **I have a good friend, but me and my other best friend always mock her out and tease her, and we both really like her, but it's so much fun to be mean to her. I don't want to hurt her and I don't think it does 'cause she (I think) knows we're kidding. But I'm not sure!**

Here are reasons that kids at my programs have told me people tease (not in any particular order):

- They don't like someone
- They do it because friends are doing it (peer pressure)
- They think it's fun or cool
- They don't feel good about themselves, so they try to make others appear worse
- They are abused at home and are taking out their feelings on other kids
- They want to be hurtful to someone
- They want to point out or are not accepting of someone's differences
- They want to get back at someone else because they were teased

Whether your son or daughter is the "teasee," teaser, or has never been involved with teasing, it is important to talk about why kids tease and the need to stop the hurt. Each child who realizes how truly destructive teasing can be has a greater chance of toning down his or her teasing and becoming more respectful.

IF YOUR CHILD IS THE BRUNT

Here are some perspectives that you can share with your child to help him or her remain positive or at least attempt to start feeling more positive if he or she is the target of a lot of teasing:

- Just because someone calls your child a name, that doesn't make it true.

   So being called a "loser" doesn't mean your son or daughter actually is a loser. If the whole group of kids your child hangs around with are referred to by others as "losers," that doesn't make your child a loser just because he or she is their friend.

How come when you're with losers you're someone, but when you're with other people you're nobody?

- No one has the power to define your child unless he or she allows that person to do so. Teased or not, kids can hold on to who they are and how they feel about themselves.
- While children cannot make someone else respect them, they can hold on to their own sense of self-respect, which is not tied to or dependent on anything outside of themselves.

It can be helpful to let kids know that we realize these perspectives are easier for us to share and much harder for them to hold on to. Let your child know you understand how difficult it can be when others continue to tease even when their responses change. Tell them you realize that teasing can hurt even when it doesn't shake their self-image and that no matter how strong their confidence is, others will be able to inflict pain if they choose. Explain that this has happened to you and happens to just about everyone, even adults.

Why do some people have no respect for themselves and humiliate themselves just to get attention?

If your son or daughter is the brunt of teasing, it may also be important to explore and discuss the possibility that he or she is behaving in ways that are annoying to other kids. For example, does he or she:

- follow kids around, like a "leech"?
- frequently copy what other kids say or do?
- tease others?
- make bothersome noises?
- spread negative rumors?
- brag or show off?
- touch private areas of his or her body in public?

If any of this is what's going on, it will likely help to reduce or even eliminate any cruelty toward your child if he or she makes the effort to behave in a more positive manner.

WAYS TO RESPOND TO TEASING

Most kids feel more confident if they at least have a menu of response choices they can call upon if faced with someone who puts them down. Here are some ideas, in no special order, that you can suggest to children who are the target of teasing:

NONVERBAL

- Ignore whatever is said
- Walk away
- Put a big smile on your face, say nothing, and just stare at the person who said something mean, keeping that big smile as wide as possible. This shows that you don't care what was said and the person didn't "get to you."
- Make believe there is a shield of armor preventing the words from getting inside. The invisible shield can also cause the words to rebound right back to the person who said them.

VERBAL

- Say, "Cut it out"

I'm always wondering how do I say cut it out? I was in a situation where I was getting made fun of. And I didn't know how to say cut it out, without hurting his or her feelings!

- Say, "Please don't say that to me again. I really didn't like what you called me."
- To someone who teases about clothes:

    "If you don't like my clothes, that's fine. I like them. I'll remember never to lend them to you!"
- To someone who teases about size:

    "I love it when you call me shrimp! Say it again . . . come on, say it again."
- To someone who often says mean things:

    "If you hate me so much, I don't understand why you're spending so much time following me around." To this your child can add: "Sorry if it may seem rude, but I'm not going to stand around here listening to you. See ya around . . . Have a great day!"
- To someone who often says mean things:

    "You really don't even know me. I'll bet if you spent time with me, you'd find that I'm really a good friend to have."
- To someone who wants to fight:

    "Hey, you might like bloody noses. But I don't. I don't want to fight you. Let's just say that you won. If you don't like me, that's okay. Don't be my friend. Let's just stay out of each other's way."

I wish that I will not have to retaliate with my fists to mean people.

Note: This is a tough situation. Many kids have said to me that talking won't be as powerful as just fighting off certain people. I'm not suggesting that kids ought not to defend themselves if someone starts pushing them around and they risk being physically hurt. I am saying that if fighting can be avoided, that should be a first choice.
- If talking directly to the person who is teasing does not work:

    Encourage kids to ask an adult for help. Besides speaking with parents, kids can approach teachers, coaches, and other staff members for help. It is best for kids to have these conversations in private. Sometimes it can make a difference if an adult steps in and helps ease the situation by changing classroom seats so the person who is being teased does not sit close to the one who is teasing.

Since it is up to the person who teases to make the decision to stop, there is no way to guarantee when and with whom each of these responses will work. If one response doesn't work, tell your son or daughter they can try another.

Here again, it is essential for kids to be reminded that they can control only themselves. They cannot control what someone else says or does. So if they tell someone to "Please, cut it out!" no one can promise that person will stop. The only thing we can promise is that the person might not know your son or daughter wants them to stop unless he or she says so. If someone continues to tease, regardless of what efforts are made to get him or her to stop, children need to be reminded that they still can stay in control of what they do in response to the teasing.

Deciding just how involved we parents ought to be when our kids are the brunt of teasing is tough. When my son was in elementary school, there was one boy who constantly bothered him. That kid teased and pushed him around, and basically made his life miserable. After my son tried everything we could think of to get the boy to leave him alone, my husband and I finally decided it was time to call his parents. It turned out that was the best decision. Whatever they said to their son made the difference, and he no longer bothered our son. If your child is the brunt of teasing, it might also help for you to discuss this concern with your child's teacher. He or she may be able to shed further light on what steps might be positive for your child to take in order to deal with this situation.

WHEN CLOSE FRIENDS TEASE, EVEN AS A "JOKE"

Sometimes teasing comes from close friends. That can make it even harder for kids to be honest about how this makes them feel. They often laugh along with everyone else when, deep down, they're feeling humiliated, embarrassed, and hurt. Silence about their true response is usually fueled by fear that if they told their friends how upset they are, that might ruin the friendship. So they may continue to laugh on the outside and not let anyone know they're really crying on the inside.

As parents, we can help by offering insight that will enable our kids to be more sensitive to what their friends might feel and not tell in response to remarks that are supposedly meant only to be "joking." We can also reinforce perspectives and ways to express difficult feelings if our kids are the ones who are jokingly put down.

Here's a sample dialogue sequence your child might find useful as a pattern for responding to a friend who teases:

Your son or daughter to friend:

> "I know I laughed with everyone when you said _____ at the lunch table. I didn't know what else to do. Really, I was so embarrassed. I need you to know that I really didn't think it was so funny. Please don't say that again."

If that friend says it again:

> "I know I already said this to you. Maybe you didn't realize that I was serious. I really don't like it when you say _____ in front of everyone. Please don't say it again. I mean it."

If the friend says it again:

> "I don't get it. We're really good friends. I know if you told me something mattered to you, I'd try to respect that. I'm having a hard time understanding why you keep saying what I've asked you not to say. You may not mean it, but I really feel hurt and embarrassed when you say that. I don't want you to say that to me anymore."

If the friend says it again:

> "This is really hard for me to say to you. You're my good friend. I have always loved being with you. But I'm not going to be with you if you continue to say things that make me feel uncomfortable. So I'm switching tables. When you're ready to not say that anymore—let me know.

This kind of dialogue progression can be applied to many other social situations, and, naturally, it can be reconstructed with your child in his or her own words. The dialogue reflects how kids can express their own feelings and remain in control of their response to whatever their friend or anyone else decides to do. So even if friends continue to tease, children can ultimately choose to remove themselves from that situation and, in my example, that particular friend. That is how we can help teach our children to retain their own sense of dignity and still leave room for others to change.

IF SOMEONE TEASES YOUR CHILD'S FRIEND

I've got a very good friend in my class. People mock her out constantly and she tells me she doesn't care, but I still hurt for her. What should I do to help her?

Kids are often faced with a difficult decision as to what they can say or do to support a friend who is being teased. One major worry is that if they stick up for the friend by actually saying something like, "Why don't you leave him alone!" or "BUG OFF!" or even "Stop being such a bully and pick on someone your own size," those people who are teasing might turn on them. The reality is that it is possible.

A safer consideration is to simply pull that friend aside and say something like:

"Don't pay attention to them. Don't let them bother you. They don't even know you. You're a great person. They're such jerks!"

While this may not change what is being said to that friend, it can help the friend trust that no matter what anyone says, your child is there for them. Children often don't realize how much of a difference those few words of support can make to those they are close to.

IF YOUR CHILD IS THE TEASER

There is more than one answer, more than one approach that might be applicable if your child is teasing someone else. I don't agree with blaming kids who tease for their cruelty; nor do I agree with attempting to make them feel guilty. Rather, I suggest that it would be more effective to approach a child who teases with genuine concern for those who are on the receiving end, and use the situation to explore why he or she might be teasing.

Here are some ways to begin the conversation with your son or daughter:

- "With all that I understand is happening between you and other kids at school, I'm concerned that you're okay. A lot of times when kids tease, they really don't feel good about themselves. What's going on? Do you feel angry, unhappy, or frustrated with something or someone?"
- "I understand that you're treating other kids in a way that is not right. It's not okay to say mean things and push other kids around. If you don't like someone, that's your choice. Just leave them alone. But I'm concerned about you. Do you have any idea what might be going on to cause you to behave that way?
- If you are within hearing distance when your son or daughter says something you feel is hurtful: "I couldn't help hearing what you said to _____. Maybe you were just kidding around and didn't mean to hurt anyone's feelings. But if someone said that to me, that would be very painful. I know I'd have a hard time."

SOME OTHER FACTORS THAT MAY BE HELPFUL TO INCORPORATE

- Sometimes kids act in ways that aren't so nice because it's the only way they think that people will pay attention to them.
- Sometimes kids try to make themselves seem like the "class clown" because it's the only way they think they can get attention. They feel neglected and feel that negative attention is better than no attention.
- Sometimes kids buckle under peer pressure. They think they won't be included or considered "cool" if they don't tease along with their friends.

Your son or daughter may or may not acknowledge that any of these possibilities actually is right on target with what they know they're dealing with or feeling. At the very least, by raising these concerns, you will let your child know that you know what's going on and what may be the cause. Regardless of what your child chooses to admit, you can take this opportunity to encourage more respectful behavior.

If you find it appropriate to consider contacting the parent or guardian of kids that you know your son or daughter is plaguing with put-downs, it may help to keep in mind that being honest is the best approach. For example, you can say to the parent of the child your son or daughter puts down:

"This is a bit awkward for me to be calling you. I understand that my son/daughter has been making life pretty difficult for your child. I feel terrible about this. That kind of behavior is unacceptable. I wanted you to know that we're working with our son/daughter and hope he/she will behave in a more respectful way. I'd appreciate it if you would let me know if my son/daughter continues to bother your child."

WHEN KIDS WHO TEASE DECIDE TO STOP

Reputation is hard to escape and outgrow.

Children who tease and make other kinds of trouble are often labeled "trouble" at school. The problem is that even when they decide to make positive changes, others may still regard them as "trouble." This might result in frustration and anger on the child's part and may ultimately lead to a return to negative behavior if the child isn't helped to understand that it may take some time and energy before people's opinion begins to change.

If your son or daughter is dealing with a similar decision to change his or her negative behavior, it's important to explain that it may take a while for other kids to trust the change. It may also help to remind kids that they can't go backward, can't change what they have already said or done that might have been hurtful to others. However, they are capable of learning from everything and certainly can decide to go forward in a more positive way. Explain to your children that they don't deserve to beat themselves up emotionally for what they did in the past. They shouldn't be discouraged by how long others may take to give them a new chance. They need to trust that they're doing the right thing by being nicer and realize that while they're not in control of when others begin to give them a new chance, they are in control of remaining nice and giving themselves a new chance.

I wish my friends
really knew what
I felt inside and
If they knew would
they still like me

I don't know what to do when
someone spreads a roomer about me because you
ask people who started it and they all say
someone different, and you don't want to
convict anyone.

I am in a group where everyone
smokes, and I guess I do when
I'm with them but I really
dont want to. What should I
do. And I want different
friends like there's a crowd I
want to get into but I don't
know what to say or do?

Just because I like someone, people
don't like me. I want to be friends
with him and with the other kids The
other kids will leave me if I'm friends
with him. What should I do? This is
pretty ludicrous situation
  From,
"Confused"

6

FRIENDSHIP AND POPULARITY

I have observed again and again that far too many children lack the communication skills, understanding, and confidence to handle effectively the daily ins and outs of their peer relationships.

Even the smoothest friendship between seemingly confident kids can be interrupted or otherwise affected by such things as jealousy, misunderstanding, fights, rumors, who "likes" whom (as a boyfriend or girlfriend), competition, disappointments, being left out, pressure to "keep up" or do what everyone else is doing, embarrassments, secrets that weren't kept, pressure to be loyal to one person or group instead of another, dishonesty, developmental differences, and the list could go on and on. Popular or not, it is the rare child who is exempt from facing many of these concerns during his or her growing-up years. And it is the rare parent who doesn't have to deal with the toll any of these concerns can take on his or her child, and be faced with how to help.

Some kids try to buy friendships, whereas others allow themselves to be used or feel they have to act in ways that are just not true to themselves in order to "belong." Kids who appeared to be right in the center of their crowd have admitted how much they worry about being regarded as a tag-along and have talked with me about how hard it is wondering from day to day if they'll be included in their group tomorrow. Thousands of kids have asked how they can tell if the friends they believe they have are truly their friends. Thousands more have shared the pain they feel because they don't have any friends.

To help your child deal with friendships, this chapter provides perspectives about relationships that might widen your child's perceived options, presents ideas you can share to help your son or daughter handle a variety of friendship situations that kids often find difficult to handle, and points out patterns children can be taught for communicating feelings that they often find hard to share.

I have two friends that hate each other. I can't stand it. What should, or can, I do?

The anonymously written cards that I have included in this chapter reflect how difficult it is for kids to be honest, even with their closest friends, and how confusing many of the social situations they face can be. While I recognize that each circumstance is unique, and that even the same situation will be viewed and handled differently by each child, it is my hope that the patterns of approaches I set forth will represent guidelines that you will find helpful when dealing with your own child's challenges.

My focus here is less on what kids may not share with their parents about friendship issues and more on what kids find hard to share with the friends they are involved with. Since it's also true that children might not approach their parents for advice on these issues, the more aware you are of what your son or daughter might be dealing with and not telling, the more helpful you can be with the subtle observations you may make and advice you may offer them without being asked.

A PERSPECTIVE ON POPULARITY

Wish I was popular.

A very wise eighth-grade boy once told me, "I'm very popular in my unpopular group!" Few kids seem to have this perspective. Few kids understand that what's most significant is how they feel with the friends they have.

What importance do you think your son or daughter places on being popular? The way children perceive how they fit in among friends and classmates can significantly contribute to, or take away from, how they value themselves.

Some kids truly don't care about being considered popular. The thought of popularity may be nice but not necessary for their day-to-day happiness. To others, popularity seems vital. Those in the latter group who aren't included may spend years feeling frustrated and disappointed as they wait and hope to be "let in" by what they consider to be the popular crowd. While being in the popular group might cause a child to feel wonderful, simply being included doesn't guarantee a sense of security and belonging.

Although I have a crowd, I still sometimes feel left out, as if I don't fit in—what should I do?

One mother told me that she walked into her daughter's room very late one night and found her in the process of writing down everything she was planning to say the next day to her new group of friends. She said, "She's been wanting to be part of that crowd for years. They're the most popular group in the school. Now that's she's finally 'in,' she seems to feel a great deal of pressure to stay in."

Since kids may or may not openly admit their feelings of insecurity, it might be very helpful for you to further contemplate your child's social interaction. If your son or daughter is part of a group that is regarded as popular, consider whether he or she:

· feels a strong sense of belonging

   If so, great. If not, you might start a conversation with something like:

   "I realize how important it is to you that you're part of that group of kids. And I'm so happy for you that you're finally hanging around with them. You've wanted to for a long time.

   But sometimes, even when kids hang out with a group, they may not feel like they're really part of the group. That can be very confusing and hard to deal with. You seem to worry a lot that if you don't call them, they won't call you. I

was wondering if you feel okay with them. How are things
really going?"

Or:

"I don't know if I ever told you this, but when I was in the
sixth grade, there was this group of kids who I really wanted
to hang around with. . . ." and go on to focus on the issues
that might parallel what you feel your son or daughter is
dealing with.

**I'm not as popular as I'd like, and whenever I'm around my
friends who are more popular, I feel useless. Like I'm weird or
something.**

Referencing your own experience rather than directing the
conversation to your child's situation can be less threatening
and still give you the leeway to share what you felt, how you
handled it, how your friends responded, and so on.

**I am kind of friends with the popular people. I want to be
better friends with them, but I'm afraid that I'll have to
be someone I'm not.**

· feels the need to behave and respond in what you feel is a
different, possibly negative way, in order to be accepted?
   If so, you might start with:
   "Ever since you started hanging out with _____, I've
noticed that you've been acting different. You've been kind
of fresh to me when your friends have come over, and I
couldn't help but hear you talk to your sister in a way that I
never heard before. I'm worried that maybe you think you
have to act tough just to be cool for your new friends.
   "You may not be doing that on purpose, but I'd really
appreciate it if you would speak with us in a nicer way when
your friends are here (you always do when they're not).
Maybe it would help you to think about how you feel about

your friends and why you might have thought you needed to sound that way.

"I know those kids are important to you, and maybe it would help for us to talk about this after you've had a chance to think about why you're acting this way."

These sample approaches may or may not touch a nerve. Even if they do, your son or daughter may not choose to admit that you're on target with your concerns. At the very least, you will have raised the subject and let your child know that you're aware of the possibility that something isn't quite right.

Depending on the circumstances and your child's response, you can then consider sharing any of the variety of perspectives I've included in this chapter that relate to understanding what makes a friend a true friend, that kids don't deserve to have to beg for friendships or compromise who they are just to be accepted. Even popular children often worry about remaining popular. Security one week can turn into insecurity the next. It all depends on what's going on. These perspectives I share may help you talk with your child regardless of his or her perceived popularity status.

I guess that I'm in the popular group, but they all have so much money, and great clothes. My best friend I don't even really like. I can't keep up with all the popular kids.

If you find that your son or daughter is not receptive to conversation related to pressure to keep up with his or her popular group, you might find it more effective to write a note that can be read privately. You can start with:

"From the way you answered me, I have a feeling that this is not an easy topic for you. It seemed like you didn't want to talk about it, and I didn't want to push our conversation. But I'm concerned and wanted to at least share my thoughts. I hope they help you to think through your own feelings."

You might end with:

"If you want to talk after you read this, I'll be downstairs."

That will help to relieve any pressure to respond yet keep the door open.

I used to be so popular.

OTHER POPULARITY ISSUES

Kids Who Don't Consider Themselves to be Popular

Many kids who are not part of the popular group feel that the people who are popular think they're better than everyone else. Although it's true that certain popular kids really do put other kids down and act as if they think they're superior, other popular kids are wonderful role models and treat everyone around them with respect.

People don't judge me, I'm very popular. I am respectful and therefore respected.

How can you tell if you are becoming unpopular?

Even when kids in the popular group act in a respectful way, there is just something about the fact that someone is "popular" that can be very intimidating to those who feel they're not.

Whether your son or daughter is the one who might be intimidated or the one who is "popular," it would be important to reinforce perspectives about how kids value themselves and the need to respect differences in others. Periodically, it can help to remind children that everyone is equal and worthy of respect regardless of differences, as discussed in the previous chapter.

How do you build up the courage to talk to popular people?

If you sense that your child is the one who feels like a "loser," you can also reinforce that no one can make someone feel worthless unless that person allows him or her (gives the power) to do so. Children need to be reminded again and again that while they cannot control what someone else says or does, they can stay in control over what they do and how they think of themselves.

Kids Who Consider Themselves Popular

I want to play with an unpopular girl. What should I do!

Ms. Pop

As I have touched upon, popularity is sometimes its own special burden for children. Worry about how popular friends will react to time spent with someone who is not in the same group can often cause confusion for someone who might be considered "in." Here are a few thoughts that you might find helpful to share with your child if he or she is dealing with this kind of dilemma:

- Each person has a right to decide who he or she wishes to have as a friend.
- If "Ms. Pop" wishes to play with "an unpopular girl," that's her choice. I hope she did! If she makes that choice, that ought have nothing to do with the time she spends with her popular friends.
- If her popular friends make an issue of the time Ms. Pop was with that other girl, she could say: "She's nice. I like her." If need be, she can add: "If you don't want to be her friend, that's okay. I do."

    One friendship need not have anything to do with another. If her popular friends like her for who she is, it should not matter who else she is friends with. When she's with them, she can appreciate being with them, and when she chooses to be with this other girl, they don't have to join her if they don't want to.

One of my friends is nice to me, but when popular kids come she thinks I am not alive. What should I do?

I hate my best friend.

During the elementary- and middle-school years, friendships may change dramatically. Children who are popular one week might become unpopular the next. Kids who were considered unpopular one year might find themselves at the top of the popularity list the following year. New friendships may develop with those your child never dreamed he or she could be close with; other friends that your child thought would be there forever may grow distant, for reasons that are hard to figure out.

Most kids are not prepared to handle all of these changes. Too many depend on being "let in" to one group or another and place too much meaning in whether or not that happens. We can help our children tremendously by teaching them that they don't have to depend on someone letting them in to a certain crowd. They have the control to start a friendship. They can form their own group. They also can choose how they would like to view being popular. What does that term mean, anyway? Discuss this with your child. I've even met kids who told me they wanted to be popular but couldn't stand the popular kids. So what's popularity, anyway? It's all that your child makes of it. Simply hearing that they do have some power in this popularity game can help your child feel less like a pawn and understand they are capable of becoming more like the king or queen of their destiny.

> It feels awful when you're trying to be popular just 'cuz you're nice and smart—people hate smart people! I just want friends! I can't help the fact that I'm a genius to everybody!

What's most important is the friendship itself. Help your child to keep this in mind. Kids are often so concerned about how many friends they have that they tend to forget the true meaning of friendship. Numbers are not as important as who a friend is and how a child feels with that friend.

HELPING YOUR CHILD KNOW HOW TO MAKE A FRIEND

I've never met a child who didn't care about having a friend. Yet I've met thousands of children who haven't any friends at all and don't seem to know the first thing about making a friend. Over the years, there have been many kids who have told me how difficult it was for them to let their parents know how lonely they really were. One boy in the seventh grade said, "I just didn't want them to be disappointed."

The need to learn the skills related to starting a relationship is not limited to elementary- and middle-school children. Some students graduate from high school having been swept along with the friends they met in elementary school. They may not have had to make a new friend in years. Many arrive on their new college campus and find that they're thrown by the fact that friendship doesn't seem to "happen" for them as they expect it will. This often causes them to think something is wrong with them or that they're at the wrong school because they just don't seem to be fitting in. It also makes them more vulnerable to behave in ways and make decisions that are not really consistent with their values in order to try to be accepted. Given this, parents need to know that any advice or insight they can share with their children on friendship, from grade school on up, might be extremely helpful.

Beyond the significance of helping young people of all ages have the awareness and realize they have the ability to take steps to start a relationship, this is also very much part of the "life skill" foundation they must establish in order to let their own comfort level dictate the risks they choose to take. Kids will be less likely to walk away from their only friends who might be doing something they feel is uncomfortable or dangerous if they don't trust that they have the power to start and develop just as strong a friendship again.

I had a close group of friends and it was hard leaving them. We all got along and there was no pressure to do anything you didn't want to do. I'm kind of nervous about how I am going to make friends who have things in common with me and won't pressure me to do things I don't want to do.

I do not have any friends at school. And I would like to have a friend.

In every school I've visited, there have been boys and girls of all ages who told me they walk through the halls by themselves, sit alone at lunch, and feel ill at ease in their classrooms. They're often the ones who are picked last (or not at all) when class projects are assigned and who rarely have a bus partner (unless assigned) for trips. There continue to be children who stand apart at recess, watching crowds of other kids talking, laughing, and planning to do homework together or something on the weekend. These children are usually consumed with the wish that someone would just come up to them, even to say "Hi." Some kids spend years feeling lonely and rejected this way, waiting for friendship to happen to them.

We need to teach our children that they don't have to wait. They have the power within them to start the process of making a friend. We can and must teach them that there are specific steps they can take to try to build a friendship.

Here's a basic plan of action that you can share with your child that he or she can use to work toward a friendship or, when ready, to initiate a boyfriend or girlfriend relationship, as well. It's a logical, practical approach that anyone can use, even those who feel quiet or shy:

> I used to be shy and never talk to people, then I asked someone to be my friend, and now we are real close friends.

STEP ONE: THE DECISION

The first step is for children to decide that they want to make a new friend or a first friend. While kids can only make this decision for themselves, it may help boost their confidence if you tell them that they are worthy of having a friend and would be a good friend for someone to have.

STEP TWO: THE SEARCH

This step involves looking around and determining whom your child might want to consider approaching. Kids can search the school bus, their classrooms, school halls, library, gym class, recess area, or anywhere else, in order to then pick out one person who seems like maybe he or she might be nice to have as a friend.

This is a great time to discuss with your child the importance of not judging people by their outside looks, clothes, skin color, size, weight, etc. Too many kids are fooled into thinking they can't and don't want to relate to someone because of their outside appearance. They need to be reminded that they can't just look at someone and know if that person could be a good friend. Rather, they need to spend time getting to know that person, time to let that person get to know them. Only then will they have the kind of information needed to make a fair evaluation as to whether they'd like to continue spending time together.

It can help to include in your discussion characteristics and indications that your child can look for prior to making the decision as to whom to approach. For example:

- Does the person seem to have a nice manner in the way he or she treats and responds to your child? If there has been an opportunity to make this observation, does this person seem respectful of others?
- Does the person seem to have a spirit about him or her? Does the person seem to have an "up" personality? Does the person smile often and seem friendly?
- Does the person make eye contact or look away when your child approaches him or her?
- Does your child feel a sense of warmth and a welcoming feeling in that person's presence, or is the feeling more distant?
- Might this person have interests in common with your child?

You and your child can add any other factors to the list that you feel are relevant. Once contact is made and your child has the opportunity to begin to get to know someone, you can refer together to the qualities of a true friendship that I discuss on page 117.

Kids may be more relaxed in their looking process if they give themselves a deadline that builds in at least a few days to check out who is around to consider. That way, they won't have to feel rushed in their selection process, but will still be geared toward picking someone out by a certain time.

I wish people would get to know me better before they judge me.

I have trouble sometimes calling up a friend and asking them to go to a movie or go into town with them. I don't

**know what to say and I don't want them to say no. What
should I do?**

STEP THREE: THE APPROACH

Now it's time for a child to go up to the person whom he or she
picked out. This can be a very tough step, as most kids worry that the
person will say "no," laugh at them, make fun, or humiliate them in
some way. Basically, the fear is rejection.

This step can also be difficult because kids may not be sure of
what to say. It can help ease any jitters if you and your son or
daughter figure out a menu of specific starting lines that are appropriate for where he or she plans to make the approach. Here are
some suggestions:

- For the school bus:
    "Hi, I always see you on the bus. My name is _____.
  What's yours?"
    "I always see you at the bus stop. I live around the corner from
    you. How about if I meet you at the corner tomorrow morning?
    Maybe we can sit together."
- For walking to or from school:
    "I always see you walking home the same way I do. How about if I
    meet you after school and we walk home together?"
- For general school interaction:
    "Do you want to study for the math test with me after school?"
    "I was thinking about walking into town after school. Would you
    like to come with me?"
    "I think we eat at the same lunch period. Do you want me to save
    you a seat at my table?" Or "Is there any room at your table?"
    "Do you want to come to my house one day after school
    this week?"

If your son or daughter doesn't feel ready to actually invite
someone to spend time at your home or spend time together, he or
she can simply begin by saying "Hi," or exchanging names, mentioning that they're on the same bus, et cetera. The opening lines you
prepare with your child can focus on just beginning a conversation

with someone he or she never spoke with before. "What did you think of the math test?" may be less scary to say for starters, and not involve pressure to go further.

It can help to remind your son or daughter that it's better to approach someone on a one-to-one basis for this first conversation. Many children have told me about instances when kids who weren't part of their group came up to them in front of their other friends and asked if they'd like to do something together. Many said they would have liked to have answered "Yes," but didn't because they did not want to have to deal with their friends' reactions. So a private approach may give your child the best chance for a positive reply. Share this with your son or daughter.

What happens if a new girl comes to your school and you want to make friends with her but the friends that you're with don't want you to?

PERSPECTIVES AND ENCOURAGEMENT

We can't know how someone will respond to our kids. The person who is approached for friendship by your child may or may not be interested. We can only promise them that if they don't at least try to take these steps, they might end up waiting a long time to start a friendship. This courage they get up to start a conversation with another kid is the way to expedite the development of friendships. Remind them of this. It can also help to let your son or daughter know that you understand it can be very uncomfortable, even scary, to walk up to someone who he or she may never have approached before. By acknowledging these feelings, you will be validating that it's normal and okay to feel that way. You might say:

"Hey, I'm really proud of you! I know talking to someone for the first time isn't the easiest thing to do. In fact, lots of adults feel unsure and scared about this, too. It's really natural and okay to be nervous. I'd be surprised if you weren't.

"The only thing that wouldn't be okay is if you let being scared stop you from trying to do what you really want to do—start a friendship.

Just having the guts to go up to someone and start a conversation is
terrific, even if that person says 'no' or doesn't respond as you hope."

Parents who respond to their child's anxieties by saying, "Don't
make such a big deal about it. Just go up to them!" might find that is
not as supportive as acknowledging to their child that they know it's
not so easy to take this step. The perspective "It's really okay to be
scared, it's just not okay to let being scared prevent you from going
up to someone anyway" is one I continue to find very helpful. The
trick here is to let kids know we know it's hard and be able to offer
encouragement anyway.

Depending on your child, you might also consider adding:

"Even if your heart is pounding so loud that you think everyone on the
top floor of your school will hear it, they really won't. But it's normal to
wonder. And it's normal for your heart to pound!"

Too often, kids think they need to wait until they're more comfortable to take the first step. Unfortunately, many wait and wait,
and because they still feel scared, they hold back and never make the
first move.

We also must explain that not everyone "connects." When someone doesn't seem interested, kids often feel that something is wrong
with them. They need to know this only means they might not have
gone up to the right person yet.

Now that the person knows someone is interested in being
friends, he or she might pursue the relationship at a later time. If it
turns out that this person isn't interested in a friendship with your
child, then your conversation with your son or daughter may well
help validate any disappointment, then turn the focus toward appreciating what courage it took on their part to take a chance.

Since kids often measure their self-worth in terms of how they
perceive others feel about them, it's critical to reinforce that if
someone truly isn't interested—someone who has never really spent
time getting to know your child—then it would be very sad if your
son or daughter takes that personally.

To put this another way: If someone who doesn't know your child
decides that he or she doesn't want to know your child, it would be

terribly sad and even silly if your son or daughter felt awful just because someone who doesn't know them doesn't want to get to know them. The good news is that there are more steps to follow, more choices.

I feel like dirt and wish that someone would be my friend.

STEP FOUR: PLAN "B" AND BEYOND

If one person doesn't work out, kids can look around again and go on to make a new choice. As with so many other concerns, this is easier for us to suggest and harder for kids to do. Especially if it took all of your child's courage to take the first step, he or she might be very disappointed if that first try doesn't work out as they had hoped it would. That's why it is so important to talk about this possibility before he or she even begins the first step.

MORE PERSPECTIVES

Although it might be painful and frustrating for your child to experience negative responses, giving up would be worse. We need to help kids understand that making the decision not to try anymore is an unacceptable choice.

Kids need to keep in mind that even if they approach twenty people and all twenty say "no", maybe, just maybe, the twenty-first person could be that hoped-for friend. Some kids develop friendships more quickly; others take more time. If children keep trying, they are likely to find the person they've been looking for who will turn into a very wonderful friend. If your son or daughter hasn't found that person yet, it doesn't mean that person doesn't exist. It simply means your child hasn't gone up to the right person yet.

We need to teach kids early on that they do have choices, do have control over the steps they take to reach out and start friendships, even if that process may take some time. They don't have to wait for friendships to "happen" to them. If they understand that they have the power within them to take the first step, that will help them become more confident.

I don't really have a question but I just want to thank you. I don't really have any friends at this point and I am mocked out. I used to be afraid of rejection but I think your talk will help me go for it. I am going to ask as many kids as possible in order to find friends. I am going to say "What the heck?"

We also need to help children understand that in order for a friendship to develop, two people need to want it. If only one person wants the friendship, that's not a friendship. No child deserves to beg for a friendship or compromise who he or she is just to be accepted.

HELPING YOUR CHILD DEAL WITH FRIENDSHIP ISSUES

The following sections will address some of the more common concerns that children have told me they have difficulty handling with friends. For each, I have offered perspectives that you might find helpful to share if your own son or daughter has a similar concern. Where appropriate, I've also included ideas about what choices your child might have to consider, and what they can say or do in order to deal with the situation more effectively.

Kids often don't even realize they have a choice in how they can respond to friends. Their ability to figure out choices and what those choices might mean will help them handle the often difficult day-to-day friendship experiences without compromising who they are in the process.

IF KIDS AREN'T SURE IF A FRIEND IS REALLY A FRIEND

How do I know if my friends are really my friends?

It might interest you to know that the above question has been written by students in elementary through the twelfth grade. Before I started my programs, I never imagined that so many young people would be so unsure about how to know if someone is a true friend. I continue to receive this question from older as well as younger students.

No matter how many friends your son or daughter has, it would be valuable to talk about the qualities of a true friendship. You might find it best to start your conversation by asking your child what qualities would be most important to them in a true friend.

After listening to what your child brings out, you can further discuss any of the following qualities that might not have been mentioned. You might find that sharing what these qualities and descriptions mean in your own friendships can add a nice, personal dimension to your discussion. These are not in any particular order and are all important to address:

- Trust
- Unconditional love
- Honesty
- Loyalty
- Consistency
- Compassion
- Considerateness
- Include you
- Respect you
- Are there for you when you need them
- Accept you for who you are
- You can be totally yourself with them
- Sense of humor, fun to be with
- Can be silly together, cry together
- Have shared interests
- Have comparable values
- Would risk telling you they're worried about you, even if that might make you upset
- Won't talk about you behind your back
- Will keep your secrets

Your conversation about qualities of a friend will not only help your child learn how to determine if someone is a true friend. It can also reinforce what to look for when trying to make a friend and can help make him or her more aware of what it means to be a good friend.

I think friends are most important in life. They stand by you when you're upset, they make you laugh, and they don't care

how you look or what you wear. I hope my friends stay my friends forever.

Since some kids behave in ways that make them hard to like, talking about the qualities on this list can further help you identify what changes might be important for your son or daughter to make in order to become more desirable to have as a friend.

I have a loud mouth. I always get in trouble.

For some kids who always seem to get into trouble, it may take time for them to make changes that other kids will trust. If this could have been written by your child, it can help to ask questions such as:

- how he or she thinks other kids feel about this behavior
- how he or she thinks this behavior might affect whether others would wish to become a friend
- what changes would be good to make

Sometimes negative behavior has less to do with not knowing how to be a good friend and more to do with insecurities, difficulties at home, etc. You might find it helpful to refer to chapter 5, p. 89, for ideas on how you can approach your conversation if you think this could be the case with your child. It can also be beneficial to talk with your child's teacher to learn if he or she shows any negative behavior in the classroom. If you need further input to help you better understand and try to respond to the needs of your child, you can find additional help from counselors and other school staff.

Many parents think letting someone know their child is having a rough time is a negative statement on their parenting. Not so. It takes strength to ask for help. Doing so is a very positive, important move you can make as soon as there is even any question that your child (or you) may need it.

Depending on what social situations you feel your child is dealing with, you might also choose to reverse the qualities and focus on how your child can know if someone is *not* a true friend. So, in your talk, instead of exploring the statement that a friend "treats you in a nice way," substitute as your focus the person who "acts in a mean way," change "will keep your secrets" to "will tell your secrets," etc.

What happens when a friend says he's your friend but he beats you up?

If your child could have written the above card, he or she may not know to say to that "friend":

"If you're really my friend, you wouldn't beat me up. I don't like it when you do that. So stop."

If the person doesn't stop, kids often aren't sure what else to do. The next step would be to say something like:

"I know I said this already, but I hate it when you hit me. It's not funny. And it hurts. So bug off. Don't say you're my friend if you keep beating me up. If you keep doing it, I don't want to be your friend anymore."

This is an example of what good friends do not do. While that may seem obvious, I've learned that it would be unfortunate to take for granted that kids understand this. We actually need to say to kids that good friends don't beat their friends up. That's not caring behavior.

From any angle, it can be very significant to spend time working with your child on making a distinction between someone who is a true friend and someone who is not. Too many kids don't know the difference.

WHAT IF KIDS WANT TO BECOME FRIENDS WITH SOMEONE WHO DOESN'T GIVE THEM A CHANCE?

When your child is seeking out a friend, he or she will most likely meet some rejection in the process. This is never easy. But sometimes another child's reaction is not personal. Make sure your child knows this. While some kids who come across as not being interested might actually be upset or preoccupied about something that has nothing to do with the person who is trying to be their friend, others truly aren't interested—at least, for that moment.

WHAT KIDS OFTEN DON'T UNDERSTAND
- It takes two people to have a friendship
- If only one person wants it, it's not a friendship

I would really like to be friends with someone, but that person is kind of cold to me. If I say hi or smile at the person, the person doesn't respond. I think the person is really fun and nice but I don't know how to become that person's friend.

· They don't deserve to beg for friendships (they're worth more than that)

Explain to your son or daughter that he or she has options when dealing with the variety of responses other children may give when approached for friendship. For example:

· If someone seems to "hate you" and always walks away, you can choose to approach that person privately and ask if you did anything to make the person mad. This may or may not get an answer. If an answer is given, it may or may not be honest. However, asking the person directly about his or her response is a choice to consider.
· It may be important to evaluate behavior. If you act in ways that the person who is approached feels are annoying, there may be good reason why that person isn't interested in giving you a chance.
· Sometimes people don't show that they're actually interested in friendship because they're concerned about what others will think.

I have been tagged with a dirty reputation, and I want to know how to clear it.

· Sometimes children who appear as though they're not interested in your friendship are really interested, but fear and discomfort may prevent them from letting you know.
· Many kids have told me they act snobby as a protection, not because they're really snobs. It's possible that in time they'll become more comfortable to the point where they will be open to get to know a person who would like to become their friend.

- So if your child is dealing with this concern, the idea is that he or she doesn't have to give up interest in someone who doesn't seem to be responding in a positive way. But it would be unfortunate for him or her to just wait around, expecting that disinterest will change. It may or may not. People in this situation should know that they can keep trying for a while, but that they also should check out who else is around and might be good to try to get to know.

IF FRIENDS ARE IN A FIGHT AND TRY TO PUT YOUR CHILD IN THE MIDDLE

My two best friends are fighting and I wish they would stop! Because I don't want to choose sides. I will hurt their feelings.

If your child is getting caught between friends who are fighting, you can help by pointing out the options available to your child that he or she might not see.

WHAT KIDS OFTEN DON'T UNDERSTAND

- They have choices
- If kids are in the middle of a fight between friends, they're allowing themselves to be in the middle
- So, although friends may want your son or daughter to be in the middle, it's still up to your son or daughter to let that happen or not
- While kids cannot control whether their friends fight, they can control what they do in response to the fighting

WHAT KIDS MAY NOT KNOW TO SAY

- "I'm sorry you're in a fight and I really hope you can work things out. But this is your fight, not mine. I don't want to be put in the middle. You both are important friends to me. . . . Don't put me in the middle."

IF A CHILD'S CLOSEST FRIEND MEETS A NEW FRIEND

If you have a best friend and you want to have another friend also. And if your best friend gets mad at you because she doesn't want you to like that other person. What do I do? She puts me under pressure. P.S. It happens to me all the time.

WHAT KIDS OFTEN DON'T UNDERSTAND

· If a "best friend" makes a new friend, that person need not represent a threat to their best friendship
· They can have several "closest" friends
· Best friends are very special, but they should not dictate the extent or choice of other relationships your child enters

I have some friends that are in one group and some more in another. But I'm not sure they like each other. And I don't know which group to sit at lunch with because the other might think I don't like them. What should I do???

· Close friends from different groups are allowed. All of the members of the group don't have to be friends with each other or even like each other. Each person can choose independently whom to hang out with. This decision does not have to be a group decision.

WHAT KIDS MAY NOT KNOW TO SAY

To a friend who becomes friends with someone your child doesn't like:

"I know you started being really good friends with _____. That's cool. I know you know I don't like them that much. [Or: "I know they don't like me that much."] So when you're with him, great. When you're with me, that will be great. I'd just rather be with you when he's not around."

[Or: "Some days, I'll eat lunch at your table, and some days, I'll eat lunch at his."]

To a best friend who gets mad about your child making another friend:

"You're my very best friend. But it's really hard when you get mad about me being friends with _____. It puts a lot of pressure on me. I'll still be your best friend no matter who else is my friend. I like _____. He's really nice. So please stop telling me not to like him."

Children often need to be reminded that just because they ask a friend to stop saying something, that doesn't mean the person will stop. If this is your child's issue, you might find it helpful to ask your child and discuss what other choices can be considered if the best friend continues to create pressure.

To a best friend who seems to have been taken away by a new friend:

"Are we still okay? We hardly ever are with each other anymore. . . . I miss you."

Or:

"This is really hard to say. Ever since you started being friends with _____, things aren't the same with us. Are we still friends?"

This is not such an easy thing to say. It also may be tough for your child to hear the friend's answer. If this is your child's issue, it can help to talk about the many reasons why kids may allow themselves to be pulled away from a friendship, the fact that friends don't have to be with each other all the time to still be close, or that some friendships don't last forever.

WHEN FRIENDS THREATEN NOT TO BE FRIENDS

WHAT KIDS OFTEN DON'T UNDERSTAND

- That it is up to each person (notwithstanding when parents don't approve of a friend, which is another issue entirely) to pick whom he or she wishes to have as a friend
- If someone is a friend, that person is a friend for who you are, not because of anyone else you have in your life

I wish that my friend would let me be friends with her worst enemies with her still being my friend.

- It's not up to a friend to control who else your child becomes friends with
- It's not up to your child to control whomever else his or her friend becomes friends with

How am I supposed to tell my friend that I don't like the people she hangs out with without her getting mad at me?

What do I do if I have an ex-friend and she won't be my friend unless I dump my best friend?

WHAT KIDS MAY NOT KNOW TO SAY

- "This is hard for me to say. I hope you won't get mad that I'd rather not spend time with _____. I know you like them a lot. That's great. But when you're with them, I'd rather not be with all of you. I hope you understand that has nothing to do with our friendship. I love you a lot."
- "It's hard for me when you say you don't want me to be friends with _____. I know you don't like her. Maybe you think if I'm her friend, that will change our friendship. You're my good friend, and you are so important to me. That won't change.

    "So when I'm with you, then I'll just be with you. When I'm with her, I know you don't want to be with her. That's okay. But please don't try to tell me who I should pick as other friends. I don't tell you who to be friends with. I know that's up to you."
- "If you won't be my friend anymore because I'm friends with _____, then that makes me wonder if you really want to be my friend. If you're really friends with me, it doesn't matter who else is my friend. I'm your friend because of YOU. If you like me as a friend, I hope you like me because of ME, not because of who else I like or don't like."

Friendship situations can be picked apart to help your child understand what they can or cannot control, what may or may not be their responsibility, what their choices are, what their choices might mean, and how to honestly express anticipated concerns to the other people involved.

IF FRIENDS ACT LIKE YOUR CHILD ISN'T EVEN THERE WHEN OTHER PEOPLE ARE AROUND

WHAT CHILDREN MAY NOT UNDERSTAND

This change in behavior does not necessarily mean the friendship isn't true or has changed. It may simply mean that the friend is insecure around other people and thinks he or she must act cool and aloof from your child. It also could mean the person is uncomfortable about what other kids think of your child or that this person doesn't even realize he or she is acting like your son or daughter is "invisible." These possibilities make it all the more important for kids who feel this way to let their friend know what they're feeling in this situation.

WHAT CHILDREN MAY NOT KNOW TO SAY

"When we're alone together, things are great. When we're with other people, sometimes it seems like you think I'm invisible. You may not be acting that way on purpose . . . but next time we're with a bunch of people, it would mean a lot if you talked with me [or paid attention to me], too."

Another choice if the friend continues to ignore:

"I don't get it. If we're such good friends, what's going on when we're with other people? You keep acting like I'm not there. It makes me feel like you don't want anyone to know that we're friends."

One of my friends is nice too me, but when popular kids come she thinks I am not alive. What should I do?

Periodically, it can help to remind kids that they can control only what they personally say and do, not how other people hear them, not what those other people decide to do in response to what is shared. Children can control what they do in response to others' actions, and that is what still leaves them in control.

IF YOUR CHILD LOSES A FRIEND
BECAUSE HE OR SHE MADE A MISTAKE

Everybody thinks I have nerdy friends, but I like my friends, but my problem is keeping them even if they are nerdy. I lost my best friend last year by telling a promise I couldn't keep. I want to start over and be a good friend but she won't even talk to me.

WHAT CHILDREN MAY NOT UNDERSTAND

They can't go backward, can't change what they already did. However, they can learn from it, apologize, and not let it happen again. They're "human." Everyone, even grown-ups, makes mistakes.

WHAT KIDS MIGHT NOT KNOW TO SAY

To the friend that was lost because a promise wasn't kept:

"I feel awful about not keeping my promise to you last year. You were my best friend, and that meant so much to me. I don't blame you for being angry and not thinking you could trust me anymore. I've been thinking a lot about how much our friendship meant and I would love to start again. Could we try?"

Children have nothing to lose and everything to gain if they try this kind of approach. As with anything else, point out that there's no guarantee as to how the other person will respond. However, if the approach isn't made, there may be no chance to start again. If it's made, at least there's a chance. What is more important, perhaps, is how your child may feel upon sharing these thoughts. You might discuss that with your son or daughter, as it can feel like a burden has been lifted after such a discussion.

It's also important to explore how that old friend might respond. He or she might say, "Okay, I'd really like to try to be close again" or "Thanks for saying that, but I don't think so." Or he or she may simply not stand around to even listen to your child's words. The possibilities are many. The more aware your son or daughter is of possible choices and potential outcomes, the more prepared he or she will be to handle whatever the response turns out to be.

WHEN KIDS ARE BOSSED AROUND

WHAT CHILDREN MAY NOT UNDERSTAND

· They have a choice in how they allow themselves to be treated

My friend makes me do things I don't feel right with, and if I don't, he doesn't play with me. How do I deal with that?

· If friends boss them around, they're choosing to allow that to happen. So they can also choose other ways to handle the situation.

WHAT CHILDREN MIGHT NOT KNOW TO SAY

· Depending on circumstances, they might say:
   "It's not fair for you to always make the rules. Let's share who gets to make them. If you make them today, I get to make them tomorrow."
· If a friend does not agree:
   "I will only play with you if we share who makes the rules. It's not okay for you to always make them. Friends don't boss each other around. Friends take turns."
· If a friend still tries to be the boss:
   Kids have a choice. Continue to spend time with that friend or say:
   "I really want to spend time with you, but it's not comfortable for me when you always want to be the boss (or make the rules, whatever applies). When you're ready to take turns, I would love to spend time with you."

When you are bossed around, it doesn't always warrant a conversation. For your child, it may simply be a matter of realizing that he or she doesn't like being bossed around and that he or she has a choice. Rather than even saying anything, you could suggest that kids could just make the decision to change their behavior and not allow themselves to be bossed around anymore.

If a child doesn't like being bossed around but is reluctant to stand up to a friend's bossiness, it may help to ask that child what concerns he or she has about what effects a change in his or her behavior would have on a friendship.

WHEN FRIENDS TALK BEHIND SOMEONE'S BACK

What if you like someone as a friend and they talk behind your back and be mean to you?

WHAT CHILDREN MAY NOT UNDERSTAND

- Good friends aren't mean, at least not on purpose
- Good friends are consistent and nice. If they say nice things to your face and mean things behind your back, they're not being a good friend.
- Everyone has a choice with regard to listening to what someone has to say about someone else. If something that someone is saying doesn't seem respectful, you can tell that person you don't wish to hear it.
- There is no guarantee that someone will stop talking behind your back if he or she is asked to stop. No one can control what someone else says or does. However, if not approached, that person may never know how you feel.

WHAT KIDS MAY NOT KNOW TO SAY

- "This is really hard for me to say to you. And, honestly, I didn't hear it myself. But a few people who I really trust have told me you're talking about me to other people in a not so nice way. If that's true, that makes me upset. If you have anything to say to me or about me, I'd appreciate if you would tell me to my face, and not talk behind my back."
- To someone who starts talking about a friend behind his back:
  "It's hard for me to listen to what you're saying about _____. He's one of my good friends, and I'd feel more comfortable if you didn't talk about him like that."

Children need to be helped with figuring out what words they can say to stand up for what they believe is right. So often, kids remain silent, not knowing what to say, fearing if they say anything, their friends will get mad or, worse, they'll ruin the friendship.

How children express what they wish to say is a key factor. The use of "I" language, talking in terms of one's own feelings, can make the difference between fueling a negative or a positive reaction. For example, in the dialogue suggested above, saying, "I'd feel more comfortable . . ." is likely to come across in a more positive way than if a kid said, "It's really awful for you to say that about _____!"

WHAT IF KIDS ARE SPREADING RUMORS?

WHAT KIDS MAY NOT UNDERSTAND

· Once rumors are out, they're hard to control
· What kids can control is how they respond to what is being said (and spread) about them
· They need to go about their life, keeping their head up high, and be able to trust that the people who count the most won't be sucked in by what is being said. If anything, good friends will check directly with any friend who is being talked about to find out the truth.

WHAT KIDS MAY NOT KNOW TO SAY

· To friends, in case they hear the rumors:
   "I know people are saying _____ about me. I just want you to know that's not true."
· To the person who might be spreading the rumor:
   "I understand that you've been saying _____ and I'd really appreciate it if you stopped."

If children remain silent and don't go up to the person who supposedly is talking about them, the talking could just continue. They need to know that the talking could continue, anyway, even if they ask the person to stop. It can help if you explain to your son or daughter that it can only be up to that person to decide to stop. But there will probably be a better chance the person will stop if your child says something rather than remain silent.

WHAT IF KIDS MAKE A TEAM AND THEIR FRIEND DOESN'T?

What if you make a team and your friend does not? What do you do?

WHAT CHILDREN MAY NOT UNDERSTAND

- While they may feel disappointed that they didn't get picked, true friends can also feel happy for their friend who made the team, or got the part in the play, etc.
- It's a good idea to talk with a friend ahead of time about the possibility that only one will get picked

WHAT KIDS MAY NOT KNOW TO SAY

- "I don't know what to say to you. I'm so sorry that you didn't make it. I feel really rotten that I did and you didn't."

WHEN KIDS ARE USED

- They have a choice. If they think someone is using them, they don't have to continue to give money, don't have to continue to allow homework to be copied or whatever other action is going on to make them feel this way.

There's a person who's mean to me, but usually when she needs something or copies my homework then she's nice.

- They need to consider why they are allowing themselves to be used. Sometimes this is testimony to how little they value themselves. Perhaps letting themselves be used is the only way they think that person will pay attention to them.
- Sometimes children allow themselves to do nice things for someone who has not been friendly to them, hoping the person will be nicer. Children need to be brought back to how to tell if a friend is truly a friend. Good friends share and help each other, but don't use each other.
- If there is a question about whether someone is using them, children need to stop doing what they think that person is using them for. Doing so can help them learn if that person truly wants them as a friend because of who they are, rather than pretending to be a friend so they could get something.
- If the person doesn't seem to want to spend any more time

together, now that homework can't be copied, that's important information about the friendship. Perhaps that person
really was only using the friendship to get homework.

· If the person does continue to be a friend, then your child
still needs to decide for him- or herself what he or she feels
is or is not okay to do for other people.

WHAT KIDS MAY NOT KNOW TO SAY

· To someone who has been copying homework:

"I've been thinking. . . . I know I've been giving you my homework
to copy, but I'm really not comfortable doing that. But I'll be happy to
spend time with you one afternoon and help you understand how to
do it for yourself." (This is a way that your child can still be nice, still
offer help, but not compromise his or her respect for the work he or
she put in and the need for everyone to do their own work.)

· To someone who has been borrowing money:

"I'm sorry. I just don't have any money to give you. I'm kind of
broke myself. Hey, when do you think you could pay me back for
what you borrowed last week? I could use it."

· To someone who is nice only when he or she seems to want
something:

"I don't mind helping you with this. But maybe you could help me
understand something, because I'm a little confused. Yesterday, on
the bus, you were saying things to me with your friends that really
hurt. Today you're acting nice. One day not so nice, one day nice.
It seems like the only days you're nice to me are the ones when
you need my help with something. I have a hard time thinking
that's okay."

Most children would probably say, "I could never say that!" Even
if they don't actually end up saying that to someone, they need to
know it's another choice. Their ability to figure out what their feelings are and how to express these feelings in a clear way is of crucial
importance.

By processing and practicing how to construct this kind of honest
dialogue, children will learn more about how to get their feelings
out. They can gain much from learning that they can be respectful

and straightforward at the same time. The more they practice saying what they truly feel, the more prepared they will be to stand up for themselves.

I don't know how to stand up for myself.

WHEN FRIENDS MAKE OTHER FRIENDS

WHAT KIDS OFTEN DO NOT UNDERSTAND

- They need not panic, be jealous, or anticipate that their friendship is going to be over just because their friend made a new friend
- A true friend doesn't have to spend every single minute with you to make sure the friendship stays strong

I wish my friend would not be so jealous when someone else comes to my house.

- True friends can have many other friends, and each friendship of theirs can be a strong one. One friendship does not need to compete with another.
- If time with a friend seems to be growing short because of their new friendships, this can be discussed. Plans simply may need to be made more in advance.

WHAT KIDS MAY NOT KNOW TO SAY

- "Please don't think that our friendship isn't just as important since I became better friends with ———. You're still one of my best friends."
- "It's hard for me when you act that way because ——— is coming over to my house. You're my best friend, but I think it's also good for us to spend time with other kids. That way, we won't get sick of each other!"

My friend has a new friend, and I feel left out because she hangs out with her friend instead of me.

Children need to understand that while it's terrific to be sensitive and caring about what a friend feels, each person is responsible only for his or her own feelings. Those who are jealous if another friend spends time with someone new, need to make peace with their own jealous feelings. The more we help our children trust that they don't have to capture friends and keep them all to themselves for them to be able to remain friends, the less restricted they will be in establishing their relationships now and in the future.

WHEN FRIENDSHIP ENDS

WHAT KIDS MAY NOT UNDERSTAND

- It's normal to feel sad about losing or ending a friendship. It's a loss.
- For a relationship to be a friendship, two people need to want it. If only one person wants it, it's not a friendship.
- If a friendship is over, both friends might as well know it sooner than later. So if your child's feelings about a friendship change, it's thoughtful and caring for him or her to let a friend know. Most children don't want to hurt a friend's feelings by telling them this.
- If a friend tells your child their friendship is over and he or she is upset, you can reinforce that although this might be painful to find out, it's better for that friend to have been honest rather than pretend to care that their friendship continues to mean what it no longer does. Remind your child that he or she can hold on to all the memories and all that was gained from that friendship, and try to appreciate that the time they spent together was worthwhile. (This is another perspective that is easier for parents to share and harder for children to accept.)

WHAT KIDS MIGHT NOT KNOW TO SAY

- "I've been trying to think of how to let you know this—without hurting your feelings. You've been such a good friend. And I can't even tell you what has changed with me, because I don't know

myself. But our friendship is not the same for me anymore. I didn't
know how to tell you that."

**I knew a lot of friends for five years. And they invited me to
their birthdays. Now when they won't invite me to their parties anymore it seems like they're dumping me or leaving
me out.**

· "It's so hard for me to tell you this. You and I have been friends since
  kindergarten. We've always been together. But I'm just not into the
  same things that you're into anymore. I've been really uncomfortable
  when we've been with each other lately. I'm just not into that
  stuff. It scares me. That's why I need to stop hanging out with you
  right now."

HELPING YOUR CHILD WITH OTHER FRIENDSHIP ISSUES

**Sometimes I am with a whole bunch of friends and I feel left
out because I don't quite fit in. Sometimes I laugh with them
but inside I really feel empty and left out.**

**I have a friend who, if I tell a secret to her, she tells everyone.
But she promises not to tell, but she has no self-control.
What do I do?**

Since there are likely to be countless issues that your son or
daughter will have to face when dealing with friends, it's possible that
the concerns I've presented will not be exactly the ones your child
must handle. You'll find that the pattern to my responses can be
applied to most situations. Here's a summary:

· Identify the issue
· Help your child understand the dynamics of the issue
· Identify with your child what he or she can and cannot
  control
· Share with your child what choices he or she has available to
  handle the situation
· Help your child figure out what each choice might mean

- Help your child identify his or her feelings, and what concerns he or she has as to what friends may feel
- Discuss if it is appropriate and/or important to express these feelings to those who are involved, and figure out specific words that can be said. (Do not assume kids know what to say. Review how to "turn feelings into words"—i.e., if it's hard to say something to a friend, kids can start with: "This is hard for me to say . . .")
- Plan to take action
- Share more perspectives with regard to how friends might respond and any other potential outcomes
- Reinforce how your child can still be in control regardless of the friend's response

WHEN KIDS DON'T LIKE OTHER KIDS

Just a quick note about situations in which children do have to make an effort to get along with others they may not like. Such a case would be when relatives are visiting and your child does not like his or her cousins. Or the cousins may be nice but unable to play basketball, or not very interested in computers as your child is. Whatever the differences are in your child's particular situation, you can help by encouraging your kids to focus more on finding something in common rather than concentrating only on what they don't share an interest in.

The perspective here is that if kids always anticipate that the cousin can't play basketball very well, and spend all their time with that cousin playing basketball, wishing he or she would play basketball better, those kids will probably always be disappointed. If they found another activity everyone enjoyed, the feeling of those visits may change dramatically. So the idea is to help your kids appreciate people for who they are and what they can do, rather than expect them to be who they are not and be continually frustrated by what they cannot do.

Summer camp groups can be another source of frustration for many kids. Whether your child is the one whom others would rather not be with, or the one who tells you that certain kids in the group are "nerds," you can help your child put this group experience in perspective. Kids often think they need to be good friends with everyone in their group. They think they need to like every single person. The reality is that they don't. It would be nice to feel that way, but it's not necessary. Simply sharing this could ease your child's anxiety about fitting in with everyone.

Not everyone has to like each other, all they have to do is be nice to each other.

You can point out that what is important is that your child learn to accept that each person is part of his or her little community. Each counts, each is equal. Each has feelings, and each deserves to feel that he or she belongs to the whole group. So rather than worrying about liking everyone enough to want to have as a friend, we can encourage our kids to just be nice to everyone and, here again, try to concentrate on what they have in common instead of only viewing them as being different. Most kids have more in common than they think and can discover this shared ground if they adopt this approach.

IF YOU DON'T FEEL POSITIVE ABOUT YOUR CHILD'S FRIENDS

What if your friend's mother won't let your friend come home with you and you only get to see them at school?

When parents don't wish their kids to spend time with a particular friend or even a group of friends, it's the rare child who will simply take that directive and completely cut off those relationships. It's more common for children to simply not bring those friends home, not talk about them to their parents, and continue to be with them whenever possible. Some kids feel guilty going behind their parents' backs, some don't.

Especially if kids are in school together, it's extremely difficult for parents to control whether children continue to have lunch together, continue to make plans after school and on the weekends. Some kids start lying to their parents about whom they are spending time with, not because they're liars or even feel good about not telling the truth, but because they don't know what else to do since they still wish to be with those friends . . . regardless of what parents have forbidden.

If you do feel strongly about wanting to restrict your child from being with a particular friend, it's certainly your right to take that kind of responsibility for your feelings and set boundaries that you feel are appropriate and safe for your child. I believe that's what parents are supposed to do, even if doors slam, "I hate you!" resonates all over our homes, and our kids are not very happy for a while. Sometimes we all need to make unpopular decisions.

If my mom doesn't want me to be someone's friend, what should I do?

However, if you're not absolutely sure that these relationships are dangerous or you're not at the "absolutely need to forbid this friendship" stage, then you're probably better off stating your concerns and giving your child the room to make up his or her mind about the friendship. For example:

"I know he means a lot to you, but:

"here's what concerns me . . ."
"here's how I see you change when you're with him . . ."
"here's how I see you treat your sister differently when she's around . . ."
"here's what scares me. . . . I understand from some other parents that
    he's been suspended for _____."

"While I appreciate that continuing this friendship is your decision,

I hope you'll be strong about what you let yourself do."

Or:

"I hope you'll at least think about this. . . . I'm worried about his/her influence."

What do you do if your friend is a bad influence on your life?

When parents express their concerns about who their kids hang out with, some kids are actually relieved. They don't feel comfortable, either, but don't know what to do about their friendship. It's usually easier to blame a parent for not being able to spend time with that friend.

What do you do if someone takes drugs and is your best friend?

Heidi, age sixteen, told me:

"When my parents wouldn't let me go to parties with these kids that I hung out with, I was relieved. I didn't know how to tell my friends that I was so uncomfortable when everyone was doing those things. It was easier saying my parents wouldn't let me go and making believe that my parents were the worst. . . ."

Kids may or may not admit that deep down they're concerned, too. The problem to them often involves the fact that if they admitted their parents were right, they would seem like a fool to stay friends with that person, knowing he or she was a bad influence.

So, all things considered, it's better to say something to your kids than remain silent about a friendship issue of this nature. If you do feel strongly enough to attempt to regulate your child's ability to be with a friend you consider to be a worrisome influence, then at least acknowledge in your approach that you're aware your child can go behind your back. You might also find it important to remind your child that your concern, your attempt at restriction, is out of love and fear for his or her safety (or whatever else it stems from). You might also discuss with your child what he or she feels would be an appropriate consequence if whatever ruling you'd like honored is disobeyed.

EXTRA NOTE ABOUT HOW YOU VIEW YOUR CHILD'S FRIENDS

Just as kids judge each other by such things as outside looks, clothes, where kids live, where kids are from, religious and racial backgrounds, past reputations, etc., so do many parents. When you make your judgments, it would be important to evaluate whether you are being completely objective. Consider how much time you have actually spent with your child's friend. If you haven't given yourself a chance to get to know this person, you may find your child will be very positive about your suggestion to have that friend over to play at your home or for dinner so that you can get to know each other better.

IF YOU THINK YOUR CHILD DOES NOT HAVE A FRIEND

My parents tell me on Saturday mornings, Why don't you go to the mall with your friends? But I don't have any. What should I tell them? I don't want them to be disappointed.

It can be very hard for kids to admit to their parents that they don't have anyone they can call a friend. Among the reasons kids have told me they hold back are feelings of embarrassment, fear of disappointing parents, and concern that their parent will be worried about them.

I have no friends. Please help!

If your child is alone much of the time, doesn't receive phone calls from peers, doesn't mention friends, and seems to prefer to stay home alone rather than be with a friend, it is important to examine what's really going on. Consider, first of all, that some kids are very social in school and truly don't feel like having a friend come over for the afternoon. They've had enough interaction with peers for the day and just want to relax, watch TV, play with a pet, spend time on their computer, and have a chance to basically unwind and "chill." Others are so fully scheduled into after-school activities that they don't have time to spend playtime with friends at home during the week. They reserve their playtime with friends on the weekend. Regardless of your child's after-school activity schedule, if your son or daughter never seems to mention a friend, doesn't make plans with friends, spends most or all of his or her time alone, then it could be very important for you to raise the subject of friendship.

If you are concerned that your child may not have any friendships, you may wish to speak with his or her teacher before bringing the subject up with your child. A teacher's answers to the following kinds of questions can give you important information:

- How easily does your child seem to relate to classmates?
- Does your child seem well liked by classmates?
- What about during lunch or recess? Is your child actively involved with other kids or alone most of the time?
- Is there anything about your child's behavior or demeanor that might cause your child to be hard for other kids to like? Or that represent cause for concern?

If teacher feedback supports your suspicion that your son or daughter is having difficulty interacting with peers, it would help to talk with your child about loneliness and share ideas about how to start a friendship.

If your son or daughter has kept silent about not having any friends, you might start your conversation by saying something like this:

> "For the past few weeks, I've noticed that you've been staying home after school, watching TV or doing homework. I figured maybe you just wanted to take it easy after being in school all day. But I also figured if you're spending time alone after school, you'll probably make plans with other kids on the weekends. The weekends keep passing by and I haven't seen you spend time with anybody your age. I know a lot of kids find it hard to say they're lonely. And a lot of kids don't know how to start to make a friend. Lots of grown-ups don't, either. I have some great ideas about how you can start to look for a friend. How about if we make a plan. . . ."

The reality is that your child may or may not acknowledge that your worries are valid. However, by bringing the subject up, you will at least let your child know that you know, and will have opened the door for discussion. That itself can be an important first step.

JOINING A CLUB CAN HELP

Aside from helping kids understand how to start a friendship on a one-to-one basis, it can be wonderful for parents to suggest that they join an after-school club or activity. You and your kids can explore together what opportunities are available within your community, such as intramural sports, Scouts, 4-H Club, and activities through a church or synagogue organization.

These activities provide a ready-made social situation in which it can be easier for kids to get to know others who are the same age and have common interests. There is usually a teacher, parent, or other adult adviser who oversees and can encourage social interaction.

WE CAN ONLY DO SO MUCH—THE REST MUST BE UP TO OUR CHILD

During the years that my kids were in elementary and middle school, there were times when they weren't included, peers who they thought were friends who turned out not to be, times when they didn't feel good sitting at their lunch table, times when they didn't know whom to call to try to make plans. I personally have felt the pain that can be so excruciating, knowing that your child is lonely and hurting inside.

I've said several times already that we need to keep in mind that we cannot live life for our children. This also applies to their ability to make friends. While we can say to our kids, "Why don't you call Noah?" or "Have you ever thought to call Keisha? She seems so nice" or "How about asking Sean to come to dinner [or to the mall with us, or to the movies, etc.]?" we cannot make friendships happen *for* them.

While that is true, there is still a great deal we can do to help our kids help themselves. I hope this chapter helps you feel more prepared to help your child to experience the richness that deserves to go along with all that true friendship can mean.

It's nice to have you talk to us like this. It straightens things out for me about my friends.

I like a different person everyday and I don't know what to do?

I can't tell my mom I'm going with a Mexican

My Father thinks He knows everything that goes on but he doesn't. I wish he could understand some of the pressures. If I told my dad what happens at parties, he wouldn't let me go to another one for the rest of my high school days.

WHAT SHOULD I DO ABOUT DATING? HALF OF THE WORLD HAS A GIRLFRIEND OR BOYFRIEND AND I DON'T EVEN KNOW WHAT'S GOING ON

7

BOYFRIENDS, GIRLFRIENDS, "GOING OUT" ISSUES, PARTIES

When would it be important to start discussions about "going out" or liking someone as a boyfriend or girlfriend? Earlier than many parents might think, earlier than many would wish. Earlier than many kids would admit.

This is a very personal issue. Each child is likely to have his or her own feelings about this, as will each parent. When my son was in the eighth grade, he wanted to go out with a girl who was in his class. He literally spent two hours pleading with her mother, who refused to consider allowing her daughter to have a boyfriend until she was in the ninth grade. Her mother wouldn't budge with this ruling. My son was forced to look for someone else, but actually did end up going out with the girl later, when they were ninth graders.

What does "early" mean? Depending on your child's level of sophistication and what's going on with his or her friends, it would probably be good to talk about this by mid–elementary school. Certainly, no later than third, fourth, or fifth grade. Yes, really. I hope this chapter will help you better anticipate, understand, and be more prepared to help your son or daughter deal with the often difficult issues, feelings, pressures, and concerns related to boyfriend/girlfriend relationships.

HELPING YOUR CHILD DEAL WITH THE PRESSURE
TO HAVE A BOYFRIEND OR GIRLFRIEND

> I hate it when somebody just wants to embarrass you and
> says you like a person when you really don't, and then you
> feel bad when the other person thinks you really like him/her
> and you really don't.

As early as the elementary level, kids are quick to tease each other
about who likes whom and who doesn't. Because children are so
easily pressured when friends are interested and they are not, an earlier rather than later conversation about boyfriends and girlfriends
with your child can help to offset the impending pressure. There
seems to be less of a problem when the reverse is true and a child is
interested but that child's friends are not. Kids often view it as being
"cool" to be interested in having a boyfriend or girlfriend.

I'm not suggesting that you rush into the nitty-gritty, heavy-duty
advice that applies to older, more mature kids and their relationships
at this time. However, you might need to help your fourth-grade
daughter understand that it's normal for her "boyfriend" to act very
nice when they're alone and tell her to "get away" when he's in
front of his friends. Your seventh-grade son may need to talk with
you about the pressure he feels because he doesn't care at all
about having a girlfriend and just about all of his friends do. Your
daughter in the sixth grade may need to talk about how upset she is
that she's taller than every boy in her class. Your eighth-grade
daughter might secretly wonder if it means she's a lesbian because
she's not interested in having a boyfriend and all of her friends are
"boy crazy" or she can't find a boyfriend when most, if not all, of her
friends have one.

> I like boys but I am not so sure if they like me. The ones who
> are attracted to me I think are gross. Do I like the same sex?
> Am I lesbian? Please help. Please.

Such discussions with kids are not meant to urge our children into
social action prematurely. Rather, the idea is to explore potential
feelings, make kids aware of the different kinds of pressures that

might arise, examine together how these pressures can be handled, and create the chance for you to offer guidance regarding how to deal with specific situations that might otherwise end up being uncomfortable and confusing for them.

What do you think about short boys "going" with larger girls? Not that I do, but I want to know just in case. What do you think of boys going with girls, at our age, to begin with?

The initial pressure that children must be prepared to face relates to the possibility that close friends may start being interested in having a boyfriend or girlfriend while they are still worlds away from wanting that kind of relationship. Unless children understand that this difference in interest levels is natural, okay, and even relates to their stage of development, they may wonder if something is wrong with them.

Why do my friends bug me about asking a girl out?

Children need to be taught that they need not fake or rush wanting a girlfriend or boyfriend. They need not push themselves to do so earlier than when they truly are ready, just to do what friends are doing. If friends are good friends, they're likely to remain good friends regardless of the existence of a boyfriend or girlfriend. Some adjustments may need to be made in how they share their time, but the friendships themselves don't have to change just because one friend has a girlfriend and the other couldn't care less. Kids often don't know this.

Just like with physical changes in their bodies, kids can be helped to understand that each person is going to be on their own time schedule for developing an interest in having a boyfriend or girl-friend. If your son or daughter is involved with boyfriends and girl-friends, it can help for you to encourage sensitivity for those who are not yet at a similar place of interest. However, since the subject of "liking someone" is one of the topics that kids find hard to discuss with their parents, it's possible that you may not be fully aware of the extent to which your child's interests are directed toward having a boyfriend or girlfriend. Whatever the situation is with your child, you can discuss the issue with him or her by opening a conversation from one of many angles.

What if you like boys and are afraid to tell your mother?

I've always been friendly with boys, not in love, just friendly, and now they're asking me out and I don't know what to say. I really like them but my mother would kill me if she knew. What do I do?

If you aren't sure whether your child has reached that stage, you might start a conversation with something like this:

> "I know a lot of kids might feel funny talking with their parents about having a boyfriend or girlfriend. You might not even be thinking about that yet. Or maybe you are, and that's okay, too.
> "But just in case some of your friends are and you're not . . . it's important that you know that's just fine. That's totally normal.
> "Some kids end up feeling very pressured, and may even think they have to make believe they like someone just because their friends do. But I wanted to make sure you know that even really close friends may not be interested at the same time as each other. Some kids start having boyfriends or girlfriends early, some not until years later.
> "That doesn't have to change your friendships."

Then, take it from there. By bringing up the subject of boyfriends and girlfriends, you're letting your son or daughter know that it's okay to talk about this and that perhaps you really do understand more than he or she might think.

If you know your child is interested in boyfriend/girlfriend relationships, you might find it helpful to say the following, just in case he or she has friends who are not:

> "When I was growing up, I was one of the last kids in my group of friends to have a boyfriend. I felt kind of funny around my friends who did, because I wondered if they were judging me. I also worried if they'd still be my friend, since they were spending more and more time with the friends who did have boyfriends or girlfriends.

"If any of your friends aren't into girlfriends or boyfriends, it may be great to let them know that whether they like someone or not, that won't change anything between you. By letting them know you still care about your friendship, that can help them feel more comfortable just in case they feel funny about being the only ones who aren't going out with anyone."

MORE PRESSURE

When several pairs of boyfriends and girlfriends hang out together after school or on the weekends, it can be awkward for a boy or girl who doesn't have a boyfriend or girlfriend to be alone with all the pairs. Children may have lots of feelings, ranging from comfortable to awkward or very uncomfortable, if all their friends are in pairs and they are alone. It may or may not be a tough situation, depending on what the pairs are doing. If they're all watching a video together, that might not be awkward at all. If they're playing kissing games or making out, that could be very awkward for those not yet romantically involved.

Even kids who are in pairs might feel awkward among other boyfriends and girlfriends, depending on what they're doing. Your son or daughter may need to be reminded that those who have boyfriends and girlfriends will also be at different stages of readiness with regard to what and how they choose to share with each other.

Any pressure related to what children will be exposed to from the other couples can be offset if you talk with them ahead of time about potential concerns as well as ways they can be handled. Kids need to discuss their limits, anticipate what circumstances they're about to put themselves in, and figure out what alternatives they can consider if the scene turns out to be one they would rather not experience. In this way, children can be prepared to reevaluate their situation and make a new decision, figuring out what other choices they may have, such as calling a parent or neighbor to pick them up, just going into another room, or taking a walk, so they don't have to stay around the other couples.

This is the kind of thinking process we, as parents, can provide to help our children develop. As with the process of trying to work out friendship situations, children need to be helped to figure out choices, what choices might mean, and what the outcome might potentially be. We can help them explore the different ways they might feel, how friends, boyfriends, or girlfriends might feel, and, where appropriate, how we as parents might feel. Their ability to realize there are choices, and to figure out options and think them through, will help children maintain personal control over what they allow themselves to do.

The preparation process we as parents can take part in also includes arming kids with questions that will help them determine what choice might be best for each situation. Basic questions such as asking a friend, "What do you think you're going to be doing?" may seem obvious to you, but may not be obvious to your child. It's always best to make sure kids know what words they need to say. Kids have taught me it would be unfortunate to assume they know how to figure that out. The lessons we can help our children learn at this level can assist them through their entire lives by decreasing their stress and increasing their confidence in any number of social situations.

HOW HAVING A BOYFRIEND OR GIRLFRIEND CAN INFLUENCE HOW KIDS VALUE THEMSELVES

I feel left out because my friends have boyfriends but I don't. I feel like I'm not as good as them because of it. It hurts a lot because no guy likes me.

Many years ago, I talked with a student after one of my assembly programs who said to me:

"I'm going to school tomorrow and am going to find a boyfriend. I don't even care who he is. I just don't want to be the only one of my friends without one."

This struck me as very sad. But our children often define themselves in terms of their relationships. If all of their friends have boyfriends or girlfriends and they don't, this fact alone can be powerful enough to influence how they value themselves.

We need to help children understand that it would be unfortunate to depend on having a boyfriend or girlfriend relationship to be able to feel special or whole, especially since relationships are likely to be up and down, on and off, throughout all their growing-up years. Like the weather, at the upper-elementary and secondary-school levels, most of these relationships tend to be very changeable, as you might remember from your own growing-up experiences. I remember classmates who would be "in love" one day, only to be "so over it" the next.

While we don't have the ability to control the weather, we do have control over how we respond to weather conditions. It's up to us whether we choose to walk in puddles, allow ourselves to get completely soaked, use sun protection, or whether we allow the weather to ruin our day. Kids also have control of their own individual end of any relationship. But many of our children aren't aware that this is a choice they can make. They're often so caught up with worrying that their boyfriend or girlfriend won't like them anymore that they opt to remain silent rather than stand up for themselves.

We can teach kids that if a relationship is "stormy," they don't have to stand out in the rain. They can seek advice from parents, teachers, counselors, and other adults in their life in order to gain insights and develop the tools to be able to protect themselves emotionally. We can and need to reinforce for them that no one has a right to power over someone else. Relationships deserve to be viewed and experienced with both parties involved considered as equals.

Most boys are disrespectful. I feel as if I am a nobody.

If children diminish and humiliate the person they're going out with, that is of tremendous concern and is definitely not okay. If kids think less of themselves, allow themselves to be diminished, don't view themselves as equals, or remain dependent on the other person in their relationship to validate their sense of worth, that also is of tremendous concern.

My boyfriend pulled a knife on me!

How do I know if I or my friend has been date-raped? What exactly is it?

Not only do we need to teach kids that abuse in any form is unacceptable, we cannot take for granted that they know what rape and other forms of abuse actually are.

Without exception, the number of hands raised by college students in every audience I have addressed throughout the United States over the past several years in response to my question "How many of you know someone who is in, or has been in, an abusive relationship?" has been staggering.

What if you were slapped and hurt by your boyfriend? How would you tell your parents if they didn't know?

The earlier we reinforce the need for greater respect within our children, for self as well as for others, the greater the chance we'll have to prevent kids from allowing themselves to be abused. They deserve to know they're worth more than that.

HERE, TOO, PARENTS TEACH BY EXAMPLE

Kids learn what's okay and what's not okay from the way their parents treat each other and allow themselves to be treated by others. Some of those lessons reinforce demeaning treatment of one partner by another. Parents can help prevent this kind of negative treatment being repeated in their children's relationships by being honest about these circumstances and reinforcing lessons related to being assertive about standing up for their self-respect, what it means to value oneself, and how important it is to let someone—if not a parent, then another adult (grandparent, aunt or uncle, friend's parent, teacher, counselor, social worker, priest, rabbi, etc.)—know when they need help.

We as parents can try our best to stay tuned in to the possible influence that relationships might have on how our kids value themselves. Do they seem to be compromising their sense of dignity and self-respect? Is there concern about any behavior or personality changes that seem to be boyfriend or girlfriend related? Is it possible that their relationship is abusive in any way?

We can say to our kids:

"I thought a lot about how I could say what I'm about to say to you. First, I want you to know that I respect that who you go out with is your decision. I hope you can trust that what I'm about to say is out of love and caring and my wish for you to be happy. I know _____ means a lot to you and you've been going out for a while.

"But, it's very painful to watch the way she treats you and hear the way she talks with you. I wish there was something I could say to you to help you trust that you're worth more than that. You don't deserve to take her meanness. The fights you've been having are taking so much out of you. I'm worried that she might be using you and that you're going to get hurt.

"I know lots of kids probably would think this is none of their parents' business, but I'm really worried that you're going to get hurt."

When I've raised difficult issues such as these with my children, I find it most effective to:

- anticipate any potential resistance
- state it aloud, so your child knows that you know
- then go ahead and say what you need to say, if need be, starting with, "This is so hard for me to say . . ."

WHEN PARENTS DON'T APPROVE OF THEIR CHILD'S BOYFRIEND OR GIRLFRIEND

What kids end up doing about their parents' concern is very individual. Parents are likely to have more influence over younger children's decisions than older ones'. Therefore, the beginning years of interest in relationships with a boyfriend or girlfriend are an excellent time to talk with your child about qualities and personality types they feel would be positive or negative. It's especially important early on to talk about what it means to treat someone with respect and what it means to be respected. From there, we can clearly explain the many forms that abuse in relationships can take.

As kids get older, it usually is harder to impose parental restrictions on the person a child wants as a girlfriend or boyfriend. Even when religion, race, or the way parents see a son or daughter being treated represents a serious parental concern, young people will often choose to see their girlfriend or boyfriend in secrecy. No matter what a parent's opinion is, it's rare for kids to give up a relationship, especially if both kids want it to continue (and especially if they see each other in school).

I can't tell my mom I'm going with a Mexican.

However, that doesn't mean we ought to remain silent as parents. Our honesty can at least alert our son or daughter to what we believe are serious concerns about the relationship or, specifically, about the person he or she is dating. Because this kind of sharing can be emotionally charged, you may find it more positive to write out what you wish to say to your son or daughter and leave a note that can be read privately, without emotional interference.

A child may put his or her back up, say that it's none of a parent's business, and not choose to listen. They may also listen very carefully, knowing that what is being said (at least from most parents) is offered out of love and meant with their own best interest at heart. Children may or may not admit that their parents' concerns have touched deep-rooted nerves. The problem often is, if kids admit these concerns are valid, even just to themselves, then what?

If you share concerns in terms of "I" language, meaning in accordance with your own feelings rather than telling your kids what to feel or what to do, your children will likely be more open to listen. If you do decide to take a hard line on restricting your son or daughter from going out with someone, you would be wise to let your child know:

- you recognize it's possible that your son or daughter could choose to continue to see that person behind your back
- you know there's only so much you can control
- that this is a matter of trust and honor
- that you know this is painful for your child, and you don't feel good about the whole situation either . . . and the last thing you would wish is to contribute to any painful feelings your child might experience

You could then say, "Knowing how we both feel and the reality of the situation, how can WE deal with this?" And then see where things go from there.

IF YOUR CHILD WANTS A GIRLFRIEND OR BOYFRIEND
(How to Help)

As with the concern about not having any friends, if your child doesn't have a boyfriend or girlfriend and wishes to have one, this need not be viewed as a negative for your child, but rather as evidence that he or she just hasn't found the "right" person yet. Many kids don't see it this way, they just see that "all" of their friends have a boyfriend or girlfriend and they're the only one who doesn't.

I like this one boy but I'm way too shy to say anything to him.

I like a girl but I don't know if she likes me. What should I do?

Kids usually don't realize that there is a step-by-step process that they can follow in order to start a boyfriend or girlfriend relationship. The process is identical to that which I shared in chapter 6 for starting a friendship. You can help by going through those steps with your son or daughter to help figure out a plan of action. Because of the big deal that kids often make about boy/girl friendships, many girls have only experienced friendships with other girls, and many boys have had only male friends. As a result, kids may view the other sex as they would someone from another planet. We can help by reminding kids that those of the other sex are also humans who probably share many of the same interests, and often are just as scared to start a conversation. So they just need to push themselves and "go for it"! (I know, I know, that's easy for us to say . . . and much harder for them to do. We can let kids know that we know that, too.)

How can you tell a boy that you really like him?

I have this really close friend of the opposite sex and I'm confused. I think I like him/her but feel like it's against the rules to feel like this.

As with making an approach to start a friendship, kids need to be reminded that they have nothing to lose and everything to gain if they try to reach out to that person. If the person isn't interested, they just need to see who else is around. And, as with starting a friendship, kids don't deserve to beg for someone to be their boyfriend or girlfriend, they don't deserve to allow themselves to be used or to buy a relationship by compromising themselves. As with friendship, if only one person is interested, that's not a relationship. So, they might as well try.

While the process of starting a boyfriend or girlfriend relationship is identical to that for friendship, there are other factors to consider that are a bit different. In a friendship, if someone is not interested, that's pretty much it. The uninterested person will probably have little or nothing to do with the kid who made the approach. However, if kids are not interested in going out with someone, they may still wish to have continued contact as "just friends." They can still spend time together and still get to know each other better. Who knows, maybe sometime in the future that person who wasn't interested in a going out–type relationship will end up changing his or her mind.

If you want to go with somebody but they don't want to go with anybody, what do you do?

So if this card could have been written by your child, a helpful suggestion would be just to work at (and enjoy) building a friendship relationship with this person, if he or she is open to doing so. They can spend time together (go for pizza, watch videos, study, go to the library, play sports, volunteer for community service, etc.) and get to know each other, with no pressure to define this as a "boyfriend / girlfriend" relationship. The better they get to know each other, the more meaningful their friendship can grow to be. And in time, maybe they'll go out, maybe they won't. But if it seems that this person is someone worth knowing, both kids will gain from all they share.

There is a girl I really like but she's always going with an older guy. I'm not sure what to do. I'm not sure if I'm cool enough or if she would even listen to me. What do I do?

No matter how many "older guys" that girl has been going out with, the boy who wrote this card still has nothing to lose by trying to approach her. If the girl doesn't think he's "cool enough," and certainly, if she won't even listen to him, maybe she's just not the person he deserves to spend his time with, anyway. It might also help to say to this boy:

"Check it out! You never know. Think of it as an adventure. She may still just like older guys. But if she doesn't want to go out with you, it doesn't mean you're not cool. It's just means maybe she's not for you. Maybe you and she could at least just grow to be friends."

AN EXTRA PUSH FOR "FRIENDSHIP FIRST"

You needn't wait for your child to be interested in going out with someone who may not want that kind of a relationship to talk to him or her about this. It would be terrific if kids learned early in their lives that probably the best way to establish an excellent foundation for a boyfriend or girlfriend relationship is to start out as friends. That way, the relationship can grow naturally, without pressure to advance, sexually or otherwise, and kids can just go one day at a time, learning about each other and building trust, confidence, and all those wonderful things that are part of true friendship.

Because it can be uncomfortable for kids to deal with the way peers may comment on friendships between boys and girls, it would be helpful for parents to encourage respect for and development of relationships with either sex. Many more girls and boys would become friends with each other if other kids would not tease and make comments having to do with "liking each other," when they simply want to enjoy a friendship.

HELPING KIDS LET SOMEONE KNOW THEY'RE INTERESTED

I like someone but I don't know if he likes me and I don't know what I should do or say to him.

This is a big issue. Many kids don't know what to say or do to show someone that they like them. In order to get the word out, or find out whether they have a chance, children often ask friends to check, get "inside" information from that person's brother or sister, or rely on notes that are passed around. These ways of gathering information are often not reliable. We can help children take control of the process by approaching that person directly. Here again, they need the words.

How do you tell a girl you like her?

A menu of opening lines you can provide your children with can include everyday kinds of topics, such as:

- "I saw you at the bus stop this morning, but you were talking about your math homework and I didn't want to interrupt you. I'll see you tomorrow morning."
- "Did you watch the play-offs last night? AWESOME!"
- "I was thinking of going to the concert on Thursday night. Would you like to go with me?"
- "What did you think of the test?"

We have to teach kids that they need only "be themselves" and talk about everyday kinds of things. To figure out which approach line might be best, it's a good idea to suggest that they consider how much contact they have already had with that person.

If there is a guy that I like and really hasn't considered me more than a friend, what can I do to get closer to him?

If kids have never talked with the person they like, just asking about an exam or even saying "Hi" can be a good beginning. Then they need to keep up the contact. Not in an overbearing, overdone way. There doesn't need to be dramatic flirting, only regular conversation. That itself will show interest. Children need to be reminded that people are usually turned off by those who come on too strong. They should know that they can relax more than they may think and they don't need to worry about sounding brilliant.

The more kids say "Hi" and ask how a person is doing, the more their interest will be reinforced. Comments such as "That was a really funny thing you said in class" or "I loved your project" can also confirm their interest in someone. "Your hair cut looks great!" is a little bolder maybe, but it's another specific example of how kids can let someone know that they're being noticed with everyday comments.

"Hi"s can then turn into sentences. Sentences can build up to paragraphs. Paragraphs can develop into conversations. Conversations can start out in between classes, expand during lunch, grow longer at recess, on the bus, or walking home, and ultimately flourish during an extended afternoon or on the weekend. We can remind our children to just take things one step at a time, one day at a time, and that they need only start with a smile, even before they say "Hi." We also need to make sure they know that establishing eye contact with the person they approach (or anyone) is important. Many kids have no idea how to show or express their interest. We can give them basic tips and reassurance as we help them learn that doing so is much easier than they may think.

HELPING KIDS DEAL WITH THEIR DECISION TO ASK SOMEONE OUT

Kids often go back and forth when deciding if they should ask someone out: "Should I, shouldn't I?, Should I, shouldn't I?" "What if he says no?" "What if she says yes?" "I'll feel like such a jerk." "What if they tell all their friends?" "What if they laugh at me?" "I'll be so embarrassed." "What will I tell my friends?"

I like somebody but I'm afraid to tell anyone because they might laugh. What should I do?

How do you tell someone that you really, really, really like her? Like, as a girlfriend!!!

Whether kids have gotten to know someone fairly well or have had little or no prior interaction, they can still make the decision to ask someone out. And that's exactly what they can say, just plain:

- "Do you want to 'go out'?"
- "Would you go out with me?"
- "I'd like to go out with you."

That's direct and certainly gets the point across. Once the question is out, kids can usually expect to get a quick answer:

- "Yes."
- "Yeah, that would be great."
- "I'd love to go."
- "Thanks for asking, but that's not good for me. Perhaps another time."
- "I'll have to let you know,"
- "Thanks for asking . . . but, honestly, I don't think of us in that way. I hope we can just stay great friends."

You and your child can add more possibilities to the list. This kind of discussion will not only prepare your child for a range of conceivable responses, but can arm him or her with what words they, themselves, can say if asked out as well.

I wish there were a way to guarantee that kids who take a chance on asking someone out could be protected from rude or insensitive responses. However, while our teaching can help make a positive difference, there's always the chance someone's blunt or unkind answer will hurt them. If more kids were taught to appreciate the courage it usually takes to ask someone out, there would probably be less anxiety involved with the decision to approach someone.

You can use this lesson also to remind your son or daughter that no matter what response they give when asked out, they deserve to feel flattered if they are asked out. And no matter who asks them, the asker deserves to be respected for putting themselves in a vulnerable position by making the effort.

HELPING YOUR CHILD DEAL WITH OTHER "GOING OUT" ISSUES

While it would be impossible to anticipate every single situation that your son or daughter will face when dealing with a boyfriend or girlfriend, let's look at some common ones and the words your child could use facing them. Here, as with the friendship issues, the general pattern of responses can be applied to other situations that may come up that aren't specifically addressed here.

If Your Child Wants to Turn Someone Down

How should you turn down a person if they ask you out and you don't want to go out with them?

As I have mentioned before, if someone does not want to go out with the person who approaches him or her, that child might still want to enjoy a friendship. So a "no" answer can also include saying something like:

> "Thanks. That was so nice that you asked. You're my good friend and I honestly just want to stay 'just friends.' I'm glad you asked, though. I'm sorry. That doesn't change our friendship, does it? I hope not."

Or to someone who is not already a friend:

> "I really want to thank you for thinking of me in that way. It's a little hard for me to say this, but I'm going to have to say no. I'll see you in class, though. I'm really glad you asked. . . . Maybe we can become friends."

While this was not the answer the asker was hoping for, it represents an honest, respectful refusal. Again, aside from being honest, kids need to be reminded to respect privacy. It would be horrible for the child who refused to turn around to friends and say, "You'll never guess who asked me out!"

When someone is asked out, that person can say "Yes," "No," or, "I'd love to go out with you. But Saturday is not good for me. How about one day next week?" Most kids tell me that they would rather know than not know if someone is interested in them. If the person says "yes" but really means "no," what kind of relationship would develop, anyway? The "relationships are only relationships if two people want it" theory applies to every relationship. Kids need to be reminded of this as well.

IF YOUR CHILD LIKES SOMEONE WHOM FRIENDS DON'T LIKE

You can help by suggesting to your child that he or she can say to that best friend who is upset about his or her choice in boyfriend or girlfriend:

> "I'm sorry if you don't like him [or her]. But I do. Now that I know how you feel, please don't say it anymore."

Or:

> "It makes me sad when you say he's a loser. I think you would feel differently if you got to know him.
>   "I really like him and I'd really like to understand why you don't. Could you please explain to me why you feel that way?"

Kids need to be taught that whom they go out with is their own choice. It's not up to their friends, unless they allow it to be. If friends are truly friends, they'll state concerns but will respect each person's right to make his or her own choice. When the issue is attractiveness of a boyfriend, "cute" is usually in the eyes of the beholder. What is cute to one person may be ugly to another. What's important is how your child views that person. It would be helpful to reinforce this for your son or daughter if he or she faces this situation. Your child might take into consideration what trusted friends think, then make up his or her own mind. This is a grown-up message, admittedly, but if we don't say this, it's possible our kids won't learn what they must about the power they have in their own life.

I want to go out with a girl, but most of my friends do not like her. What should I do?

WHEN YOUR CHILD'S FRIEND SPENDS MORE TIME WITH A BOYFRIEND OR GIRLFRIEND

When kids are more and more interested in a boyfriend or girlfriend relationship, the time they spend with a boyfriend or girlfriend can cut into the time they spend with their friends. That seems to be the natural way things happen. If your child is feeling that a friend is not spending as much time with him or her for that reason, you might encourage your son or daughter to simply say to that friend something like:

> "You really seem to be happy with _____. I'm glad for you. The only thing I miss is the time we used to spend. Maybe we can plan to do something."

That friend may or may not alter the amount of time spent with your son or daughter, but at least your child will have gotten those feelings out in the open. More than likely, by mentioning these feelings your child will be able to at least confirm that the friendship has not changed, it's just that the friend now has a girlfriend or boyfriend.

I can't get close with my best friend anymore. His girlfriend is my cousin, which makes it even harder. Help.

I would also suggest that you encourage your son or daughter to look around for someone else with whom to spend time. Here again, you will be helping your child figure out what he or she can control and what cannot be controlled.

Your child can only control what he or she expresses to that good friend about wishing to spend more time together, but cannot control what that friend chooses to do about those feelings. No child has to sit with "left out"–type feelings, because all kids have the power to start a new friendship and not wait around for someone to make time for them. This is a point that might be especially helpful for you to share.

Sometimes the reason kids spend more time with a girlfriend or boyfriend without balancing it with other important people is that they think they need to be with that person constantly or else they might lose the relationship. If your child is the one in a relationship, you might remain aware of how much time he or she is spending with a boyfriend or girlfriend as opposed to seeing close friends. It can help to discuss this as well. You may simply make the observation of how happy you are that your child still spends a great deal of time with his or her good friend whom you like so much. Or, if that is not the case, you may raise the point that you don't see your child's good friend around that much anymore and ask when he or she will be coming by again. Then continue the discussion to include issues such as balancing time, choice versus obligation, and fear of losing a friend, boyfriend, or girlfriend as that relates to time spent with that person. Children can benefit from being reminded that they don't have to be with someone every single free minute for the relationship to be meaningful and stay intact. This is no different for "regular" friendships.

IF YOUR CHILD LIKES SOMEONE WHO ISN'T INTERESTED

If you like someone and they like your best friend, what do you do?

The point to reinforce here is that your child can control only his or her side of the "liking." It's up to the other person to like your child back in that way or not. So, what your child can control is the decision to continue the friendship as is, and therefore still keep that person in his or her life—if that person wants the friendship, too. As with friendships, children need to be reminded that they don't deserve to have to beg for someone to like them, don't deserve to have to compromise who they are or allow themselves to be used, and don't deserve to have to try to buy a relationship—with their body or anything else. If someone doesn't like your child, he or she needs to be encouraged to look for someone else.

If the person whom your child likes actually likes your child's best friend, that doesn't change the suggestion to maintain a friendship. If your child airs any thought about trying to "take away" that boyfriend or girlfriend, discuss it. Usually that is viewed as a pretty ratty thing to do. It is a sure way to put friendship in jeopardy. Talk with your child about this, and what feelings are prompting this reaction. Then think of something positive to do. One choice would be to let the friend know about these feelings. Your child may choose to say to his or her best friend, "You're so lucky! I'm really jealous. I wish he liked me. But if he can't like me, I'm glad he likes you."

Why do people try to break up people's relationship with their girlfriends and boyfriends?

Even when people break up, it may be helpful to suggest that your child talk about his or her feelings with a good friend before going out with someone that friend just stopped seeing. Explain that this is not necessarily about asking for permission, but out of courtesy. It's a statement of respect for their friendship. Most kids will agree that it's not worth taking a chance on ruining a friendship because of a boyfriend or girlfriend. Friendships can last for a lifetime, while most boyfriend and girlfriend relationships, at least those in elementary and secondary school, are much more short-lived.

My friend is mad at me because she thought that I kissed the boy she likes when she told me she didn't like him anymore.

Another reason to suggest that even younger children wait before starting a relationship with someone who just ended one with someone else is that the person may be interested not as much in your son or daughter as in the idea of having a "relationship." Older students refer to this as a rebound. For some kids, it's a matter of saving face in front of "the whole school." Since young people unfortunately may tend to view a breakup as a negative statement about their self-worth (thinking that if they were really special, that person would still be going out with them), a quick, new relationship (with anyone) might be their attempt at proving to their peers as well as confirming to themselves, "See, I'm still cool" or "I'm still desirable" or "I'm still valuable."

A NOTE ABOUT BREAKUPS

Young people need to understand that when breakups happen, it is not a statement on how special either person is. Rather, it means that the relationship wasn't working as it needed to, didn't feel as it needed to for either or both people. As with friendships that end, a breakup with a boyfriend or girlfriend can be very painful. This, too, is a loss that will take its own time to heal. This is another time that validating your child's feelings can be very important. Kids often feel they should be past their hurt feelings after a very short while, especially if their boyfriend or girlfriend appears to be just fine. If your child was going out with someone who is in his or her classes, or hangs out with the same group as he or she, discuss that your child might find it awkward or difficult to be in the presence of the "ex" and certainly find it hard to see attention given to someone else. Your child might appreciate knowing what words he or she could say to that "ex," such as:

"Is it as weird for you as it is for me?"

"I really hope we can still be friends. But first I need to get used to not being your boyfriend. So let's cool it right now. I'm going to need a little time."

Depending on the circumstances and what your child feels, you can construct related dialogue together, reinforcing how to turn feelings into words and how to actually express those words even if your child is uncomfortable. Your son or daughter might also find it helpful to talk about what his or her former boyfriend or girlfriend might be feeling.

These kinds of discussions can help your child anticipate and be more prepared to face these situations as well as help to confirm that his or her feelings are very normal. It can also help to remind your child that he or she can gain from every relationship experience. Kids can take forward into new relationships what they learned about interaction that was positive and can try to avoid repeating what they learned was negative.

IF TWO FRIENDS LIKE THE SAME PERSON

If two friends like the same person and that person hasn't decided yet whom he or she likes, it could prevent a great deal of hurt if the friends would approach each other first and say something like, "We both know we like _____. I just want you to know, whoever she ends up liking, the most important thing to me is keeping our friendship." Close friends might even decide that, perhaps, because one likes a girl or boy more than the other does, that's the one who ought to get the chance to go out with him or her. However, it's still going to be up to that boy or girl to choose between the two friends. It's also possible that neither friend will be picked to be a girlfriend or boyfriend. The important issue in these touchy situations is to help your child see that open communication can help address these situations before they come between him or her and a friend.

IF YOUR CHILD IS PRESSURED TO DO WHAT HE OR SHE DOESN'T WANT TO DO

My boyfriend wants me to do things that I don't want to do.

By the time many kids reach middle school, peer pressure in relationships is already a significant issue, one they often don't know how to handle. The choices and words to say that you can discuss with your child are pretty clear-cut: "Yes" or "No," "I'll think about it," "I'm not ready for that, please don't push me," "Please don't touch me there. I don't want you to do that again." The communication may be verbal or nonverbal as long as your child is clear. "No" has to mean no. If he or she says "Yes," it's very important for your son or daughter to assess what that can mean, where it can lead, and what the possible consequences are. If the answer is "No," the same assessment can be made.

What should you do when your girlfriend says I want to have sex!

Some perspectives: A boyfriend or girlfriend can ask, but it is still up to your son or daughter to make the decision as to how he or she will respond to what is being asked. Since kids cannot control whether someone else respects their limits, values, or their own sense of readiness, they need to understand that they can control respecting themselves. That leaves them in control. The point is, your son or daughter has a choice. Too many kids don't understand this.

You might find it helpful to explain that there is a difference between being mad and being disappointed. It's one thing if a boyfriend or girlfriend is disappointed because a partner did not wish to go further sexually, as he or she would have wished. But being angry about this is a different story.

I'm thinking now of a student who came up to me after one of my school assembly programs and asked if I could talk with her for a few moments. She explained that she had a new boyfriend who was pressuring her to have sex with him, and she didn't know what to do.

She told me that she did not want to have sex with him but was afraid he would break up with her if she just left her answer as "no." She had started going out with him just five days before. Yes, FIVE. So instead of completely refusing, in answer to his "Well, then when?", she told him she'd have sex with him in two more weeks. At this point I said, "It sounds like you ought to DUMP HIM!"

I went on to offer perspectives about how she deserves to value herself and realize that what she shares with him of herself is rightfully her choice. If he does not respect her limits, that's important information. I asked her if she really wants to go out with someone who doesn't respect her. (No, she didn't.) I also said that if he broke up with her because she wouldn't give in, that would mean to me that he was probably going out with her for what he could get rather than for who she is. If that's the case, he would have been using her. She's better off knowing that sooner than later. I don't know what this girl ultimately chose to do, but I hope our talk reinforced the fact that she had options and could exert control over the situation.

All of our children need to hear these important statements when or before they go out with someone. They should be reassured that their bodies should be respected, and that the motives of any person who pushed or threatened if they did not have sex (or generally, go as far sexually as the boyfriend or girlfriend wishes) should be questioned.

REPUTATIONS

People always call me a slut because I go out with so many people from other schools.

Another important issue to discuss with your son or daughter is how others might perceive and judge relationship decisions. Kids need to anticipate that their peers might label or characterize them because of such things as:

- the number of relationships they're in
- what other kids think of whom a person is going out with
- rumors about how far they go sexually

While in an ideal world it would be great if people respected privacy and each person's right to make his or her own relationship decisions, the reality is that kids talk about each other. They judge, and especially if those judgements are negative, word tends to spread very quickly. It usually doesn't take very long for such talk to be "all around the school." Labels are tough to handle and very difficult to shed. That's another reason why we need to encourage our children to honor their own values, hold on dearly to their own sense of self-respect, and be true to who they are when they decide what to allow themselves to do.

The following card, written by a seventh-grade girl, is another testimony to how important it is to make sure we help kids understand all of this.

> I have a problem. It is about sex. My mom never talks to me about it. My boyfriend wants to have it but I don't know what to do and I am very scared that if I don't have it he will break up with me. But what if I get pregnant? Please advise. P.S. My boyfriend is in the ninth grade and I love him very much.

You need not wait until your son or daughter has any interest in a boyfriend or girlfriend in order to share your own views, values, and beliefs. If your son or daughter has reached the upper-elementary-school level and has not approached you with questions about sex, it is important for you to approach your child.

I have received more anonymous sharing cards from middle-school students than I care to count that read, "I'm pregnant," or "I think I've been date-raped," or "I've been touched in places that I shouldn't be. . . ." Our kids won't know what is totally inappropriate for them to be doing unless we discuss with them what it is in the first place. Our discussions can help them understand our definition of appropriate boundaries, ways to avoid or get out of risk situations, how to deal with pressure, and so on. Since kids are not likely to ask, again, it's crucial for us as parents to create the chance to tell them, anyway.

PARTIES

My father thinks he knows everything that goes on, but he doesn't. I wish he could understand some of the pressures. If I told my dad what happens at parties, he wouldn't let me go to another one.

I debated whether I should begin this section with one of our major fears—what kids won't tell us about their parties, what's really going on. What I have to share I know will include some parents' worst fears. The truth is, what goes on at parties sometimes scares even the kids. Many kids actually wish they could talk with their parents about these kinds of things. But, as this student states, they're often too afraid because they sense if they do, they'll never be allowed out again.

What's going on at your kids' parties? If you haven't asked, you might start with:

> "I figure that a lot of kids think that if they told their parent what really goes on at their parties, they'd be grounded until their thirty-sixth birthday. . . . I really am concerned, though. The word at the PTA meeting was that kids in our town are drinking a lot of alcohol, and parties are getting out of control. I'm worried about your safety. And I love you too much to be silent about this. Will you talk honestly with me?"

Hopefully, your child's answer will be "Yes." If not, you can still share your thoughts, feelings, and concerns in writing or aloud. If your child does not choose to respond, it's reasonable to ask that he or she hear you and your concerns.

Parents' biggest worry about parties is that they include sex, alcohol, and other drugs. There is the great fear that kids are going to get out of control, and that something terrible will happen as a result.

As parents we can't always control what goes on when our children are out, but there are some steps we can take to increase our children's safety. We can form "parent networks," we can make rules like "no parent home, you can't go there for a party." We can work actively with our kids to help them believe the risks are real and know how to pick apart situations to determine what choices they have when faced with a situation that might be tough. We can enable them to tell the difference between which choices are safe and which aren't. And we can keep them in our prayers.

Think about the conversations you have already had with your son or daughter about getting together with friends. What constitutes a "party" in your mind? Have you established boundaries as to how many friends are allowed in your home if you happen not to be there? How accessible is any wine, beer, or liquor you might have in your home? Do you smoke pot or use other drugs, and could it be possible that your kids know where your stash is hidden? I've heard too many stories from kids who told me they knew much more about what their parents did behind closed doors than their parents ever realized. Think about this when you decide what to share with your child about your own habits, what your personal thoughts are about alcohol and other drug use, the decisions you make regarding them in your life, and your honest concern and thoughts about your child's use of them. This kind of sharing can add a further dimension to the bond that can continue to grow between you and your child.

When our son and daughter were younger, I often called in advance to double-check if a parent actually was planning to be home for the party either of them planned to attend. I told my kids I was calling so they would be aware that I was following through with our concern. They weren't thrilled, but eventually we were able to transition to an honor-type system.

Did we get through the teenage years avoiding the dreaded big *Risky Business* "party of the century"–type fiasco? No, we did not. All seemed to have been going pretty smoothly as far as respect for our household rules was concerned. That is, until one weekend when my husband was on his annual fishing trip with the guys, and I was spending the night with the wives of the guys who went fishing.

Our kids, then in high school, told Emma, a friend of our family who was staying at our home with them while we were away for the weekend, that my husband gave them permission to "have some people over." She bought into it.

The living-room furniture was evidently emptied and piled into the dining room. Not only did kids from our town come, but kids in a few of the surrounding towns got wind of it and they came, too. Our son and daughter admitted that they never expected so many people to come. It just seemed to get out of hand. And because it got so crowded, and people got so out of control, they got scared, couldn't take it anymore, and actually left. Yes, they left all the out-of-control people in our home.

Thank goodness our son's best friend was there. He and a few others took charge and, with Emma's help, cleared everyone out. I happened to call around eleven that night just to say hello, and found out what was going on. I don't even want to try to describe how I felt when I got off the phone. You can be sure that my husband and I talked extensively about this experience with our son and daughter in the weeks that followed. The offense that this party represented was so overwhelming that we weren't even about to try to think of an appropriate punishment. We mainly talked. Our kids said they knew it was a terribly wrong thing to do, they acknowledged how much of a risk they had taken, and it never happened again. So they say.

We were lucky. To our knowledge, no one was hurt, either at our home or on the way home. The law now makes parents responsible and liable if anything like an accident happens—in our home or even to people on the way home from a party at our home—as a result of drinking alcohol or use of other drugs in our home, even if we weren't home.

What is also important to discuss with our children is not only the potential destruction that can take place if too many kids are together for a party and get out of control—and not only the potential parental liability, which can be very serious—but also how being out of control under the influence of alcohol and/or other drugs can result in devastating outcomes, such as date or acquaintance rape, drug overdoses, and alcohol poisoning. Add consequences such as fighting and other forms of violence. Kids have described a variety of troubling alcohol-related experiences that took place at parties, such as when one boy punched another in the face because he thought he was "hitting" on his girlfriend, or when one boy punched his fist through a glass windowpane because he was so upset that his girlfriend broke up with him.

The reality is that, especially when parents aren't home, it's possible that there will be kids who will go further sexually with their boyfriend or girlfriend than was planned and certainly further than their parents would have wished. Even when parents are home, if kids want to go further, they often can find a way. Ideally, it would be great if all our children had within themselves a respect and control for boundaries, so that even if parents weren't home, they would honor the limits that they know are appropriate and safe.

I'm in a heavy situation: A lot of my friends are drinking and doing drugs, even my ex-boyfriend. I don't wanna try it but I kinda do. I'm scared it might mess me up.

Even if we establish clear boundaries with our kids, it still may be hard to control where they actually go and what they allow themselves to do. As we all can do, children can learn from experience. My theory is that if we're lucky enough to survive a mistake, we can grow stronger from the lessons it teaches us.

When kids lie to their parents and say a friend's parent was home at a party when that wasn't the case at all, or lie about where they actually spent their evening, I don't believe that these kids should be branded as "liars" (at least, most of them should not). Bending the truth in those circumstances is often the only way they can figure out how to have the freedom to do what they want with their friends without parental interference. That doesn't make these lies okay. Lies enable kids to put themselves in potentially dangerous, risky situations. They also raise serious questions about the whole issue of trust. I'm not suggesting that your child is going to lie. It's just important to remain aware of that possibility and, if you do become aware of it, to use that situation as an opportunity to discuss your feelings, the risk of the action to your child, and your child's feelings. A punishment may also be appropriate to consider, but more important is to try to discuss what happened, why, and the importance of preventing it from happening again.

IF YOUR CHILD'S FRIENDS SHOW UP WHEN YOU'RE NOT HOME

You can also prepare your child to know what to say in specific situations, such as if more than the agreed-upon maximum number of friends show up at your doorstep when you're not there. For example, your child can know in advance to say:

> "I'd love to let you in! But my parents would ground me forever if they found out I did. I'm not supposed to. They said three friends, at the most, if they're not home. And I already broke their trust last week. So I'm really sorry, guys. I just can't let you in. Please don't give me a hard time with this. I'll call you later."

Kids need to know that a great excuse to get out of uncomfortable situations is to blame it on their parents.

IF YOU'RE THE PARENT HOME
WHEN YOUR CHILD IS HAVING A PARTY

Kids usually get very embarrassed if their parents parade in and out of the party they are having. That's probably why a lot of kids prefer to go to parties at the home of a friend. They may not want to deal with their parents' interruptions. They also may not want their parents to be aware of what they're doing. In fact, the decision to stay overnight at the home of a friend is often their way to avoid having to come home in the shape they were in at the end of the evening.

With regard to parties at your home, you're in charge. You, as the parent, have the right to establish rules that your children and their guests must respect. If they don't, you can establish ahead of time what will cause you to ask your child's friends to leave (and how you anticipate they will be able to get home). Whatever your boundaries, whatever your concerns, it's best to discuss them with your child before friends arrive. You can give your child a choice. If your son or daughter doesn't feel it will be possible to conduct the party in accordance with what rules you have set forth, he or she can decide it's better not to have the party. How parents approach party rules is a personal judgment call that parents can decide only for themselves.

Bottom Line

The reality is that we probably cannot anticipate every single issue that will arise that relates to a party situation in our own home or at the home of a child's friend. The best we can do is stay aware of the potential dangers, keep the communication lines open, and establish boundaries for our own children that are consistent with our values and beliefs as well as what we know to be safe behavior.

Will your child make a mistake? Break a rule? Break your trust at some point in the growing-up years? Probably. But just as we need to forgive ourselves for being human, we also need to help our kids understand that they can learn from every experience, and that mistakes are not sins. We can hope they'll go forward much wiser for all they learned (and not repeat the mistake).

Beyond anything we teach our kids for their own safety and survival, unless they own it—meaning, believe it for themselves—they may still take chances we don't even want to think about. The next chapter, on peer pressure, choices, and risks, will further help you help the kids in your life develop a safety mind-set and be able to take greater control over what they allow themselves to do.

How do you talk to your parents about drinking or smoking if you know they'll get you in trouble or be mad?

dont
What if you really ↓like sex, but it's the only way you can make friends.
Theres this girl wants to do it with me, but I can't turn her down because she will tell everyone I am immature.

I think I am Pregnant!
what do I do - I havent
told no one.

what DO you do If
A feiends on drugs
& you Know it But you
Dont want them to
get in trouble

8

PEER PRESSURE, CHOICES, AND RISKS
(Alcohol and Other Drugs, Sex, Smoking, or Anything Else)

When our kids are tested by peers, it's likely that we won't be around to whisper over their shoulders, "Please don't!" or "Wait a minute, are you sure you know what you're getting yourself into?" If someone starts moving their hand, will they allow that person to go further sexually or not? If the person who pulls up in a car to pick them up has been drinking, will they get into the car or not? Will they drag on the cigarette if it's passed to them? Will they take their parent's car on a dare?

The reality is, kids may have literally only a few seconds to make serious choices, some of which may have life-or-death consequences. And they'll probably be faced with making them completely on their own, based on their own perception of what risks are involved. For most parents, that's scary. It is to me.

While we cannot expect to be with our children at the exact moments they are pressured to make difficult choices, there is still much we can do. This chapter is devoted to offering ways you can help your child be more prepared to identify, understand, and control risks when dealing with pressure from peers.

Before going on, I want to mention that not all peer pressure is negative. On the contrary, peer pressure can also inspire and challenge kids to accomplish what they may never have otherwise been able to achieve. Peer pressure can create a positive learning experience, one that teaches kids about who they are, reveals to them what they believe, and gives kids a chance to prove to themselves that they can honor their own values. These things in and of themselves can provide a boost to our children's self-confidence. Another positive effect of peer pressure is that it can teach kids who their real friends are. You might find it interesting to ask your child to think of peer-pressure situations that turned out to be a very positive influence on them. Also encourage your child to consider ways he or she might have been a positive influence on others.

In this chapter, I'm going to concentrate only on what worries parents most about peer pressure, the kind that can lead to negative consequences. Since the potentially dangerous exposures seem to be starting earlier and earlier, we need to be even more prepared to help our kids have the knowledge, inner strength, and skills to avoid and prevent unwanted, unthinkable outcomes. Since all kids are at risk, I figure time and space are better spent on helping them deal with the difficult influences they might encounter in order to prevent negative outcomes. The good outcomes are much easier to handle.

WHEN TO START PREPARING
KIDS TO HANDLE PEER PRESSURE

If you're thinking, "My child doesn't have to deal with this yet," it may help to realize that peer pressure takes many forms. If it's not alcohol, other drugs, sex, or smoking, maybe your son or daughter will be pressured into taking candy from a store without paying, or sneaking into the movies. The list of possible peer-pressure situations could fill volumes.

> I was in a club but then I was not, because I did not do something the club was doing.

Think about it. If someone your child wants as a friend asks to copy the child's answers during an exam, that's peer pressure. When a group of kids shout, "Chicken" or "Oh, you're such a baby!" to your son because he didn't want to ride his bicycle fast down a steep hill, that's peer pressure. If your child's friends start saying mean things to someone in the school yard during recess and your child doesn't want to go along with what they're doing, that, too, is peer pressure. If you have instructed your child not to go through a shortcut on the way home, but her friends are going that way, and tell her, "Aw, c'mon. Your parents will never know," that's peer pressure. Ask your son or daughter to come up with other situations.

> **When I was in the fifth grade, a good friend of mine always swore, and I felt very pressured to swear along with the group, but I just couldn't, so they made me feel very left out. What could I have done?**

Every child will be tested by peers in one way or another. Every child will have to deal with peer pressure. It's part of growing up. Therefore, the time to start preparing kids to face peer pressure is as early as possible. As soon as your child starts to talk, you can start teaching him or her how to turn feelings into words. You can encourage self-expression, nurture respect for others, and help your child understand what it means to own what you do.

One of my roommates from college is the director of a fabulously innovative day-care school associated with a university in the Boston area. I spent a morning with her observing classes and was intrigued by one incident I'll never forget. A boy was playing in a large sandbox (in the classroom itself). He wore a huge witch's hat, was stirring a "brew" with an oversized spoon, and had a variety of cups surrounding him, each containing something to put into the brew. As he was busily shaking each of the contents of the cups into his brew, stirring with huge circular motions as he added each ingredient, I saw what I anticipated as "trouble" coming toward him. Another little boy (these were three-year-olds) had started walking toward the sandbox, and I had a feeling he was planning to intrude.

Sure enough, as the child making the brew sensed that the other boy was approaching, he turned around in the sandbox to face him and started to cry. At that point, my roommate said to him, "Use your words, use your words!" Miraculously, the boy in the sandbox stopped crying almost immediately, paused for a moment, and said directly to the boy who was coming still closer, "STOP THAT!"

That was several years ago, but I can still picture the scene as if it were yesterday. I was struck by the power of what it can mean to start teaching children at a young age what words they can say when faced with an uncomfortable situation. When the boy who was approaching heard "Stop that!", he actually stopped and walked away. It was great that he listened, but it doesn't always work out that way. At the very least, the child in the sandbox had been armed with the tools to stand up for himself.

Based on all that kids have shared with me, I know that far too many pre-teens and teens don't have the inner strength and ability to communicate as clearly and stand up for themselves as well as this three-year-old demonstrated, witch's hat and all. Even if it were only one child who didn't have the capacity to stand up for him- or herself, that would still be too many.

BEYOND THE FACTS, BEYOND OUR "DON'TS"

It's not enough to tell our children, "Don't." No matter how much they understand that what they're about to do is wrong, unhealthy, dangerous, and could get them into trouble, their need to belong may be so powerful that they may do it, anyway.

> **If you were pregnant and you were only thirteen and three months along, would you tell your mother, even though your mother has warned you that if you ever got pregnant she would kill you, or something threatening, and your best friend is the only one that knows, and she said she would help you through it? What would you do? PLEASE HELP ME!**

With all the prevention-oriented educational programs that have been in place for so many years, one would think that kids would have "gotten it" already. You'd think they would understand that if they allow themselves to take risks, they could potentially pay dearly in all kinds of unwanted and devastating ways. But the reality is that there are still kids for whom it takes a tragedy to prove the risks are real. For some, even the impact of tragedies wears off in time and they go back to taking risks. There are still those who believe the risks are real but think the consequences happen to "other people" in "other places" and couldn't possibly happen to them—until they do. There are kids who believe the risks are real but do not value themselves enough to take a hard line on what they know ought to be their limits. And there are still kids who are playing Russian roulette with their decision making.

There is no question that it is absolutely crucial for our kids to understand every updated bit of factual information related to such concerns as the effects of alcohol and other drugs, how HIV and other sexually transmitted diseases are transmitted (and how they're not), and what they need to be aware of to prevent pregnancy and date or acquaintance rape from taking place. They need to know that smoking cigarettes and cigars, taking snuff, and chewing tobacco can all lead to very serious illness. As a basis for healthier, safer decision making, they must have their facts straight. We can surely help by providing this information.

Can we have sex? Yes _____ No _____

However, the facts alone are not enough. And if we only give kids factual information and tell them "You better not do this or else . . ." that is likely not to be enough to make a difference in what they choose to do when no one is looking over their shoulders. Kids tend to take chances. They're especially concerned about fitting in, being accepted, and not losing a boyfriend or girlfriend. They're also curious and concerned about being considered cool, and many think they're invincible. It's the rare child who will actually follow a parent's boundaries exactly as given. I'm not suggesting that's okay, I'm just saying that we need to know what's really going on.

I realize I'm suggesting the possibility that it may not be wise to take everything your child says as complete truth. There is a delicate balance that I honestly found difficult to establish with my own kids. That is, the balance between trusting and being even a little suspicious or trusting and doing a little bit of investigating just to double-check that rules my husband and I had set down were not being broken. Since so many thousands of kids across the country had made me privy to what they often couldn't tell their parents, that fueled my thoughts about what my own kids were really doing and not telling me. They eventually called me on this, and I agreed to work at my ability to take things at face value unless proven otherwise. It was really tough. I'm sure this is all an art form! Well, as long as I'm dealing with "truths," the truth is that I silently did do a little more checking than anyone might have realized. I always felt the stakes were too high to ignore my intuition at certain times. You have to come up with your own comfort zone with your children—your rules and fears and boundaries, and their requests, desire for freedom, and the risks they'll take. It's also important to realize that regardless of how much "checking" any parent might do, there are certain things that it may not be possible to find out unless your child decides to tell you.

How do I explain to my parents I'm not a child and tell my mom what me and my boyfriends do when we hang out?

Wherever your comfort zone is, just keep talking with your children and sharing your feelings, listening and responding to theirs whenever possible. Because beyond the facts and our "don'ts," our children's life skills need to be strong. To me, life skills include communication, social skills, decision making, and coping skills. However, even with a solid foundation of accurately understood factual knowledge and life skills in place, if a child doesn't value him- or herself, the child might still not be capable of acting on that knowledge and utilizing those skills.

I have been out with five boys and had sex with all of them. Is that normal for one school year? I didn't love any of them but they just put so much pressure on me, I had to. This is my problem. What should I do?

To go one step further, with accurate knowledge, excellent life skills, and a strong sense of self-worth, kids might still take serious chances if they don't believe the risks are real. All of these components must be in place if we are to hope our kids will take control of their risks and make safer, healthier choices for themselves now and throughout their lives.

COMMUNICATION SKILLS

We can help kids figure out many different responses to possible pressure situations—from drinking or smoking to sex, to stealing, to teasing or cheating—so they can be as ready as the three-year-old in my roommate's day-care school. You might wish to add the following to your own list you share with your child:

- "No."
- "*No*, thanks! If you want to, go ahead. I don't."
- "I don't think any of us should be doing this." (Usually harder for kids to say.)
- "I don't like when you push me to do things like that. Please lay off. If you're really my friend, you'll stop pushing and respect that this is my choice."
- "I need to go home right now."
- "Please don't touch me like that."
- "No. Don't touch me there."
- "That makes me really uncomfortable. Please stop!"

I had a sexual experience and I'm scared. I regret it and want to take it back. What should I do?

We need to teach kids that nonverbal responses, such as putting up a hand to signal "stop" or moving someone's hand away, can also be very effective. This is a good time to reinforce the fact that kids can control only what they personally say or do. They cannot control another person's response to what they say or do. But, again, each child can decide how he or she wishes to deal with the other person's response. That's the way each child can stay in control. Many kids still don't understand this.

Remind your child that even if the other person does not stop, he or she can get up, move away, or call home (or a neighbor, relative, or friend's parent) to arrange to be picked up if he or she is at school or somewhere else. Also, if your son or daughter can't think of anything else to get out of an uncomfortable situation, he or she can say something like, "My mom won't let me" or "Sorry, I wish I could. But I have to baby-sit."

We also need to acknowledge the fact that it's normal and okay for our kids to feel uncomfortable. Just because they know what words to say doesn't mean it will be easy to say them. It may be very hard to get the words out, but it's important to get them out, anyway.

Here's a perfect place to remind kids about how they can "turn feelings into words." They can simply start with "This is hard for me to say. But I need you to stop . . ."

I am nervous for seventh grade because I don't want to be pressured into drugs or smoking by older kids. And I don't know what to say or do. I am scared. What should I do?

Ideally, our kids will be able to learn to anticipate uncomfortable situations in order to avoid putting themselves where they don't want to be. However, it's likely that at some point along the way, they'll have to think fast and come up with something to say to quickly get away from a situation they don't want to participate in. If they have a menu of sentences that they've learned ahead of time, just in case, they will never be lost for words and can concentrate on removing themselves quickly.

SOCIAL SKILLS

How do you tell a friend you don't want to do something without hurting their feelings or losing them?

Kids need to have strong social skills—meaning, they need to be confident that they know how to make new friends (refer to chapter 6). We cannot hope that they will walk away from dangerous situations involving their only friends, and/or their boyfriend or girlfriend, if they don't know how, and don't trust that they are capable of starting again.

Kids also need for us to reinforce the perspectives that go along with being faced with making choices that differ from what their friends are doing and, in some cases, choices that their friends might not like.

We must remind them and talk with them about what a true friendship really means. We need to challenge our kids to think about and discuss with them what kind of statement it would be about a friendship if someone didn't respect their right to choose which activities to be involved in and which to avoid. And what they think a relationship would be based on if someone broke up with a girlfriend or boyfriend because they wouldn't go further sexually. This is also a good time to reinforce concern about how kids value themselves and the fact that while they cannot control whether someone else respects them, they can control respecting themselves.

DECISION-MAKING SKILLS

First, it's important to remind kids that they have a choice. They have a right to say "Yes" or "No." They have a right to choose. While this may seem obvious, as I've said before, many kids don't realize this is so. We then need to help our children learn to pick apart situations, identify choices, figure out what choices mean, and anticipate potential risks in order to make effective decisions.

HELPING KIDS FIGURE OUT CHOICES

Since it would be impossible to anticipate every peer-pressure situation that your child will face during the growing-up years, you can teach him or her a general pattern of approaching decisions that can apply to most situations. Here's the basic range of choices your child would have to consider when dealing with any kind of peer pressure. Your son or daughter might:

- not give in to pressure, and walk away from the situation
- not give in to pressure, but stay
- give in to the pressure
- not give in to pressure and speak up, tell friends that what they're doing is not a good idea, will get them into trouble, is dangerous, etc.
- tell someone (an adult)—call for help

To be more specific, and to give your child practice in how to figure out choices, your son or daughter can suggest an incident that he or she has already experienced to use as an example, or you can create an example based on what situations you might be concerned your child will have to handle. For instance: What choices might your child have if everyone at a party is drinking beer and your child doesn't want to drink? Add the fact that everyone is saying, "Oh, come on. Try it." Here are choices your son or daughter might have to consider:

- Give in to the pressure and have a beer
- Tell them something like, "No, thanks" or "I already told you no, please stop asking"
- Hold a glass that is tinted so everyone thinks it contains beer
- Take a beer and periodically spill some out, giving the impression that you are drinking it
- Tell everyone that they're drinking too much and really should stop
- Leave the party

You and your child can discuss these choices and add any of your own. The more your child has a chance to practice figuring out choices in all different types of situations, the more prepared he or she will be for whatever will come up in their life.

Role-playing the situation with your child can be a terrific way to explore what might happen as a result of one choice over another. This kind of interaction can also give your child a chance to reinforce what words can be said in the face of discomfort or danger and what kind of control is feasible for him or her.

That people would stop telling me what to do and let me decide for myself.

HELPING YOUR CHILD FIGURE OUT CONSEQUENCES OF CHOICES

Simply knowing what the choices are is not enough. Your child needs to know what each choice might mean so he or she will be able to anticipate the possible results or risks of each one. Using the party example where everyone was drinking beer, you and your child might consider a number of different choices and their possible consequences.

If your child gives in to peer pressure and has a beer, he or she might:

- not respect him- or herself for giving in to the pressure
- be more accepted by those at the party
- feel a greater sense of belonging at the party
- feel sick or get drunk from the beer

- behave in a way that is out of control
- like it, then what?
- get into trouble because parents will find out
- not drive home safely (for older kids who are driving)

If your child tries to tell friends not to drink, those friends might:

- stop and seriously consider what your child is saying
- think your child is a ridiculous wimp, goody-goody, nerd, etc.
- tease and make fun of your child for trying to stop them

If your child leaves the party, he or she:

- may be teased and talked about after leaving
- may have great self-respect for being confident and strong about making the "right" decision
- may jeopardize being accepted, or being included at other parties
- may risk losing those friendships
- won't get into any trouble for drinking
- will no longer be in an uncomfortable situation
- will be understood by friends
- will be respected by friends for taking such a strong stand
- will learn who is a true friend and who is not

If your child holds a tinted glass or takes a beer and keeps spilling some out, he or she:

- may feel accepted and relieved because friends think he or she is drinking beer
- may be embarrassed because some friends might discover it's not really beer/or catch him or her in the act of spilling it out
- may feel privately ashamed to lack the confidence to say "no"
- may feel secretly out of place, pretending to do what other kids are doing but knowing that's not the truth

Why is it so hard to be accepted?

If your child stays at the party and says, "No, thanks":

· friends may understand and respect the request
· friends may continue to say, "Oh, come on . . ."
· friends may tease and not feel your child is part of the crowd
· he or she may feel proud to be strong enough not to give in
· he or she won't get into trouble (although if a party is "busted" for drugs, all kids at that party, whether they're using them or not, can be brought in)
· driving home will be safer (for an older child who is driving)

For each choice, I did not put the possible consequences in any particular order. It might be very interesting to ask your child how he or she would order the possible outcomes. What consequences would be the biggest concern? What would be the least?

HELPING KIDS UNDERSTAND WHAT OWNERSHIP MEANS

We have a greater chance that kids will be more serious about their decisions if they realize that whatever they decide to do, they must own. Early on, we must hold them accountable for what they allow themselves to do. That will help to reinforce the reality that what they do is their own choice, and therefore the consequences are their responsibility.

During an assembly I was presenting for fourth-grade students at a school in the Midwest a few years ago, one of the boys blurted out something that caused an interruption, and was immediately reprimanded by his teacher. He looked at me and said, loud enough for everyone to hear, "But my friend made me say it, my friend made me say it!"

I then asked him, "But *who* said it?" He paused, looked back at me, and answered, "I did."

We can and must acknowledge to our children that they will be faced with all kinds of pressure. Even their closest friends might try to urge them to do something that might not be comfortable or safe. They need to know that no matter what anybody says to them, it's still up to each person to decide what to do in response.

HELPING KIDS BELIEVE THE RISKS ARE REAL

I mentioned in chapter 7 how dramatic the show of hands always is when I ask high-school and college audiences, "How many of you know someone who is or has been in an abusive relationship?" The response is just as staggering when I ask:

- "How many of you know someone who was date-raped?"
- "How many of you know someone who became pregnant before she wanted or planned to be?"
- "How many of you know someone who drinks or uses other drugs and drives?"
- "How many of you know someone, personally, who has been seriously injured or has died as a result of drinking or use of other drugs and driving?"
- "How many of you know someone who has had a sexually transmitted disease?" "More than one?"
- "How many of you know someone who is HIV positive?" "Or has full-blown AIDS?"

Whether there are fifty, several hundred, or more than a thousand students in the audience, I frequently hear an undercurrent of laughter when they observe that just about every hand was raised in response to my question about drinking and driving. But without exception, there is absolute silence as hands are raised in response to my next question, which relates to knowing someone personally who experienced an alcohol-related serious injury or death.

When the consequence is personalized, it's always a different story. Students get much more serious. Some cry. What I do at those moments is call them on it. There is no arguing about what has just taken place. They heard the laughter, they felt the silence. I find that this is usually the best moment to let them know I respect that bottom line, whatever they choose to do is their choice, their own call. But the issue is, what are they really doing? I let them know that I know each student can only answer that question for him- or herself. You can have a similar discussion on responsibility with your son or daughter.

The following card was written at one of my programs by a male high-school senior. I only hope he kept his word.

On weekends I tend to drink and drive. I don't feel that I am drunk but I'm under the influence of alcohol. The story you told me went straight to my heart. I will not allow my friends or myself to operate a car when drunk.

Although younger kids won't be driving cars, they may have older brothers, sisters, relatives, or friends who do. Unfortunately, the news reports continue to be filled with stories about alcohol- and other drug-related accidents and deaths. In addition, there have been many grief-ridden stories in the media about teenagers who gave birth and left their newborn infants in bathrooms to die, or be found and cared for by someone else. These terrible tragedies can add fuel to discussions with your child about safe choices, abstinence, and how important it is to be able to come to a parent for help no matter how bad a situation seems.

Sometimes I feel pressured into, say, going further than I wanted to because I'm afraid of losing him. The same with drinking. I mean the pressure is not really bad, but I feel I have to because everybody does.

Incidents of rape are usually in the news. While those crimes are usually stranger related, that's a springboard for talking with younger kids about preventing date or acquaintance rape, sexual and other types of abuse, and encouraging safety-mindedness in relationships and in general. Stories on kids with guns and other weapons in school, gang fighting, reports about children shooting other students and even parents, can all provide an opening for prevention-oriented discussion with your child.

In science class we were working on packets. Everyone was cheating. Everyone! My friend and I were comparing notes together. Other people came over and asked to cheat. I said no but my friend said yes. So I left. I then felt very bad. What should I do or have done?

There are other consequences in the news that relate to honor and betrayal, cheating, stealing, and breaking other kinds of laws.

These are also important pressures and concerns that we must help our kids deal with, not only during their growing-up years but for the rest of their lives. Talk with your child about them, what the pressures were, if he or she can relate in any way, and what decisions he or she would make in a similar situation. When experiences happen in your hometown that can represent teachable moments, and can make the experiences and related lessons even more personalized for you and your child. What is especially important with these incidents is that our kids get the idea that the consequences are real. They don't just happen to "other" people. We can also say that no matter how remote any city or town might be, no matter how beautiful and seemingly insulated a community may be, if someone takes a risk, he or she needs to be ready to face very real consequences.

It seems unconscionable that we need to talk with kids at such a young age about all of these things. But with the exception of the few cards I specifically indicated were from high-school students, the rest of the cards I've shared in this book were collected at my upper-elementary- and middle-school-level assembly programs.

I have a drug problem.

The cards speak for themselves. To me, they scream! If we want to help with prevention, we need to reach kids earlier than when they might be exposed to all of these pressures and choices. That means we have to talk with our children when they are still in elementary school.

How can I talk to my parents about the sexual stuff or about my sex life?

I am concerned about my friend because he smokes cigarettes at his bus stop. I told him about what would happen but he does not listen. What should I do?

Kids need to be brought to the point where they believe the risks are real, not only because their parents say so, not only because they're taught about risks in health classes, or are reminded to be cautious by the media, but because, in their gut, they know this to be true. Until they own those feelings, they may still take terrible chances. So how else can we help kids believe that for themselves?

The process of helping our children transition to the point where they view risk taking as the danger these words imply is just that—a process. It's a matter of building on every opportunity. Through reading books and talking openly with our sons and daughters, we can consciously try to help them value themselves more, become more self-confident, build stronger life skills, and talk about their feelings. Lots of talking.

On top of all that, I believe we need to further clarify for our kids what taking a risk actually means. In order to do that, I have figured out perspectives that can help you and your child pick apart what it can mean to take a chance and have unwanted consequences happen. One would think this is common sense; however, the responses from students as well as parents tell me otherwise. This is a very helpful exercise.

I've watched thousands of faces respond to these perspectives with private nods, with knowing looks. I share them with you in the hope that you will find they will make sense to your own son or daughter. I've shared these thoughts with my son and daughter on more than one occasion. At the very least, they seemed to listen seriously. Remember, all of this is a process; none of it is a one-time discussion.

I'm fourteen. Am I old enough to be sexually active?

PUTTING THE CONSEQUENCES IN REALITY-BASED PERSPECTIVE

I'll use a common concern as my example for this series of questions and answers that illustrate how we can put into perspective the consequences someone may face as a result of the decision to drink and drive. You can say to your son or daughter:

- "Can I promise you that if you ever drink and drive, you'll definitely get into an accident?
  "No. But I can promise you that you might."
- "Could you get into an accident the very first time you drink and drive? Possibly."
- "The ninth time? Possibly. The fifty-first time?

Hard to say. The hundred and fiftieth time?
Maybe."
- "Could you get away with it each time? It's possible. But it's also possible that the second time you do it, you won't make it home."
- "The point is, every single time you take a risk, it could be that time that the accident occurs, that time that you completely lose control."
- "Can I promise that it will happen? No. But I can promise that it might. And if this is something that you would never want to happen—ever in your life—then I suggest that you cannot take even one chance."

In order to prevent and avoid unwanted consequences, our kids need to understand that each time they take a particular risk, the unwanted consequence could happen. When I'm also dealing with the concern about unwanted pregnancy, I broaden my words of caution:

- "If this is something that you would never want to have happen in your life, or you would absolutely not want to happen in your life right now . . . then I suggest you can't even take one chance."

All it takes is one risk, one time, for an unwanted result to happen. That's the message. On top of offering those perspectives, I believe we need to add:

- "What will it take for you?"
- "Will it take losing a best friend in a drunk-driving accident to prove that no one is exempt? That if people take risks—you, me, anyone—there could be unthinkable results?"
- "Will it take a pregnancy?"
- "Will it take actually knowing someone personally who is dying of AIDS?"
- "What will it take . . . ?"

You can add your own questions and then follow with:

"I know what I wish your answer would be . . . but I also know that you have to find your own answers. I'm worried about you. I love you so much. I just would never want anything bad to happen to you."

RISK REDUCTION—OUR OWN
EXPECTATIONS NEED TO BE REALITY BASED

Through all we share with our kids, we need to help them reach a point where they take seriously, for themselves, the need to question: "At what price do I do this? What are my risks?" And "If my friends or boyfriend or girlfriend don't respect my right to choose, maybe I need to reevaluate how important they are in my life."

I'm not suggesting that upon hearing all these perspectives, our kids will automatically and immediately choose to eliminate all of their risk taking. Rather, by asking questions, challenging them to think, giving them another way to view what could possibly happen, we have a better chance of helping them understand what taking a risk actually can mean to them. And if they understand all of this for themselves— with a foundation of valuing themselves and the skills to act upon reality-based evaluations of risks—we've got a better chance they will take more serious control of what they allow themselves to do.

WHEN KIDS MAKE MISTAKES

Kids find it very hard to admit to their parents that they've made a mistake, gone against their rules, violated a trust, or made a poor choice. It's usually not that our children want to lie, but more a choice to hold back the truth. Reasons for holding back include fear that parents will be disappointed, shocked, angry, have less trust in them, respect them less, and possibly even judge friends as being a bad influence.

It's understandable that kids might be fearful of admitting to their parents that a girlfriend is pregnant, they have an alcohol or other type of drug problem, they stole something—or any other serious concerns. What they often don't understand is that they can still be loved, they're still valuable, they're not bad people just because they might have had bad judgment. Our kids deserve and need to have adult support and guidance always, but especially in serious circum- stances that are too hard to handle alone.

While it's true that there are some parents who would not be there for their children, I'd like to think most will. Unfortunately, many kids don't have the courage and don't trust that they can take the chance to find this out with their own parents. The more you let your child know how aware you are of the many difficult things kids might be faced with growing up today, the more you will help to increase the possibility that your child will feel you're approachable when they have had a troubling experience or just want to discuss their thoughts about one.

Don't wait until a mistake happens to talk with your child about the reality that everyone makes mistakes—grown-ups as well as kids. Be sure your child knows that mistakes are not sins, and that he or she can learn from every experience, and, in fact, that sometimes what may seem like the most awful mistakes can turn out to be the most positive and powerful life lessons. We need to tell our children that as long as they are lucky enough to survive a mistake, they can learn what they need to know and do differently so they won't make the same mistake again. A mistake can enable them to go forward that much wiser.

Consider what feelings might cause your child to hold back difficult information from you. Then let your child know you're aware that there might be times when he or she might think you would be too upset to learn something that has taken place. Then reiterate what I've already said many times: "Worse than what you believe would be the worst thing you'd have to tell me, would be if you felt you couldn't." Confirm you'd rather know than not know. That somehow you'll deal with whatever it is that may come up—together.

You might find it helpful to tell your son or daughter that although you may be upset when you hear their news, if you're given a few moments to recover from the shock, he or she can absolutely count on you to be there for them. (Sound familiar? There's a pattern to all of this!)

How can you make a bad reputation into a good one?

Also, it can be helpful to remind your child that no one can go backward. However, you may want to add that people can decide to let things go. That means each of us has the option not to hold a grudge and not to punish oneself for years over a mistake that was made. Parents and family members also need to know how important it is to let a mistake go, however terrible or unfortunate it might have been, and kids themselves need to be encouraged to forgive themselves. Too many children are held back by bad feelings about themselves for something that happened in the past that they cannot ever change. Family and friends need to be urged to let a child put a terrible mistake in the past and allow him or her to start life anew. The past is history. Kids usually hate it when parents don't allow them to let go of a mistake they made. When parents keep bringing it up, that makes it even harder for a child to let it go and move on. The mistake should be acknowledged and discussed fully, then dropped unless your child raises it again. While it's possible that certain mistakes may effect serious life changes for children, and can also have a lasting impact on their parents and family, it's the issue of having made the mistake that can be dropped. After addressing it with your child, it's important to concentrate on trying to help him or her go forward in the best possible way.

It would probably be wise to forewarn our kids that people at school may not be as forgiving. Reputations often last for years and don't contribute to good feelings. But your child cannot control what other people think. Your child can only control the personal choice to go forward differently.

What do you do when you're pregnant and everybody knows and they tease you about it?!

These lessons are not easy to give and not easy to learn. They are not easy for adults or children. However, if we don't make the effort to identify the feelings that could be involved here, we may miss out on having the opportunity to help our children through very rough times. It's important to mention to kids that while friends can be a great source of support when times are difficult, it's also crucial for them to seek out the help of an adult. If they don't feel they can go to their parents, they need to consider someone else. You can mention other relatives and close friends whom you trust. Then add teachers, staff, counselors, social workers, psychologists, family doctor, hot lines, and certainly their priest, rabbi, or other clergy whom you know, like, and respect. Actually let your child know you hope he or she would consider going to them if ever he or she chose not to come to you.

When you are abused, how do you tell someone about it?
How do you tell someone you can trust?

"I'D NEVER DO THAT"

Even when our kids vow that they'll "never ever do that," and truly
mean it when they say it, the reality is they still might. They often
don't realize how much harder it will be to handle a particular situation when they are actually faced with it. They may not understand
that it's much easier to say, "I'd never give in to pressure from my
friend" when sitting in a cozy living room with their parent. When
face-to-face with that friend and that pressure, you never know what
will happen.

No matter what, I will never drink or smoke.

OUR APPROACHABILITY

"I'm scared for you" will likely be heard differently by kids than "You
better not do that!" I think it's worth repeating that what I have
found makes a big difference in how kids hear us is to let them know
that we know "they're going to do what they're going to do." We
know that we're not going to be with them when they "go out" with
someone. We're not going to be physically present at their parties.
Even if the party is in our home and we are at home, we're still going
to be in a separate room most of the time. We're not going to school
with our kids. So, what they do is going to be their own decision, as
they are the ones who will be face-to-face with the pressure and have
to decide how to act.

I don't suggest you imply to your kids that "anything goes," just
that we are reality based with regard to what we know we can control
and what we cannot control. We still need to clearly state what
boundaries we feel are appropriate for our children. We need to
establish clear rules. We need to talk about consequences related to
breaking our rules or breaking our trust, and share whatever we feel
we would want our kids to factor into their own decision making.

We also need to realize that trust must go both ways. It's better to
establish trust with our kids rather than fear. Many kids don't think

their parents are allies. Consider what your kids would say about whose side you're on.

If we come off as caring, not preachy, and truly listen without judging, we have a better chance that our kids will come to us no matter what. We also need to be consistent, honest, and not rush our answers if we still must take time to think things through. It's perfectly fine to say, "I need to think about this. I'm not sure. How about if we meet in this chair in an hour!"

It can always help to reinforce the "turning feelings into words" concept (chapter 1) so that even if kids are scared, they can know to start with, "I'm really scared to tell you this . . ." or "This is really hard for me to tell you. I know you told me never to do this, but . . ." If you give your child those kinds of opening lines (using examples that identify the possible reasons why he or she might worry about coming to you), you will in essence be giving your son or daughter permission to tell you anything.

I get stoned every day and I don't know how to stop.

It can also help to anticipate that many kids will figure that you're saying, "Be careful" simply because parents say those things. So they may end up humoring you, placating you with, "Yeah, I'll be careful," and then go ahead and do what they planned to do, anyway. They do this not necessarily because they don't want to listen to us, but more because they're just being kids.

I still say things like, "Please take it easy on the way home" to my own kids, who are now twenty-nine and twenty-seven. The difference for me today is that I know to follow with, "Parents need to say those things!" I'll then get a knowing smile. But I'll feel better because I know they will at least have heard me. That gives me a little more peace of mind.

I've said this already, but I want to emphasize that it bears repeating to your kids periodically. What I have found to be very valuable is to say to my son and daughter, "Worse than what you think would be the worst thing you could possibly tell me . . . worse than that would be if you felt you couldn't."

I want to run away from home because my dad drinks and my parents always fight. What should I do?

How do I get all my friends to stop pressuring me to get laid?

You can try to zero in on what you think your child could be experiencing with friends and what you know is going on at home, to further touch nerves and give permission for talking about whatever you are mentioning. So if you're concerned that your child is sexually active, you might approach your child with:

"I realize that a lot of kids find it very hard to talk with their parents about sex. Kids who have already had sexual experiences wonder if they should let their parents know. I just want you to know that I'm here for you—I know you know how I feel, that I hope you wait until marriage to share yourself so closely—but if you end up making a different decision for yourself, I hope you'll still trust you can come to me. There's a lot that would be important for you to understand. So I'd rather know than not know."

Or, if you think your child is involved with drugs, you might say:

"A lot of kids probably wouldn't tell their parents if they were involved with drugs. Maybe they're afraid their parents would turn them in, or force them to commit themselves into a rehab program. I just want you to know that while I would probably have to learn what the best way to help you would be—if ever you have a problem with drugs, I'd rather know than not know. More than anything, I would want to help you in any way I could."

Or:

"I've been walking around trying to think of a way to talk with you about this. I've had a feeling lately that it's possible you have a drug problem. I have to believe that's a really tough thing for any child to admit to a parent. But if that's true, I want to help you in any way I can. . . . Please, be straight with me."

I wish there were a way to guarantee that our kids would be honest with us. It's possible that no matter what we say, some kids will be in denial, some will still feel too scared to tell us the truth about their drug problem or any other issue. We can only do the best we can to stay tuned in, accessible, become more aware, be good listeners, and continue to let our kids know how much we care.

We can say things like, "I feel like turning you upside down and shaking you! I have a feeling there are all sorts of emotions in there that are just waiting to come out." We can encourage our child to talk with us aloud and write journals. And we can seek the advice of our spouse, significant others, other family members, teachers, counselors, social workers, and other professionals. The rest is up to our child.

IF KIDS ARE WORRIED ABOUT A FRIEND

This is another concern that kids find hard to share with their parents. Very often the reluctance to say anything about helping a friend with a problem has to do with not wanting to get a friend in trouble. Kids are also worried about getting the friend mad and actually losing that person as a friend. Children are also worried that parents, knowing that a friend or friends are involved with something dangerous, might restrict them from spending time together.

We can help our kids by offering more perspectives and asking some pointed questions, such as: Would your child rather have an angry friend than an out-of-control friend or a dead friend? Would it be okay to stay silent if a friend is having a very difficult time emotionally? Discussion can follow to help kids understand the importance of letting an adult know.

I like telling kids the story of what happened at a Girl Scout conference where I spoke with an audience of teenage girls.

I was told ahead of time that one of the girls in the audience had just returned from rehabilitation for a drug problem. The girl who told her friend's parents was also going to be in the audience. Supposedly, the girl who had a drug problem stopped speaking with her friend after that friend informed her parents about the problem. That was the background I was given before starting my presentation.

As with every other educational program I conduct, I gave the audience a chance to write anonymous questions, issues, and any-thing else of concern. When it came time to read the cards aloud and discuss what was written, one of the cards read something like, "I just came back from rehab for my drug problem. And I just wanted to say, 'Thank you, friend.' "

I still get the chills thinking about how powerful and confirming that must have been for her friend to hear what she wrote. It had to have been a very difficult decision for that girl to go to her friend's parents. The reality is that she cared enough about her friend's well-being to risk their friendship in order to get her help. That took a lot of strength. Here's another place where we need to discuss with our kids the meaning of "At what price silence?"

KIDS CANNOT STOP *FOR* A FRIEND

Kids are likely to find it very painful to know that a friend is doing something that is self-destructive. Children often do not understand that only the person who is doing whatever it is—whether smoking, drinking alcohol, using other drugs, taking sexual risks—can decide to stop.

However, that doesn't mean your child cannot seek help. Here are some choices you can suggest that your child consider if he or she is worried about a friend:

- Talk with the friend and urge him or her to go for help
- Encourage the friend to speak with his or her parents
- Offer to go with the friend to speak with someone who is trained to help (not to go into the session with the friend, but rather to wait outside for support)
- Offer to keep the friend company when he or she speaks with a parent
- Talk with you (parent) about how worried he or she is about that friend, and get advice about what to do to help
- Talk with a teacher, counselor, social worker, or other adult about what would be most helpful to do

It can also help to share ideas with your child about what can be said to that friend: For example:

- "I wish you wouldn't smoke anymore. I'm really scared for you. I know you said you could stop anytime, but I heard that stopping is harder than anyone thinks. You really are taking a big chance."
- "This is really hard for me to say to you . . . but I'm your best friend and I'm going to tell you the truth. I'm so worried about you. I'm so upset and really angry about what you're doing to yourself. Please, please, let your parents know you need help. I'll come with you to talk with them."

Kids usually don't know what to do to if they're worried about a friend. Even if your child has not mentioned any such concern, it would be good to let your son or daughter know that if ever there is such concern, he or she could come to you. You can also discuss other choices, such as those listed above.

Worried about a friend that keeps doing things to hurt her. (Drink, smoke, etc.) I don't know what to do or say because she won't listen.

It's important to teach that silence is not an option (for concern about your child's friend, or if your child is concerned about him- or herself). Reinforce to your child how important it is to make sure an adult learns about serious concerns such as that. At the very least, your child can write an anonymous note and leave it with a teacher or school counselor, stating how worried he or she is about that friend and why.

It would also be good to tell your child that professional staff know how to proceed in a private, appropriate way in order that a friend in trouble will receive proper help. And certainly let your child know he or she can come to you with any of these concerns.

WHEN KIDS WORRY ABOUT A PARENT

SMOKING

My parents both smoke. I don't like it when they do it. I'm scared they'll die. What should I do?

If your child could have written this card, it might be a good time to approach your child and talk about his or her possible concern. Kids have often expressed that concern over a parent's health, as well as a great deal of frustration because they don't know what else to do to get the parent to "listen to them" and stop.

As with worries about a friend, kids need to know they can't stop a dangerous behavior for their parent, either. With regard to smoking, we need to explain to kids that the only way a parent will stop smoking is if that parent makes the decision to stop. Again, many kids don't realize that they don't have the power to stop for someone else, not even their parent.

If you smoke cigarettes, cigars, or pipes, or chew tobacco, it's very possible that your child is worried, whether or not he or she has said anything to you. It may help him or her if you bring up the subject. You can also take this opportunity to teach your child about how hard it can be to stop. Kids often think that stopping is no big deal. If you have tried to do so and are still smoking, that can make it even more real.

ALCOHOL AND OTHER DRUGS

If a parent drinks alcohol to excess, or uses other drugs, children worry. Even little kids who may not be able to express themselves clearly are likely to still worry. It may seem like they're oblivious, but don't count on it. If there is a drug problem in a family, or even what seems like excessive drinking to a child, figure that it's going to take its toll on the children in one way or another.

Most kids in this kind of situation think they're not supposed to tell anyone about what's going on. They often think they're the only family dealing with this kind of a problem. If a parent hasn't actually told a child not to say anything, kids may just, deep down, feel that they shouldn't let anyone know. It may be years before they tell anyone how painful their feelings really are.

How do you handle drugs in your family?

When a parent has a drug problem, kids may be afraid to bring friends home. These children are likely to be fearful that parents will be out of control and even fight in front of friends, and they may feel ashamed and scared that friends might learn that their parent drinks.

Kids may think they are somehow at fault for their family's problems. Children with such a concern may think if only they could do something differently, if only they could be the best, maybe their parent will stop the drinking. They may try hard to be the best in school, the best in sports, and the best in everything else in order to solve the problem they perceive. The more those kids might try to be "the best," and the more their parent drinks, the more those children might feel that they're just not doing enough.

Other kids may act out in a negative way at school. They may get into trouble in class, get into trouble with the law, begin to drink alcohol and use other drugs. That may be their only way to get attention. The negative attention may be better to them than no attention. Some kids, especially if they're young, might just be very quiet. But that doesn't mean they aren't aware that something is not right. Still others may act as if they're hyperactive, running around, making jokes, and may not be taken seriously. These children may not be able to tell anyone that their behavior is in response to their nervousness about what's going on.

Worry about a parent's drug problem can come out in these and other ways. Kids who are living with this situation need appropriate help. If you know there is an alcohol or other drug problem in your family, you may have already taken steps to help your son or daughter deal with this, and perhaps you're also getting support for yourself.

If this is your situation and you haven't yet taken any steps to get help, you might explore what counseling is available at your child's school and in your community. You can also contact organizations such as Al-Anon or Alateen and other alcohol- or other drug-related support groups. Aside from providing helpful information, these groups can help to confirm to your child that he or she is not alone, as well as help to draw out difficult emotions that might otherwise remain hidden.

I can't cope with my dad's drinking. What can I do?

Please don't wait for your child to approach you about this. Most kids don't know what words to say to let their parent or family know how they feel. You know what your circumstances are. If there is cause for your child's concern. Open the door for communication—

if you haven't done so. You might start with something like the following:

"I know we haven't talked about what's been going on here. I guess I just didn't know what to say to you. I've been so upset myself that I didn't think of how hard it must be for you . . . and how you might be hurting inside."

Then just take it from there.

If you know that there is alcoholism in your family history, that would be another reason to learn all you can in order to do what is feasible to prevent history from repeating itself through you, your kids, or other any future generations. There is a vast amount of literature on helping children and families of alcoholics you could explore and share with your children, and support is available in most communities for alcoholism and other drug-related problems.

THOUGHTS ABOUT SHARING WHAT YOU DID AS A KID

Usually this is a tough call for parents. My feeling is that there is no reason for you to share this information just for the sake of sharing it. If there's a purpose behind it, that makes much more sense. Here are some thoughts about some very basic areas of concern.

IF YOU DON'T WANT YOUR CHILD TO SMOKE, IS IT WISE TO LET YOUR CHILD KNOW THAT YOU STARTED SMOKING IN JUNIOR HIGH?

Yes. If your purpose is to prove that it is foolish to think that it's no big deal to quit. If you want to teach your child, by your example, that it's much harder to control this habit than you ever thought when you were a kid. If your message is, "Don't even start," then the fact that you're still smoking is a powerful statement. Hopefully, it can be even more powerful by what you teach your child through this discussion. If you're concerned that, upon learning that you started so early, your child will think, "Well, if Dad could do it, why can't I?" then you can say that up front. For example:

"I'm not telling you this so you can think because I did it that early, it's okay for you to do it. That's not it at all. It's an awful habit and I hate that I'm still smoking. But I've never been able to get myself to stop."

If You Don't Want to Encourage Your Child to Drink Alcohol, Should You Admit You Snuck Liquor from Your Parents' Cabinet in Tenth Grade?

I'd probably skip the part about sneaking into the liquor cabinet and just concentrate on the effects liquor has had on the way you felt, and how it affected your ability to stay in control. If, through sharing your own experiences, you are able to support the message you wish to give to your child, then it's worth mentioning your early experimentation.

If you would not like your child to drink liquor as an early teen, it would not be the best idea to say you did the same thing and handled it fine. If you can't support the need for your child to be cautious about drinking, what would be your point in bringing up the topic?

If You Want Your Child to Abstain from Sexual Intercourse Until Marriage, Should You Admit That You Had Intercourse for the First Time When You Were Sixteen?

If you shared yourself sexually years before you wish your child to, you can say exactly that. You might start with:

"Honestly, I was fifteen when I had intercourse for the first time. I wasn't sure if it would be right to tell you that, because the last thing I would want would be for you to think, 'Mom or Dad did it, so what's the big deal if I do it.' But what I learned will hopefully make a difference to you."

Then go on to share anything from your own experience that can add fuel to what messages, beliefs, and values you wish to nurture within your child. For example, if your early experience taught you that it would have meant much more to wait until marriage, that would support encouraging your child to be strong about abstinence. Your experience can be an excellent base for discussing ways to handle and prevent sexual pressure situations: This is what happened to me; this is why I gave in to pressure; this is what I hope won't happen to you. Hopefully, you can teach your child the benefits of what you learned from the consequences you faced.

Should You Let Your Child Know That You Used Drugs?

If you had a difficult experience because you took drugs, that can be very important to share. Here again, if anything, your negative experience may well encourage your child not to repeat the same mistake you made.

What if Your Child Asks You Before You're Ready to Tell?

But what if your child asks you first about your use of alcohol or other drugs, cigarettes, or exploration of sex? Tough call. Just the other night, I was speaking with an audience of parents and their upper-elementary-school children. At the end of my presentation, a parent came up to speak with me privately and asked, "What are your thoughts about being honest with my kids about experimenting with drugs when I was growing up?"

I shared with her the thoughts I have already expressed to you about using her past experience as a springboard for reinforcing limits, caution about consequences, etc.

She then said, "What if I didn't have any negative experiences? I had no problems with what I did. I was fine. Do I actually tell my child that?"

This is another tough call. We agreed that the age of a child would be a consideration. It may be important to hold off being so honest with a younger child (we didn't define "young") in order to maintain a consistent message about "saying no." An older child (we didn't define "older," either) might be more capable of putting the truth about a parent's past experiences in perspective. One possible response you could make would be:

"I wondered what I'd say to you if you ever asked me that. I'll be honest with you, I did try it. But the last thing I would want is for you to think that because I did it, that means it's okay. It's not. . . ."

That can lead right into a discussion of how kids are kids, and most kids think consequences happen to other people in other places. Talk about how children often think they're invincible. Then tell your child that this is not the case. They often think nothing can happen to them—until it does.

I want to have sex with my boyfriend. Should I?

I got my girlfriend pregnant. What should I do?

So I would turn the discussion right back to concern about believing the risks are real. I don't know that it's so terrible to admit that you didn't believe the risks when you were young, either. You can also consider saying that no one ever challenged you with questions such as, "What would it take for you to believe the risks are real?" or "Does it have to take a tragedy to prove that every time you take a chance, the unwanted result could happen that time?" (Refer to page 191 earlier in this chapter.) You could go on to say that you feel lucky that you got away with experimenting with drugs and suffered no terrible consequences. Now you realize you took some scary chances. You can build on the discussion in any direction that seems as if it would best meet your child's needs at the time. Hopefully, what you choose to include after admitting that you did use drugs at a young age will make it clear that just because you did it then doesn't make it right for your child now.

HELPING YOUR CHILD BECOME MORE SAFETY-MINDED

Can you get pregnant without actually having sex but just by fooling around, by doing everything but that?

Even if kids are intent on being responsible and safe when making decisions, they still may put themselves at serious risk. Misconceptions, misinformation, lack of awareness, or naïveté can make your children more vulnerable than they might imagine. When they are making split-second decisions in areas such as sex, alcohol, and other drugs, there is no room for misinformation or lack of awareness, no room for error in judgment. The stakes are too high, physically and emotionally.

I'm scared about growing up. How can I prevent this from happening?

Beyond having a solid base of factual understanding, kids need to be able to apply that knowledge to their own real-life situations. They need to develop a "safety mind-set" to serve as their built-in, early-warning alarm system. Their "safety check" will cause them to pause, step back, and seriously ask themselves, "What's safe? What isn't?" and "Am I sure I want to allow myself to do this?" Then they can carefully weigh what choices they have, consider what each choice might mean, evaluate the risks, and then be prepared to determine what decision is safest for them to make. Sometimes, they may need to be ready to do this processing in a matter of minutes (or less).

For example, if kids are at a party where there is alcohol, and a guy who has already had several beers suggests to a girl that she take a walk outside with him to "get some air," warning sirens need to go off in that girl's head. If she's "thinking safety" and has her prevention facts straight, she'll know that date rape ought not be talked about without including alcohol in the same sentence. If she's smart, she'll know it's not wise to let herself go out alone with him even if she does know him, and especially if she doesn't know him very well.

One of the crucial components in being able to develop a "safety mind-set" within our kids, one they will actively (and actually!) engage, is to help increase their ability to identify what circumstances warrant caution. A list of all that children need to understand would be too extensive for this book. Therefore, find resource material on each subject, from sex and alcohol to cigarettes and other drugs, in books or on the web to share with your child.

WHEN DO YOU START TALKING ABOUT ALL OF THIS?

As with growth and development, the answer is to try to talk with children before they might have to deal with these experiences. We need to tell them what they may expect before they're faced with the pressures and decisions, before they find themselves in situations where they must make choices to prevent taking these kinds of risks.

I realize it may seem unconscionable to have to teach kids about these difficult things so early. But the truth is, children are feeling the pressures related to sex, alcohol, and other drugs at a younger and younger age. Kids must be ready to deal with this, for their well-being and their survival. As their parents, we can help ease the pressures children will face by giving them the information and support they'll need to handle the situations.

Think about it. Take the need to talk about how to prevent pregnancy, for example. If so many kids at the middle-school level are saying, "I'm pregnant," then we need to teach them about sexual intercourse and the related risks before they leave elementary school.

Is it bad that I've already had sexual intercourse at this age? My age is twelve.

The only way kids will know how to prevent pregnancy is if they know how pregnancy happens in the first place. How else will they know what they should avoid and how to control their risks in the most effective ways possible?

When talking with your child about sexual intercourse, it can help to anticipate that when you finally do share the ultimate information about what it is, your child is likely to feel a range of emotions—especially if this is the first time your child has heard it. Watch your child's face carefully. Most kids say to me, "Gross! Ugghhhhhhhhh!" If they don't say that, most are thinking it. Either that, or they may be thinking, "Not my parents. Well, three children, they must have done it three times!" This is a natural response.

It can help to let kids know that if they cannot relate to this information, or cannot even imagine it, it's not for them to relate to, not for them to imagine yet. We can reinforce that it is adult information, about adult sharing. We need to say, as parents, that sexual intercourse is definitely not for kids, but that we are sharing the information with them for their own knowledge and safety, since they may find some kids they know will become sexually active very young. And they may find themselves faced with sexual pressure.

Many parents find that this is a good time to mention what abstinence means. Children can then be told that they can just put this information away in the back of their mind and not even think about it until they're at a more mature age. We can tell them that since they now know what sexual intercourse is, they can be much more sure of what is totally inappropriate for them to do. And no one will be able to fool them or pressure them into thinking it's appropriate, because they will know it's not.

After you explain sexual intercourse to your child, you can then talk about such concerns as sexual pressures, your child's power and right to make his or her own choices, the concern about teenage pregnancy (kids usually have excellent ideas as to why so many teenagers become pregnant each year—it's another good springboard to talk about peer pressure), concern about alcohol and other drugs, the need to establish limits and respect the limits of others, and your own beliefs and values related to when you feel sexual sharing is appropriate. Your discussions can be embellished further as you go along.

Keep in mind that the sharing of safety-minded information with your child is a building process. None of this is a one-time conversation. The more we talk openly with our kids, the more opportunities we will have to nurture self-confidence, strengthen life skills, and help them develop a "safety mind-set," one that they can actively engage to handle all peer pressure and other life situations they face as they grow up.

We need to be sensitive, supportive, consistent, and as aware of what our kids are facing in school and with their friends as is possible. Our guidance, our efforts to further build upon our children's knowledge base with accurate information, and the conscious work to help kids believe the risks are real, will hopefully enable them to establish safe limits—and have the capacity to stick to them. Beyond that, all I can suggest is that we keep our children in our prayers.

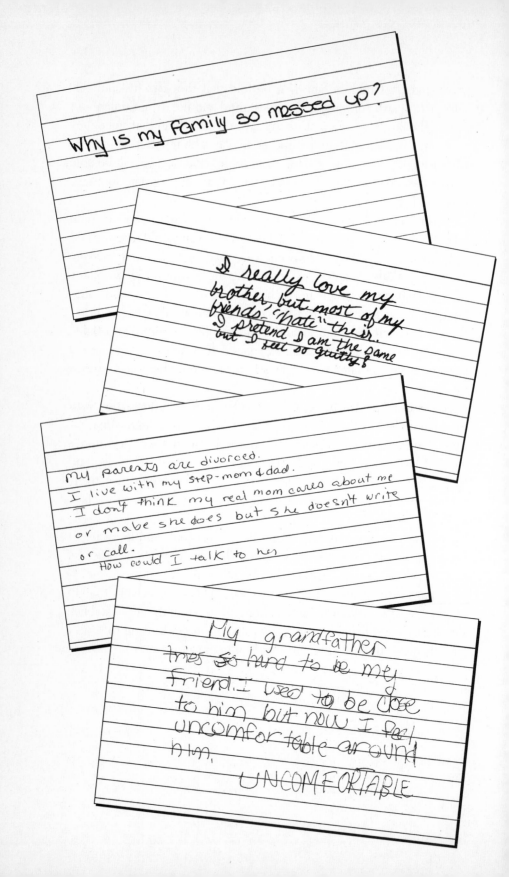

Why is my family so messed up?

I really love my brother, but most of my friends "hate" their. I pretend I am the same but I feel so guilty!

my parents are divorced.
I live with my step-mom & dad.
I don't think my real mom cares about me
or mabe she does but she doesn't write
or call.
How could I talk to her

My grandfather
tries so hard to be my
friend. I used to be close
to him but now I feel
uncomfortable around
him.
UNCOMFORTABLE

9

FAMILY RELATIONSHIPS

There are vast numbers of kids who walk around secretly feeling sad, lonely, unwanted, and frustrated, not knowing how to let family members know they wish they could be closer to them. Because kids keep these feelings hidden, parents may not have any reason to believe they exist. It often takes failing grades, truancy, heavy involvement with alcohol or other drugs, pregnancy, running away, or attempted suicide to prove to parents that their seemingly happy child is really yearning for attention, and needing badly to feel loved.

Sometimes there will be no drastic measure, no inconsistency in a child's behavior, no hint that he or she is hurting inside and that the feelings of distance from the family are taking their toll. Those hurts may not be acknowledged until years later, or maybe never. This is not a matter of feeling guilty or finding blame. Rather, we need to be aware of the possibility that an outward appearance of well-being might not be a true reflection of what our kids are feeling inside. We cannot be calmed into complacency by the fact that our family is able to spend time together. Physical togetherness doesn't guarantee and must not be confused with intimacy. It's possible to be with someone and feel even lonelier than when you are by yourself. The depth of loneliness can even be more devastating when felt in the presence of those with whom we are supposed to be the closest. Many children and adults feel this way.

I wish to be closer to my parents.

Family closeness can't be bought. While kids may like to have piano lessons, new bicycles, computer games and new clothes, those are just "things." Material things and activities are not substitutes for love. They don't provide security or console kids when they're sad. They don't offer guidance, set boundaries, or encourage. They don't teach kids how to learn from their mistakes. They don't forgive. They don't teach kids to value human life.

My father is never satisfied with what I do.

Family closeness also doesn't depend on the frequency of visits from grandparents or if holidays are celebrated together. It depends on whether kids feel good about the time spent together with family and the way family members interact with and respond to each other. It depends on whether kids are able to express to their family what they feel and need. And positive family feelings depend on whether we understand our kids, and whether our words and actions tell each of our children that he or she is accepted, appreciated, and loved.

I feel great about myself. I have no trouble with friends or family. My life is wonderful. I always feel like smiling.

There are, of course, kids who appear happy and actually are. They feel great about their parents, get along with brothers and sisters (most of the time), and generally feel wonderful about their family life. But even when family feelings are good, family life is not issue-free. Closeness must always be worked at. Closeness will always be tested.

There will always be issues that are sensitive to confront and areas where family feelings could be even more positive. These are the concerns that kids often find difficult to share with parents, siblings, grandparents, and other family members. When kids keep their feelings hidden, that can potentially sabotage their family relationships as well as diminish how they value themselves.

Why do I always feel as though I'm getting compared to my sister?

The sharing cards included throughout this chapter further confirm how much kids hold back regarding family issues and the varied nature of their concerns. Each is slightly different. Each is important for you to see the many types of issues that can come up, and what we must help our kids identify, unlock, and learn how to express. I'm hoping these cards, along with the insights and suggestions offered, will help you better understand and more effectively respond to the concerns that each of your children wish you and other family members would understand.

RELATIONSHIPS BETWEEN BROTHERS AND SISTERS

"I HATE MY BROTHER [OR SISTER]. . . ."

I want to kill my brother. How do I go about doing that?

While I know that there are lots of kids who say they can't stand their brother or sister and think they mean it, when it comes down to it, they'll usually stand by them when life is tough. They'll be protective if other kids are out to get them, and they'll genuinely worry if their health is in question.

There are also kids who say they "hate" their brother or sister but know they really don't feel that way at all. Sometimes, pressure from peers can be a strong influence on how kids treat and relate to siblings.

I hate my sister! What can I do?

If you hear your child say, "I hate my brother [or sister]," you might ask where these feelings came from. When did they start? Did the brother or sister actually do anything to make your child feel that way? You might also say that you're sorry he or she feels that way, that it certainly makes you sad, but you do respect each of your children's right to his or her own feelings. It might help to follow by telling your son or daughter that you're not expecting or asking your kids to be best friends, even though that would be great. However, it would mean a lot if they could at least be nice to each other.

It would be a good idea to approach your kids individually before bringing them together to talk about how they might try to work at their relationship. That will give you the chance to ask if the child who has been negative would be willing to cooperate. While the hope is that your child would be open to the idea of getting along better, you never know. If there is any objection, you may need to wait a while longer before bringing your kids together to have this conversation.

There is a distinction between saying to our kids:

"Oh, don't be ridiculous. It's horrible for you to say you hate your sister! Sisters are supposed to love each other. I don't want to hear that anymore. . . . Now, go make up."

And saying something like:

"I know that you have some pretty strong feelings about Jenny. I can't force you to love Jenny. I wish you could both appreciate what you have in each other, and maybe someday—when you get a little older—you'll be able to. But right now, if that's how you feel, I can't force you to love each other. But I am going to ask that you not be mean to each other."

It can help to encourage your kids to focus on looking for the good in each other, and to center on what they have in common rather than only dwelling on things that are different or that they don't like.

I have a younger sister that everyone likes. She's only a few years younger so she goes to school here. All my friends like her more than me. I like my sister but I feel like she's stealing all my friends. I know that she hates me. I wish I could hate her.

Siblings might love to make a "you bug me" list. You can suggest that they each write down what bothers them about their brother or sister. A more positive approach might be to ask them to write down what they think would make them feel better about each other. Tell them to be as specific as possible.

> **My brother is five years younger than me and he always tries to hang around with me and my friends. I love him very much and want to share a lot of things together, but I always don't want him to hang around with me and I also don't want to hurt him. What could I do?**

Your kids might also find it very helpful to write lists that identify "what I wish I could say to my brother or sister" or "what I wish my brother or sister would understand."

As with other lists of concerns, two columns can be created: one, things that cannot be changed and need to be accepted, such as the fact that they must share a room; and two, a list of what can be worked at and changed, such as who gets to pick television programs or how they act in front of each other's friends.

If television-program picking is an issue, then kids can be encouraged to make schedules together so they can agree on who picks what program and when. If the source of their problem includes behavior in front of friends, they can talk about what changes would make them feel better when friends are over.

We can be facilitators and help our kids learn how to interact with each other. For example, we can sit our kids down and say, "Ricky, will you please tell Danny how you felt when he said that in front of your friends?" Ricky and Danny can then take it from there.

> **My sister came home from college a couple of days ago. She still has two years to go. Now she complains about everything I do and my mom does. It gets me mad because we were close before she left. I find it hard to talk with her but I want to be close again. It seems as if we don't have anything in common anymore. Help!**

Too often, kids feel hurt or frustrated and don't let their brother or sister know. They may also wish they could share more and be closer, and feel too uncomfortable to say so. We can remind our kids how they can turn feelings into words so they'll be able to say things like, "I really wish we could be close like we used to be before you left" or "I don't like it when we fight. I wish we could be friends" or "I really wish we could be closer. There are lots of things I wish I could tell you, but sometimes I'm afraid you'll tell your friends or your boyfriend instead of keeping it private." Kids can either write their feelings down or say them aloud.

While we can't make their relationship happen for our children, we can help pave the way for those feelings to develop. We can encourage honesty and openness and help set the tone for cooperation and respect. We can help strengthen communication skills, teach our kids what it means to listen and actually hear each other. We can create opportunities to facilitate discussions between our kids so they can more honestly relate to each other and work out their differences. And we can help kids understand that unless they express their feelings, their sister or brother might not have any idea what is bothering them.

Our kids may need to be reminded that while they can pick their friends, they're stuck with family. What they got is what they got! So part of this is all attitude and a decision to accept sisters and brothers for who they are instead of spending so much time and energy being disappointed because of who they're not. Our children deserve to concentrate only on the best in each other and learn how to let the rest go.

IF KIDS THINK PARENTS COMPARE OR FAVOR ONE CHILD OVER ANOTHER

If a child perceives that parents are comparing or favoring a brother or sister, that can lead to resentment, not only of the parent, but also of that particular brother or sister. It could also cause kids to feel they don't or won't ever measure up, that they're not as good as their brother or sister.

Whether or not a child's perception is actually valid does not diminish the potential impact. If a child believes it, that's what counts. What might each of your children believe?

Why is my sister such a brat? How come when she does something to me she doesn't get in trouble, and then when I do it back my mom yells at me?

Here are some questions that would be important for you to consider:

· Do you yell at your kids? A lot or a little? Is your yelling directed at any one child more than another? Do you reprimand one child more often than another? Do you tend to let a younger child get away with things, but have higher expectations for an older child? Might your child think that you favor one child over another? Does it seem that one child is always to blame? Could any of your children think you're comparing them to each other?

My little sister gets more attention than me. When my mom and sister fight they make up in ten minutes. But when I fight we never make up.

Depending on what your child responds with, you can discuss your own perception or what your child can do to address the situation, or both. For example: If you don't believe you are comparing, and your child believes that you are, it can help to turn your own feelings into words. You might say:

"I'm so sorry you think I'm comparing you. I'm not. I love and appreciate both of you. You can never be Matthew, and he can never be you. Each of you is special. It's very hard for me to know that you feel that way, when I'm not trying to compare you at all. I don't know what else to say to you to help you believe I'm telling you the truth."

The child who wrote the following card needs to make a similar statement to her sister:

My sister thinks that our parents love me more. She says that our parents always take my side. It's not true! What can I do about it? I try to tell her they don't take my side but she doesn't listen!

If you realize that you have been comparing or favoring one child over another, let your child know that you're aware this has been the case. While you can't erase what has already taken place, you can apologize and tell your child you intend to make some changes. Hopefully, your child will hear and appreciate what you are saying.

It's possible that your child will secretly wonder if you'll follow through. Until you make some changes to prove out, it may be hard for some kids to trust that you mean it.

My younger brother and sister get away with murder. If I do something wrong I get in so much trouble. My mom says, "You're the oldest and must set an example for your brothers and sisters. I don't think that's fair. It isn't my fault I'm the oldest.

WHEN SIBLINGS FIGHT

"Did not!"
"Did too."
"I did not!"
"You did too."
"I'm telling. . . ."

Does this sound familiar? Why do kids still fight? Still tease each other, sometimes mercilessly? Act in such a humiliating way in front of their brother's or sister's friends? Probably the answer is not as difficult to come up with as we might think. Perhaps it's mainly just because they're kids! And they're acting "just like kids." Much of the time, they actually think fighting is fun.

Me and my sister fight all the time and I would love to get closer.

Still, that doesn't give kids license to humiliate each other and permission to make each other miserable. Kidding around is one thing, causing deep-rooted sadness and alienation is another. They don't always know the difference, and too many kids try to hide those inner feelings, making it appear on the surface that they're cool and can take it.

Some fighting between brothers and sisters is natural. It's not always necessary to try to stop it. Unless there is physical force or verbal abuse that could end up with someone getting seriously hurt, we might be better off allowing kids the freedom to work out fights on their own. Even then, it's wise to remain aware of what's going on, and stay reasonably close "just in case" the fighting gets out of hand.

Several kids have told me that because of interference from parents, their fights got worse and lasted longer. The decision to step in is a personal judgment call, taking into consideration the nature of the fight, the specific circumstance, and which siblings happened to be involved at that moment. It can help to keep in mind that even when fighting sounds awful to us, it may represent entertainment to our kids.

But not every kid thinks that way. There are many who wish it would stop and don't know how to let their brother or sister know how much they're hurting. And so they suffer, silently.

Here, as with every other issue that kids must face, they need to be helped with the words. They need to have a perspective about what they can and cannot control. They need to understand that even if they get the words out and say "I don't want to fight anymore," that won't guarantee that their sister or brother will stop. It can only guarantee that their sibling now knows they wish them to stop. Beyond that, we need to help strengthen our child's ability to respond differently in order to stay in control.

Kids need to know that it takes two people to fight. If only one person is fighting and the other isn't, that's not a fight. Kids can choose not to allow themselves to be sucked into the fighting. This, too, is a choice they can make. They can even say something like, "This doesn't seem to be a good time to be with you. I'm sorry you're so upset. I'll see you at dinner."

I know, this is easier said than done. And it's likely that kids who want so badly to get along with siblings will still feel some degree of hurt when they're mean to them. But, just as with friendships, kids don't deserve to have to beg for a brother or sister to like them. They need to know there's just so much they can control.

WHEN OLDER SIBLINGS MOVE OUT

If you have a child who is going off to college, is joining the military, or is moving to another town or state, it's likely that your younger son or daughter might miss that sibling terribly. The feelings, along with the fear that this will mean that their relationship will change, are often left unexpressed.

How could I get closer to my brother in college?

I didn't learn until about five years ago that my youngest brother was devastated when I went to college. He was only eight at the time and I didn't have any idea that he felt the way he did. He told me, "The worst day of my life was when Mom and Dad's car disappeared around the corner and took you away to school."

At eight years old, my brother, like many children, had a great many feelings that he kept inside. If your older child is planning to go away to school or move out for other destinations, it may be very helpful to talk about these kinds of feelings with your younger child. It also would be important to let the departing older child know how much it would mean to keep in active contact with that younger sibling. Before leaving, it could also be so reassuring if your older child told the younger one that he or she will be missed a great deal. That no distance, no time away from each other, is going to change what they have together.

Your older child can be encouraged to call home and just ask for the younger sibling. He or she can send that younger sister or brother cute and funny things in the mail. Even a short note saying, "MISS YOU!!" can be wonderful confirmation that the older sibling truly meant what was said. It doesn't need to take much to make a big difference in how a younger child could feel. Other messages, such as "I'M DOING GREAT!!", can also give greater peace of mind to a younger sibling who is worried over whether the older sister or brother is okay.

It might interest you to know that older kids also have feelings about leaving younger kids. They may be saddened by the fact that they're going to miss the everyday little changes that are going to take place as their little brother or sister develops. This can especially be of concern when younger siblings are at the infant or toddler stage, during which growth can be so dramatic over shorter periods of time away. They would probably appreciate receiving current pictures, detailed, "blow-by-blow" descriptions of the fact that their little brother started to climb out of his crib, took his first step, had his first piece of pizza, and so on. You, as a parent, can provide these.

WHEN KIDS SHARE A ROOM

I have no privacy. I'm thirteen and share a room with my eighteen-year-old sister. The room doesn't have a door! There's no other room in my house I can have, and my sister isn't going to college for a few more years.

Kids who share rooms with each other usually have a range of issues that they may or may not admit, at least not to the sibling in their room. A "what I wish we could change" or "what really bothers me" list might reveal the kinds of things that both (or all) kids involved need to and can work at together.

If your kids don't wish to make lists, you might find it helpful to schedule a discussion with all parties involved. You can facilitate and help your children draw out what they need each other to understand. As with anything else, some things will simply have to be accepted as given, and other things will be able to be worked at. However, even if space is a "given" and cannot be expanded, the furniture might be able to be rearranged or a curtain added to increase privacy.

When my sister and I shared a room, we placed our desks opposite each other and our beds were head to head, facing away from each other, with a thin piece of furniture between them on which we were able to put a lamp. By facing away from each other, I was able to have the flexibility to stay up later and read. I had a gooseneck lamp that I pulled very low on my side of the dividing piece of furniture so I wouldn't keep my younger sister up. Just making some furniture changes might feel different and help to ease tensions between your children who are sharing a room.

The following represent "sharing a room" issues that kids have told me they often have difficulty dealing with:

- Privacy when friends visit
- Privacy on the telephone

- Being able to concentrate on schoolwork when a sister or brother wants to do something else in the room
- Volume of the stereo, choice of music
- Keeping belongings separate and private
- Differences in age
- If a sister or brother is very messy and the other is neat

Your kids might find it helpful to look at this list and add other issues of their own. It might also be wonderful to ask your kids to list "what I love about sharing my room." Your kids might include such things as:

- It's great to have company, especially when I'm scared at night
- It's really special to be able to talk together in the middle of the night
- My brother listens to my problems and gives me good advice
- Sharing a room has made my sister and me feel closer

Many people also keep positive feelings hidden. They may go out of their way to tell someone they're upset, but don't necessarily bother to say, "I appreciate you." Our kids can learn to share positive feelings by our example, as well.

BLENDED FAMILIES, BLENDED FEELINGS

Whether kids are adopted, live with a foster family, are part of a blended family that includes children from different backgrounds, live with a stepfamily, live with a gay or lesbian parent and his or her partner, or live with their biological parents—all children deserve to feel good family feelings.

Some children find it hard to feel good about their family because of what other kids say about being "different." Here again, cruel remarks, teasing, and disrespect of any kind are not acceptable. This is another area we can and need to work at to help kids accept and respect differences.

We also need to make sure kids know that whether or not family members are directly, biologically related to each other, they can grow to love each other and feel like they are loved. Being directly related does not guarantee that family members will love each other or even get along. What counts the most is that the family environment be loving, supportive, and nurturing.

We need to make the opportunity to teach our sons and daughters to appreciate that families can blend together from many different places and become one. Differences deserve to be embraced and respected. Kids deserve to feel lucky about their families instead of embarrassed or ashamed because of what other people say. We can teach our children to be kinder, more respectful, more appreciative of what "family" really means. Beyond our specific conversations about this, we continue to teach powerful lessons by our own example.

FAMILY HURTS, FAMILY STRESSES, FAMILY ISSUES

This section offers a sampling of the many different situations and parent reactions that can rob kids of the chance to feel good about their family life. Each one has a slightly different lesson about what kids wish parents would understand . . . and what kids often find too hard to share.

IF A PARENT IS UNDER STRESS

And what worries me is when my mom is always under stress. What should I do?

When a parent is under stress, children often worry. They worry about the toll this might take on their parent's health. They often feel that it's difficult to be around their parent, especially if he or she is hyper, edgy, easily triggered into an outburst, and it doesn't take much for the parent to lose control. Kids may make plans to be away from their home as much as possible so they don't have to deal with the pain of seeing their parent so stressed out.

It can be a very helpless feeling for kids to know how stressed a parent is and not have the ability to help ease the tension. Just as parents can't "live it" for their kids, kids need to be reminded they can't live life for their parent. The best they could hope to do is talk with their parent, urge him or her to slow down, or, if warranted, get some professional help.

If you have been particularly stressed lately, it might help to acknowledge this to your child. To state that you're having a rough time may not change the rough time, but it could take the edge off your child's secret reactions. By opening the door for discussion about this, you will have invited your child to let you know how worried he or she is about you. You might even find that your child will come up with very creative ways to reduce some of the stress.

WHEN PARENTS YELL OR FIGHT

Whenever I talk to her she yells. On a calendar I've marked every day my parents yell at me. For the last five months they've yelled at me every day. When they yell at me what should I do? I usually cry.

Yelling can be very difficult to take. Constant yelling is even worse. It can make kids feel awful about being around their parent, awful about coming home. Please take another opportunity to think about how you respond to your kids. Could this be you? If so, take a deep breath. Take a step back. Reevaluate what signals you need to give yourself in order to control yourself before reaching the point where you bellow out at your kids.

Your child would probably appreciate it if you approached him or her and said something like:

> "I've been thinking . . . and I realize I've been yelling at you a lot. That doesn't feel good to me and I can't imagine that it feels good to you. I'm so sorry that I've yelled like that. I'm going to work at talking instead of yelling."

When the yelling is between parents, kids often fear divorce. Sometimes, especially if there is stress in our lives, we tend to take out the anxiety on those who are closest. Fighting doesn't necessarily have to mean divorce or that there is any kind of problem between parents. Kids don't usually know that. Especially since most kids know a lot of families that have dealt with divorce or separation, it's natural for them to worry this will happen to them, too.

If you know you're fighting a lot, it would probably be a relief to your child to talk about what's going on. If you're just stressed out about other things, tell him or her that's the case and that you're sorry that it has been so stressful around your home. If there is cause to worry about your marriage, let your child know that, too. As I've said many times already, kids usually fear the worst. If "the worst" is a reality, they might as well know it and have your support, rather than walking around worrying about this, alone.

Some parents think, "Well, if my child were that worried, he or she would say something to me about it." Not so. Even if the fighting is absolutely blatant, it's very hard for kids to ask parents about what this might mean.

WHEN PARENTS LISTEN BUT DON'T SEEM TO HEAR

I want to get closer with my mother. I want to tell her that I love her, but I just can't. I know she loves me a lot, but we don't relate very well. I try to talk to her, to share with her my problems, and feelings, and she tries to listen, but she never really hears me.

What is said so clearly and poignantly on the previous anonymous sharing card is exactly what this child might find helpful to say directly to her mother. Turning feelings into words, she could say:

"Mom, I want so badly to be close to you. I wish we could relate better. I know you love me a lot. It's so hard for me to tell you how much I love you. I know you try to listen when I share my problems with you. But I don't get the feeling that you really hear me."

Will that mother be capable of hearing what her child is expressing? Hard to say. At the very least, the child is saying what he or she truly feels. The hope is that the mother will respond differently. There's no guarantee. However, if this child stayed silent, the mother might never know that her child felt that way.

WHEN KIDS STAY HOME ALONE

When I stay home by myself I worry about strangers, robbers, kidnappers, and the doorbell ringing.

If your child is latchkey or is at the stage where he or she is able to be left alone at home, he or she might be very relieved if you bring up these worries voiced in the card above. You might also mention that lots of kids are worried about those kinds of things. They want to be at the "grown-up" stage of being left alone, but are still a bit scared. Then you can talk strategy with your child. You can help to offset your child's fears with a concrete plan of action for the kinds of circumstances that represent a concern.

For example, you can say: No answering doorbells no matter who it is (unless it's a neighbor whom your child knows or a relative, etc.). Or if someone says he or she is a plumber and had an appointment to come ("Your mom must have just forgotten to tell you"), still don't open the door. Open the door only for someone your parent told you about. No exceptions.

Rules can help ease your child's peace of mind. "What ifs" can be gone over: If someone calls, tell your child not to let them know he or she is home alone. Keep a few lights on so it looks like several people are home. Also assure your son or daughter you will check in by calling periodically. Make sure your child knows to call 911 if there is a problem.

JOB LOSS, DEALING WITH DEATH

My dad lost his job. I've been teased in school a lot. My grandmother died five months ago and our family still hasn't gotten over it.

Job loss, illness, and death are all stresses that families deal with on a regular basis. Those kinds of experiences often make it hard for kids to concentrate on their work at school, hard for kids not to worry about their parent, and hard for them to feel good about family life and life in general.

Since ups and downs are part of life, a time period like this is an opportunity to teach children about coping, about the strength that can come from being able to trust that you're there for each other.

With regard to a parent's job, becoming unemployed offers the chance to remind kids about the attitude "a door closes, a window opens" and, by your example, teach what it can mean to be resourceful and not give up. The family can get together and talk about what each person can do to help. Kids usually feel terrific knowing that there is actually something concrete they can do to make a difference.

About dealing with loss of a grandparent, I don't know that any words can take away from such sadness. However, it can help to talk about how lucky your family was to be able to share all the time you did have . . . and that all that a grandparent shared is something they can keep within them forever. This is usually a very difficult topic for kids as well as adults.

If your kids are not talking about their grandmother's or another close friend or relative's death, please don't think they don't have feelings or are not thinking about it. Rarely will that be the case. It's more likely that kids are worried that talking about their grandparent will make parents more sad. Or they may just not know what words to say. It would probably be very helpful to bring up the subject.

For all of these family stresses, many families are comforted by the power of prayer. It may also help to encourage your child to view each experience, however difficult, as a gift, a challenge, an opportunity to grow closer, a chance to develop new strengths. Difficult life experiences can also help family members learn to appreciate that the most important things can't be bought and no matter what happens, all that has been shared can't be taken away.

If you truly are there for each other, that's something that can help get your family through any difficulty. So can encouraging patience. The child who wrote this card needs to know that five months is not a very long time since his or her grandmother's death. It takes time to process and get used to any major change, especially if that change involves the loss of a loved one.

A few months ago my aunt died and my uncle is getting remarried with a person who has two children. I can't seem to accept them as relatives so soon after.

Add the fact that families don't have to deal with tough times alone. There is professional help available in every school and community. It's a statement of strength to say, "I'm having a rough time" and get help if need be. That's another important lesson that kids need to learn.

IF YOUR FAMILY PLANS TO MOVE

I lived through this issue myself. It was one of the more stressful and painful times for us as a family, as it would have meant moving when our daughter was about to enter her senior year in high school. That's not what you're supposed to do, at least not if you can help it.

We never moved, much to everyone's relief. But the process we went through for months—dealing with how she was ever going to leave her best friends, start fresh in a new school where everyone had grown up together for years—was something that certainly drained us, and caused her to be terribly upset, worried, sad, and angry.

What we emphasized with our daughter, and what might help any kids who are facing the possibility of moving, is that they need not ever lose the most important people in their life. Will day-to-day life be different without that friend to hang around with? Of course. Will kids miss their best friends? No question. But if kids want each other in their lives, they can grow with and treasure those friendships forever. Even long distance.

> I am worried about my friend. Because now all she does is cry. And talk about her old friend that moved. Please HELP.

E-mail, letters, phone calls, taking turns with visits, and making audiocassette tapes are all ways you can suggest your children keep in touch with a friend if they or someone they know has moved. Kids also need to know that even if months go by without contact, that doesn't have to mean the closeness is gone and the friendship is over. Life is usually hectic, people get caught up with their own schedules and responsibilities. It can be hard to keep in constant touch.

But if the feelings are there, they will be there, contact or not. Rather than telling kids, "It's going to be okay. Stop worrying, you'll make new friends!" it can help to validate the sadness and how tough it can be to move.

It's also possible that moving will be exciting, an adventure. It might even turn out that kids will love their new school and feel great about their new home. But before a move takes place, while the anticipated environment is still an "unknown," it can be so scary to think about leaving what has grown to be part of you, and what feels so safe and familiar. While it may not change the feelings kids may have about moving, to at least acknowledge them will help kids realize they're understood and not so alone.

ANOTHER KIND OF FAMILY STRESS, DIFFERENT HURTS—WHEN PARENTS SEPARATE OR GET A DIVORCE

My parents are divorced and I'm sad all the time. What do I do?

The following sections will address some of the common concerns related to divorce that children have told me are difficult to talk about with their parents (or anyone). If these experiences apply to your life, it is my hope that the insights offered will help you dig further below the surface to better understand what your child might be feeling and not telling you. If you aren't and have never been involved with divorce, separation, or stepfamily relationships, you might consider sharing these thoughts with someone you care about who is.

Since many kids have asked me how to be there for friends who are dealing with divorce in their family, I'm also hoping that these insights will enable you to help your own child be more sensitive to what a friend might be going through.

WHEN DIVORCE TAKES PLACE, IT CAN TAKE ITS TOLL ON CHILDREN OF ALL AGES

My parents were divorced when I was two. I still do not know how to approach my mom or dad on the subject. I live with my mom and my dad lives alone. I visit him each weekend. How can I approach them?

Most kids take divorce pretty hard. They have a difficult time expressing feelings that they feel are usually too sad, too painful, too confusing, and too scary to get out. No matter how many years ago the divorce took place, it's still likely that kids are carrying around a lot of deep-rooted feelings that remain locked in their hearts regarding the separation of their parents.

All kids, of any age, may be silencing feelings that it would be important to share with their mother, or father, or both. It's possible that parents are silencing their feelings, too. Based on all I have learned from children and parents who have had to deal with this, I respect that this is not an easy topic. Parents who plan to separate might find it would help if they said to their children, either in writing or aloud, something like:

> "I know you know Mom and I don't have very good feelings about each other. Things have been nasty, just not nice. It's been terrible for both of us, and probably awful for you kids. But I want you to know we both still love you. What is happening between your mom and me is not your fault. And we hope you will be able to trust that each of us will still be very much a part of your life, even if we're not a part of each other's."

P.S. My parents are going through a separation. I have many questions. How can I explain the questions to them?

KIDS NEED TO KNOW THEY'RE NOT TO BLAME

Kids may feel guilty and think that their parents' separation or divorce is their fault. They may also blame their sister or brother. It's not enough to tell kids, "You're not to blame." That needs to be said, but unless a parent clarifies why it's impossible for children to be at fault, they may not fully believe it. It's important to offer an explanation in terms your child can relate to, personally. For example, you can help your child realize that just as parents don't have the power to make friends for their kids, kids don't have the power to make their parents' relationship better. Parents can make suggestions as to what kids could say to become better friends with someone, give kids ideas about what words they can say to start a friendship, but they can't do it for them. They also can't make a boyfriend or girlfriend relationship happen for them. That can only be between the two people involved. Explain that the same goes for parents. Children can say, "I love you both, please don't get separated." They can say, "Please make up. I don't want you to get a divorce." But it is up to parents to be able to get along or not. Their children can't do that for them.

It would also help to make sure kids know that the way parents get along has nothing to do with their making the honor roll, cleaning their room, doing the dishes, or agreeing to baby-sit for their younger sister or brother. There's nothing children need to feel they should or can be doing to make things different for their parents. They don't have that power.

KIDS MAY WONDER ABOUT WHOM TO TELL

My parents are getting a divorce. Should I tell a lot of people or very little? I already told two of my best friends.

Your child might not let you know:

- that he or she is unsure about whether to tell friends that you are separating. Reasons may include feeling ashamed or worrying that the news will spread around the school, or your child may just not know what to say. (Reinforce that it is usually a comfort for children to share what's happening in their family with at least a few close friends. If their most important friends know, kids won't have to walk around school pretending that everything is fine.)
- how hard the experience of your divorce is to handle. Children often don't want to further upset their parents and may remain silent about their difficult emotions. (Reinforce that experiences such as divorce are too hard to handle by themselves. Stress the importance of talking with a trusted adult, such as parents, grandparents, aunts and uncles, a friend's parents, teachers, coaches, guidance counselor, school psychologist or social worker, priest, rabbi, etc.)

WHEN A PARENT MOVES OUT

My mom left me and my brother at our friend's. She said she will be back soon. Hours passed and my dad came home from work at five. He brought me and my brother home and we found a note on the table. She left my dad. I was so mad. What should I say when I see her again?

It's one thing to anticipate the possibility of what will happen when parents separate or get divorced, and another thing to actually be faced with the reality that one parent has moved out. Many children view this as a dreaded next step in the process of their family's separation. However, if there has been a great deal of fighting, nastiness, or constant bidding for a child to be on one parent's side, some children may consider it to be a relief.

In either case, there are several serious concerns a child might have at this point. Depending on the arrangement, they might wonder or worry:

- What will this mean for me?
- Is this going to be forever or for just a little while?
- Whom will I end up living with?
- Will I have to move?
- What if I want to live with one parent and they make me live with the other?
- What if I have to choose between parents?
- If I live with one parent, how will the other feel about me?
- What will I tell my friends?
- How will we afford to live?
- What went wrong with my parents' relationship?
- Didn't they love each other when they got married?
- Maybe I shouldn't ever get married; I don't want this to happen to me.
- How can I let my mom or dad know how I feel? Should I?

I wish grown-ups could stay together. Ever since my mom and dad separated, my mom changed, and so did my dad.

**My dad thinks the only thing he's good for is sending money.
My mom started smoking and feeling she needs extra love.**

In light of what you know is happening, consider what your child could be feeling. What could your son or daughter be worried about? What could he or she fear? What changes might be expected to take place? What choices are going to have to be made? If your child has not approached you about any of these areas of concern, it is important to approach your child. Acknowledge that you realize divorce is something that is hard to talk about. You might even say that you understand many kids in this situation may be totally confused about what to ask, what to say, and whether or not they would hurt a parent's feelings by letting them know how they really feel. Encourage honest sharing, and share honestly with your child, even if what you must say will likely be hard for your child to hear. Your child will probably be worried anyway—and might as well know what's really going on.

WHEN STAYING IN TOUCH WITH A PARENT IS HARD

When a child wants so badly to hold on to a parent's love, there can be such sadness, heartache, and confusion when there is little or no communication.

My father never calls. I always have to call him and he never writes.

Children may wonder or worry:

- if their parent's silence is a statement on that parent's love for them
- if they should let the parent they live with know that they would like to contact their other parent
- if saying they would like to contact their other parent will cause the parent they live with to be angry, question their love, or think they might prefer to live with that other parent

Children have also talked with me about the pain and disappointment they feel when parents don't seem to remember birthdays and other special events. As a parent, it's important to know that this is how your child might react to silence. Even if a parent left when a child was a baby and hasn't been in touch for years, children may still feel strongly about noncontact. Not calling or writing doesn't have to be a statement on a parent's love. There could be many factors, such as a parent's own difficulties, that can make it hard to be there for anyone else. The problem is, kids often take it as a measure of love. Complete silence from a separated parent also makes many kids confused about whether they should love their parent.

If you're a parent who is not living with your child, try to take the time and make the effort to communicate what your feelings are to your child. If you need some space, some time alone without contact with your child, it can help to explain that to your son or daughter to assure him or her that it has nothing to do with the child. If you are taking care of your child most of the time, talk with your child about his or her other parent and how to get and stay in touch, if that's possible. If you open the subject up for conversation, you are sure to save your child a lot of the stress, wondering, and worry.

> **I am really close to my mom and my parents are divorced and I would like to spend more time with my dad, but I'm so afraid of hurting my mom, even though she has told me it was okay. What should I do?**

It would also be important to talk with children about the fact that even if they do send their other parent letters or E-mails, or are able to talk on the phone, that doesn't guarantee that the parent will respond to their contact. It can be very frustrating to children when they are the ones doing all the calling and contacting.

> **I wish I could know my dad. I write to my grandma and grandpa. I ask about my dad and they don't tell me.**

Sometimes there is a reverse situation. It may be that the parent continues to make active contact and the child doesn't want it to continue.

What should you do if your parents are divorced and you don't want a relationship with your father for many reasons, and you've already established that with him, but he won't leave you alone? He keeps calling and bringing up the past about the divorce and only talks about the money he earned for us and how everything is always about him, he doesn't get the point that everything's not always about how great he is, and I wish he would 'fess up to what he did.

More Feelings That Children Find Tough to Share—When Parents Become Single

Children find it very difficult to let a parent know:

- that they would rather live with their other parent
- that they don't want to live with either parent
- how very hard it is if they're given the choice of whom they wish to live with
- that they want and need more attention
- that they want to stop fighting and get along better
- how sad they are, how much they care, and how confused they are about knowing what to say to console a parent
- that they're worried if their parent is going to be okay
- they feel awkward having their single parent attend school events such as "Back to School Night," knowing that other people are going to notice only one parent is present— especially if both always attended. (Again, kids may wonder what they will tell their friends and be concerned about their reactions.)

I don't know any magic words that would make saying this to a parent easy for a child. However, I can suggest how to help a child know how to get the words out, even if it's hard. Kids can say, for example:

- "This is so hard for me to say. . . ."
- "I didn't know how to tell you this. . . ."
- "I love you both and I don't want to hurt either of you. But I really

want to stay at my school with my friends. And if I stay with Dad,
that means I can. I love you, too, Mom. So I don't want you to think I
don't by saying I'd rather live with Dad.

WHEN A PARENT STARTS DATING

Children may not let their parents know:

- that it is hard to adjust to or accept that a parent is seeing
  someone else and often represents a smack in the face of
  reality for them
- that they're jealous or upset about the time their parent is
  now spending with a boyfriend or girlfriend versus time
  spent with them
- that they don't like a parent's boyfriend or girlfriend

**My parents are divorced. I hate the person my mom's
dating. What do I do?**

When a parent starts dating, children simply may resent having to
share their parent. Sometimes the resentment that they feel trans-
lates into rude behavior toward that boyfriend or girlfriend. Kids may
think they hate the person, and in reality it's possible they do. But it
also could be that they just aren't ready for their parent to be so
involved with someone else. It may be too hard for children to see
their parent with another man or another woman that is not their
parent.

It is very difficult for kids to let a parent know that they don't like
a boyfriend or girlfriend. They usually don't know what to do with
those feelings. If you're divorced and are going out with someone, it
may help to talk with your child about how he or she feels about that
person. This is not about asking permission. Kids need to know that
just as they make their own decision about a boyfriend or girlfriend
or what friends they choose, whom a parent wishes to spend time
with is a parent's choice. Rightfully so. Hopefully, kids can feel good
that their parent is able to spend time with someone who treats him
or her in a loving way and offers companionship.

However, by anticipating that there could be an undercurrent or even a more obvious resentment that your child has for a person you are dating, you could save a lot of angst if you would meet those possible feelings head-on.

When your child visits you, whether from across the country or around the corner, consider what you do with the time you share. How do you let your child know you're interested? Do you spend more time with a boyfriend or girlfriend than with your child? What activities do you plan? Do you always include your boyfriend or girlfriend in these activities with your child? How much alone time do you spend with your child? What kinds of things do you talk about? If you don't know how your child feels about the time you are able to spend together, it may be important to ask. Depending on your conversation, you might consider making some adjustments to acknowledge your child's requests, worries, and concerns.

> **When my mom's boyfriend is over at our house, she pays more attention to him than to me. I try to give her hints to spend more time with me but she doesn't seem to understand them. How can I tell her that I don't like this situation?**

WHEN CHILDREN GO BACK AND FORTH BETWEEN PARENTS

If a child spends a portion of the week with dad and the rest of the week with mom, their visiting time together can be confusing in situations where:

- a child experiences different values, different rules, and a whole different way of life in each environment
- when parents compete (i.e., give extra privileges, allow a child to stay up much later than usual, allow a child to watch a video that was forbidden in the other parent's home)

> **What do you do when your parents always try to compete against each other? They're divorced.**

If you anticipate that there might be dramatic differences between home environments, it would probably be very helpful if you talked about this with your child. You might also feel it important to talk with your former husband or wife so there can be a reasonable degree of consistency in regard to serious life lessons.

(I realize that this may not be possible, but just in case, it may be well worth thinking about.)

WHEN KIDS GET PUT IN THE MIDDLE; WHEN ONE PARENT BAD-MOUTHS THE OTHER

Even if divorced parents are at odds with each other, even if there is jealousy, resentment, or real hatred between them, many kids would be relieved if parents stopped airing those feelings in front of them. They wish parents would just be more respectful of each other and not try to put them, the children, in the middle.

> **My parents are divorced and my father often puts my mother down. I get very upset but I don't know what to say. I'm afraid to say what I really feel.**

As the child who wrote this card so clearly states, "I don't know what to say. I'm afraid to say what I really feel." This is an ideal place to reinforce how that child can "turn feelings into words." For example:

> "I'm a little afraid to tell you this . . . but, Dad, every time you say those kinds of things about Mom, I get very upset. And I don't know what to say. I'm always afraid to tell you how I feel. Please don't say those things about Mom anymore."

This child can then add anything else that would be important for that father to know. Can we promise kids that their parent will definitely stop the put-downs if they are honest about their feelings? No. But parents may have no idea how upset kids are unless they take a chance and tell them.

The same building process for expressing feelings that applies to kids with their friends can apply to kids with their parents. If, after the child shares these feelings with his or her father, he puts the mother down again, the child can say:

"Dad, I don't know what else to say to you. I know I already told you I get upset when you talk that way about Mom. I really mean it. I love being with you. But I don't want to be with you if you talk that way. Please, I don't want to hear it anymore. I love both of you."

One would hope a parent would listen. But that's not always going to be the case. In light of that reality, children need to be taught that while they can't control what their parent says, and they may not be able to control when they are required to see their parent for visitation, they can control how they respond to their parent. Kids can try to be strong about not allowing themselves to be influenced by what is said. They can wait to listen to both sides before making their own mind up as to what seems right. They can try to keep a perspective about their parent's motivation for saying anything negative.

> My parents are divorced—my father and I are very close, but he lives with another woman and I admire her very much but my mother is trying to get me to hate her. I don't know what to do.

If you are separated or divorced, in what way do you refer to your ex-wife or ex-husband? What could your child feel about the things you say regarding his or her other parent? Have you bad-mouthed that parent to your child? Put that parent down in any way? Have you ever put your child in the middle of fights between you and your ex-wife or ex-husband? How about the way you talk about someone your ex is now dating? Or your child's new stepparent? Do you push your child for information about what's going on in your ex's home?

All of your answers will help you determine what kind of pressure you might be putting on your child and how uncomfortable your child might feel. Hopefully, these sharing cards from kids will add to your understanding of how potentially disturbing and destructive negative pronouncements about your child's other parent can be.

WHEN A PARENT REMARRIES

While some children feel wonderful about their new stepparent, others resent and dislike that person. It's very hard for kids to tell parents that they don't like the person they're dating or that they have a problem with their new stepparent. Kids may feel helpless in the face of a very significant life change, and fear their parent will be hurt if they say anything negative about their stepparent.

My mom remarried and she wants me to love my stepfather but I can't feel close to him. How can we feel close?

If you are planning to remarry, your child might be very relieved if you initiate the discussion regarding how your child feels about this person and what he or she wishes could be worked out with regard to their relationship. By keeping these kinds of feelings secret, children are denying themselves and their new parent (or parent-to-be) the chance to work out concerns. They're also missing out on the chance to get support that can be derived from talking things out with their parent. Reasons kids have told me for not feeling good about their new stepparent include:

- Doesn't seem to want to get to know me
- Says bad things about my other parent
- Tries to boss me around
- I don't want to move
- My mom can't spend as much time with me
- Now I can't crawl into my mom's bed in the middle of the night
- He favors his own children
- She doesn't even care about me

Feelings that children find hard to express to stepparents include:

- that they want to be closer to a stepparent
- that they don't know what to call their stepparent
- that they're afraid to love or even like their stepparent for fear that their "real" parent will be jealous, angry, or feel less loved
- that they think their stepparent favors his or her own children
- that they feel neglected by their stepparent

Many kids might have a more positive stepfamily beginning if they felt they had permission to have a close relationship with their new stepparent. It would potentially eliminate much confusion and guilt if parents would offer their child encouragement such as:

"I hope you'll give your new stepfather a chance. Maybe he will become a good friend, and will feel like a dad to you. I know you love me, and I love you very much. I'll always be your father. And I hope we'll be close for the rest of our lives. But you deserve to be as happy as you can be with your new family. Being close with them doesn't take away the love we have with each other."

What if your parents are separated and you have a stepdad and you really love him and you want to call him dad. What should you do?

If you're a stepparent, it may help for you to do some soul-searching as well. How have you related to your stepchild? How much alone time have you spent trying to get to know each other better? Is it possible that your stepchild would say that you've been mean to him or her? Neglectful? Not interested? Have you favored your own children? Could it be perceived that way? Is it possible for you to be more approachable? Softer? Kinder? Do you feel close to your stepchild? If not, have you at least said, "I'd love for us to be closer. I'd love for us to at least try to become friends."

I have a stepfather, but I don't call him daddy, and somehow he feels left out and that I don't care because of that, and I was wondering how could I deal with it because I just can't get close to him and don't want him to think that it is his fault.

STEPBROTHERS AND STEPSISTERS

I have a stepsister who I want to be friends with, but she doesn't seem to like me.

Children need to understand that new families might be able to get closer sooner if they were helped to realize that there is probably no such thing as instant comfort, instant closeness, instant family love. Stepparents and stepchildren will need to take time to get to know each other, to become more approachable and more comfortable with each other. Even if new families actually feel close fairly quickly, it will still take time to learn about each other's needs and begin to understand each other's feelings.

By the same token, time alone won't bring families closer. Family members need to acknowledge to each other that they wish to become closer and agree to work actively at accepting each other. Family meetings can help (refer to the last section of this chapter). Bottom line, it can help to reinforce with your stepchildren that:

- they don't have to become best friends with each other; the first step is to be open to get to know each other
- the most important thing is for everyone just to be nice to each other
- closeness between a stepparent and that parent's child should not be misinterpreted as "favoring"
- no matter what past relationships kids may have had (i.e., they might have known each other at school), they can decide to give each other a new chance
- there will probably be many emotions to deal with, feelings that need to be worked out and memories of how family life used to be that might hurt. That's natural.
- it's not a child's fault that his or her parents got a divorce. It's not a child's fault that a parent decides to remarry.
- everyone has an adjustment to make and every adjustment takes time. Adjustments may be easier for some family members and harder for others. Some families adjust sooner, others take longer. Closer family feelings can be worked at individually and collectively, one day at a time.

I have a stepbrother, but when I talk to him I can't talk to him as a real brother. What do I do?

IF GETTING ALONG IS DIFFICULT

How do you go through life living with a stepmother who ignores you and hates you and makes life miserable? I've tried talking to her but it doesn't help. Help!

Sometimes relationships in stepfamilies, as in "original" families, just aren't good. For example, if a stepparent has an alcohol or other drug problem, or if a stepparent is totally insensitive to a child's needs, or if the stepchildren absolutely hate each other and feel miserable about their life together, the family dynamic can be strained at best and full of fighting at worst.

If there seems to be no remedy that you can work out yourselves, it can be very positive to seek out those who can offer support and guidance (another family member, such as a grandparent, aunt or uncle, school guidance counselor, school psychologist, school social worker, school administrator, priest, rabbi, etc.). Going for help is not a statement of inadequacy. It can be a source of strength and can offer insights and tools to help family members live together in a more peaceful and potentially rewarding way. Everyone should be reminded of this last fact as well.

DIVORCE CAN INFLUENCE HOW OLDER KIDS VIEW MARRIAGE

Many older kids whose parents have separated or gotten divorced have told me of their fears regarding finding the "right" person and marriage. The following card written by a college student speaks for itself:

Wanted to say that I am scared to death that I won't find the right person for the rest of my life and will slip into a marriage like my parents.

It would be important to anticipate that older kids might remain silent about these kinds of feelings. If you've had difficulty in your marriage, it's possible that your children will take that as a warning for them to shy away from commitment to a long-term relationship. Because of your experience, your kids might question getting married.

Remind your kids that they're not you, not their parents. They're not their sisters or brothers. They're not their friends. They can only be themselves, and each person has the capacity to establish one's own relationship with another person. No two people can relate to each other exactly like anyone else. Divorce and separation are not "catching." What happened between their parents does not have to have anything to do with what they are able to establish with another person in their own relationships.

If anything, kids can take whatever negative and positive lessons they learned from their parents and incorporate what they now know not to do—and what they learned works best—in a way that will work for them.

As your kids get older, you can talk together about the various positive ingredients that can be part of a good relationship, such as (these are not in any order):

- Mutual trust and honesty
- Caring
- Sensitivity
- Respect
- Friendship
- Being able to have fun and be silly
- Being able to be serious
- Accepting the other person for who he or she is
- Good communication
- Attentiveness
- Common interests (although not every single interest needs to be the same)
- Compatible goals and attitudes about where to live, sharing incomes, whether or not to have children, how many children to have
- Compatible values and religious beliefs
- Shared hopes and dreams

While some of these ingredients are likely to be reevaluated, such as how many children people might wish to have, other components are in the basic priority category.

While you can explain to your child that each person needs to make that priority list for him- or herself, things like caring and communication and respect (and other components like that) ought not be compromised. Of course, substitute whatever you feel are your own priorities. It might be very interesting to ask your child what he or she thinks is of greatest importance in a relationship. This conversation can be very helpful in determining what qualities to look for in a boyfriend or girlfriend.

Kids might feel good to know that their parents probably loved each other very much and were committed to spending the rest of their lives together when they got married—even though their dreams didn't work out the way they might have hoped. Children can gain strength from learning that every parent and every child has the ability to dream new dreams and find new, supportive family feelings to replace ones that didn't work.

GRANDPARENTS AND OTHER RELATIVES

How do you talk to old people without feeling uncomfortable?

Relatives can add a wonderful extra dimension to any child's life. In fact, some kids feel closer to a cousin than to their brother or sister, closer to an aunt than their own mother. They may tell secrets to a grandparent that they would never tell anyone else in the world.

> I was so close to my grandmother. I could tell her anything. I am close to my grandfather but not as. It is just harder to tell him private things so I just don't. Some things I used to just talk to my grandmother about I just keep inside. I'm not saying that I'm not close with my parents. I'm very close with them but some things that I used to just talk to my grandma about I don't tell anyone and my feelings just get kept inside me.

Many kids love their relatives and feel very lucky. Others wish they could trade them in. How do your kids feel about relatives in your family? Do they:

- put up a fight every time the family plans to get together with relatives?
- stay on the telephone for hours with friends while an elderly aunt visits downstairs?
- call their cousins "wimps" behind their backs and feel

frustrated or embarrassed when they have to include them with their friends?

It can help to talk about the many feelings kids could have about different relatives. It also can help to let kids know it's normal for kids in the same family to have different feelings about and a different relationship with the same relative. One daughter may absolutely love an uncle who seems distant and grouchy to another. A little cousin who teases everybody might seem like a pain to most, but may have a special place in your son's heart.

Kids need to be taught that just like with sisters and brothers, relatives can't be picked. They can't go to a "relative store" and switch their uncle who smokes smelly cigars for one who doesn't smoke. They can't trade in their aunt for one who cooks better and asks fewer questions, or pawn their cousins for others who can play ball. The sooner kids start accepting relatives for who they are instead of judging them and wishing they were someone else, the sooner they will have a chance to feel more positive about relating to them. This is no different from the need to accept and put differences in perspective with friends, classmates, the new kid who moves in down the block, or anyone.

WHEN RELATIVES COMPARE OR FAVOR ONE CHILD OVER ANOTHER

Just as comparing and favoring one child over another can undermine relationships between siblings, they can cause resentment and hurt relationships with cousins. Here again, even when relatives don't say anything, kids may feel they're being compared. The more attuned you are to even the most subtle possibility of comparison, the better.

GETTING CLOSER TO GRANDPARENTS

Kids can have a deep, special bond with grandparents that can never be replaced by anyone, including parents. Whether fishing, playing a card game, or sitting in the yard watching them plant flowers, time shared with a grandparent is a treat that kids usually remember for a lifetime.

Unfortunately, not all relationships with grandparents are so positive. As much as grandparents may seem magical to many kids, they're human like everyone else. They have frailties and hang-ups, and may not have time or interest for their grandchildren.

Kids often do not know how to relate to grandparents and other older relatives. They may feel uncomfortable, not know what to say, not know what to share to be able to get closer to them. Circumstances that kids have told me make it difficult for them to be close include when a grandparent (not in any order):

- favors their brother or sister
- is overprotective
- speaks with a mouthful of food
- has bad breath or body odor
- is impatient, short-tempered, or gruff
- doesn't seem interested
- is too nosy
- is very frail, ill

My grandmother two years ago had a stroke. I love her but it's hard to cope with her. How can I handle this?

- is very senile and hard to relate to
- lives far away and rarely spends time with them
- lives nearby but never makes time to be with them
- is more interested in talking about himself or herself than getting to know the grandchildren
- is always correcting them
- doesn't seem to accept them for who they are

My grandmother is coming next month. I never met her before. Instead of being happy, I feel worried about her coming. What should I do?

You can share this list with your child, or, perhaps even better, ask your child to make his or her own list first. Then consider together what might be able to be worked at, and what must be accepted as something that cannot change.

If you evaluate what circumstances exist in your family life, that will help you to identify some of the feelings that your child might not feel comfortable expressing. For example, if a grandparent is living at your home or is visiting for an extended period of time, you can anticipate the possibility that your kids might resent not having as much private time with you (even if your kids absolutely love their grandparents). Or, if a grandparent is ill or in a nursing home, figure that your kids might feel uncomfortable, sad, or anxious. They may not know what to say when visiting. They also might be very worried that their grandparent only has a short time left to live.

> **I'm worried about my grandma. She has cancer. I am feeling bad. Can you tell me what to do?**

Most kids find these feelings difficult to talk about. They may worry about hurting a parent's feelings if they say anything that might be considered negative about their grandparent. They may also be concerned that a parent will be angry, will tell the grandparent what was said, will not understand. It can be a relief for you to bring any possible concerns out in the open. Doing so can give you the chance to let your child know that whatever he or she is feeling is important—and important to you. You can then help your child understand how to deal with whatever represents a concern. Hopefully, this will help pave the way for your child to be able to grow closer to his or her grandparent.

So often, kids just don't know what to say to their grandparents and other relatives. They may think they don't have anything in common. Here are some topic ideas you can share with your child that can help to build bridges between the ages:

WHAT KIDS CAN ASK GRANDPARENTS AND OTHER RELATIVES TO SHARE

- What was it like growing up?
- What was different between then and now?
- What was it like without television?
- Were your parents strict?
- How did you get along with your parents?
- How did you get along with your brothers and sisters?

- Were you close with your family? Was your family close? Who was your favorite relative? Why?
- Did you hang out with a group of friends?
- Did you play a sport? What was your favorite?
- What was your favorite activity?
- What about boyfriends or girlfriends? When did you have your first boyfriend or girlfriend?
- What was the most embarrassing thing that ever happened growing up? The saddest? The most special memory?
- What would you do differently if you could grow up all over again?
- What do you wish someone had taught you earlier?
- Did you ever do anything you regretted doing?
- What were your biggest fears?
- What did kids pressure other kids to do?
- Could you talk with your parents about sex, dating, or anything else like that?
- What were your dreams? (Did you want to be an actress?)
- Were your grandparents around when you were growing up? What did you love to do with your grandparents?

Also:

- What was your first job?
- What were the wars like?
- How did inventions change your life?
- What is your favorite food? Favorite flavor of ice cream?
- What are your favorite recipes? (Baking or cooking is another great activity grandchildren can share with grandparents.)
- What's your favorite music? Favorite song? Favorite color? Favorite dance step?

You and your child can add to this list. It can be wonderful to video- or audiotape these conversations between grandparent and grandchild to preserve these special moments and capture stories that can never be told by anyone else in quite the same way.

What kids can talk about with their grandparents or other relatives:

- School
- Friends, boyfriends, girlfriends
- What they plan to do during school vacations
- What they think they want to do when they grow up
- Their favorite music
- Their fears, their dreams
- What makes them sad
- What they wish they could change
- How hard it is to talk about certain things and why
- How special it is to have their grandparents in their life

There are endless topics to explore and activities that can be shared. The first step is to learn how your child feels. If the feelings aren't as close as your son or daughter would wish, you can suggest that the first step is to let their grandparent know how much it would mean to become even closer. Your child can say this in writing or aloud.

Just because grandparents and other relatives may be older doesn't guarantee that they would know how badly their grandchild (or niece, nephew, etc.) wishes to get closer. Sometimes, kids need to take the first step. Our sensitivity and all of our suggestions can help.

If Grandparents Are No Longer Alive

If you have already had open discussions with your child about a grandparent who has died, it can help to reinforce that you would be happy to answer other questions and talk further about that grandparent's life. If you haven't had this kind of talk together, it's possible your child is walking around, silently wishing he or she could bring up the subject.

Many kids hold back the feelings and questions they would like to share about a deceased grandparent. Reasons vary, but include being scared to make their parent or other grandparent upset, and feeling too uncomfortable to say anything.

How should I approach my father about his father's death? I never knew my grandfather at all.

Whether your mother or father died recently or before your child was born, it could be very important for you to let your child know that it's okay to talk about him or her. You might take out old picture albums and share stories about your parent's life and all that you feel would be special to know. Your child might deeply appreciate being given a picture of that grandparent to be able to keep in his or her room.

Your child might feel relieved if you mention that you know this is not an easy topic to bring up, and that you hope he or she will ask any other question, anytime. You can also say that it means a lot to you that your child is so interested in your parent, that it feels good to you to talk about him or her.

> My grandfather died the day after I was born. Obviously I never got to know him. Whenever I ask my parents about what he was like they always give me an excuse that they're too busy. How do I get across to them that I have to know something about him? After all, he was my grandfather who I would have liked to know and love.

Many schools have "Grandparent Day" for kids to invite their grandparent to school for the day. Kids whose grandparents are no longer alive may feel sad and left out. You might consider suggesting that your child "adopt" a grandparent, perhaps from a local senior citizen center. Many senior citizens would love to share this kind of experience. Both kids and senior citizens can be enriched by what they share.

Kids may find it very meaningful to visit a nursing home. Parents can encourage their kids to pick out someone whom they would like to visit every once in a while. Kids can bake for that person, make pictures, write poems, and ask all the questions that were suggested to help them get closer to a grandparent. They don't have to miss out on the enrichment that can be derived from a close relationship with someone who is older.

FAMILY MEETINGS CAN HELP

You don't have to wait for major changes, fights, and frustrations to knock you into the realization that your family can gain from actively working together to strengthen understanding and improve relationships. Every day, each of us learns something new about ourselves. Every day, something happens to make our kids confident, unsure, scared, stronger, frustrated, confused, upset, pressured, joyous, or sad. There's always something to share, always more to know about the people we love.

How do you say "I love you" to your parents?

I wish fathers would be more considerate and understanding.

Family meetings (call them what you wish) can be a great way to learn more about each other. The idea is to get together on a regularly scheduled basis (e.g., every other Sunday night) in order to provide a forum where family members discuss feelings, identify frustrations, deal with individual topics that each person wishes to have addressed.

My mother is like a drill sergeant. Whenever she wants me to do something she expects me to do it in two seconds. What should I do?

This doesn't have to be problem oriented. You might use the meeting to share stories from your own childhood. Your daughter might share with the family what she felt when she stayed home alone, and the entire family can make suggestions to help her deal with it and feel better. Stepfamily members can take this time to get to know each other better and discuss any new family issues that might be of concern.

How do you deal with problems at home that you can't really talk about?

Family meetings offer a chance to create an even stronger support system. Kids may feel awkward when they begin to share, especially if this kind of interaction is new. You might encourage more
open responses if you have a "sharing box" in which family members
can write topics that they wish to talk about at the next meeting.

**One night I tried to kill myself because my brother was
causing trouble for me and my mom and dad always took
his side.**

With younger kids, you might start the discussion with questions
such as, "What made you happy this week?" or "Did anything make
you sad?" For all kids, open-ended questions will give you a better
chance to draw out more than a one-word response.

If your kids tease each other regularly and aren't very close, it may
take them a while to get comfortable enough to take a chance at
sharing serious feelings. It is important for your family to establish
strict ground rules about things like not interrupting the person who
is talking, not making faces, not making fun, or not intimidating each
other in any way. Each person needs to be encouraged to listen
without judging. And everyone must agree that what is shared during
the meeting must remain private.

For family meetings, turn off the television, turn off the stereo,
and take the phone off the hook or let an answering machine take the
messages. If you make it clear that this is your private time together,
your family might be happily surprised and forever grateful to find
that in time, sincere efforts to share on everyone's part can actually
help develop trust and closeness.

The first step is to realize that no matter how any family relationship has been in the past, family members are capable of saying,
"Let's start from today. I really love you and I wish we could be
closer." Or: "Let's start from today. This is new for all of us. It would
be great if we could get along better and feel more like 'family.' Can
we try?"

I Love School i come to School to learn
not to be made fun of I like school
because I learn alot at school.
I have some people makeing
fun of me I have a freind
that make fun of me

Some teachers in the school are
childish. If an event happens they don't
end it there but carry it to the future,
They spread the news to others leaving
bad reputation for us, It's hard
by words trying to face a future when it's already
others written especially when it's negative.
How do I put up with this?

Your Paraent expects you to always
get A's even sometimes when they
ask, why a A and not an A+.
Sometimes when you feel
great about a B or D+ and
your paraent puts you down
and you suddenly feel
TERRIBLE about yourself.

My friends always
asks me if she or
he could copy off
of my homework,
and I let them because
if I dont she wont
be my friend
I know that its not
right, Next time she
asks me for my homework her
again what should I say?

10

SCHOOL

Some kids can't wait to go to school each day. They enjoy their classes, feel great about their teachers, and love the chance to be with their friends. Others can't even think about school until they get past the dreaded bus ride where they worry about how much teasing and humiliation they'll have to endure. Still others have late-night or early-morning stomachaches that they hope will keep them from ever having to get on the bus so they can avoid going to school. There are kids who may at some point fall into all three categories and everywhere in between. How kids feel about school depends on a variety of factors. Sometimes those factors have nothing to do with their achievement or how much homework they have to do.

Higher grades can make kids feel proud and confident, motivated to work even harder. But as a factor in feeling good about school, achievement of higher grades may not be enough to counteract the potentially negative effects on children of any whispering behind their back as they walk through the halls, always sitting alone at lunch, being a teacher's pet or peeve, not making a sports team, not having a boyfriend or girlfriend, not being considered popular, or being more or less developed than most of the other kids.

I really hate it when you're going down the hallway and you can just hear people talking about you. It makes you feel unwanted.

All kids, no matter what their levels of achievement, will have some feelings about school that will make them feel better or worse about themselves, better or worse about fitting in, more or less motivated, or more or less confident. School can be a haven, the only place where a child might feel warmth or even a hint of love, the only place a child might be nurtured. Or school can be a living hell. For some kids, it's hell from the first day of kindergarten on.

I get a lot of pressure from my parents about my grades!

This chapter is dedicated to exploring what kids often feel and may not tell about various aspects of school life. It is my hope that what I've shared will strengthen your ability to help your child feel even more positive and be able to experience a more enriched life at school.

Teachers judge you by your grades. How can I change this?

I hate school.

PAST INFLUENCES ON YOUR CHILD'S FEELINGS ABOUT SCHOOL TODAY

It may be very helpful to consider the following:

- Has your child been disciplined for disruptive behavior? (Often, infrequently, never?)
- Does your child have at least one close friendship at school?
- Is your child part of a group? Do you sense he or she feels secure or like a tagalong?
- Has your child been accepted or left out, harassed or treated well?
- What has been the nature of your child's relationships with teachers? Have teachers been the nurturing type or strict

and less encouraging? Has your child felt positive, negative, or indifferent about teacher relationships?

- Has schoolwork been hard or easy for your child?
- Have expectations for achievement been realistic? Could your child have experienced performance pressure?
- Would your child say he or she is smart, average, or below average?
- Has your child's achievement level been, in your opinion, more or less at his or her level of expectation?
- What is your child's achievement level in comparison to that of brothers or sisters? Cousins? Friends?
- Has your child been placed in special classes, such as advanced or remedial?
- Has your child been actively involved with after-school clubs and activities?
- Has it seemed as if your child has been organized in his or her approach to schoolwork or frenzied at the last minute?
- What is your child's attitude toward test taking?
- Has your child taken advantage of getting help that has been available from teachers or tutors?

Your examination of these areas of concern will help give you a better sense of what might be contributing to or taking away from your child's positive feelings about going to school. These questions can also be an excellent springboard for your discussion about school with your child. Your son or daughter's answers can help determine areas that might be worked at as well as experiences that he or she needs to put in the past in order to go forward in a better way.

TEACHERS

FEELINGS ABOUT TEACHERS INFLUENCE FEELINGS ABOUT SCHOOL

The experience kids have with a teacher can have tremendous impact on their ability to believe in themselves and their attitude toward learning. Kids who feel their teacher is kind, loving, caring, fair, and genuinely interested in their well-being, usually feel very positive about their classroom experience. They feel safe and understood, and are likely to look forward to being there. Those safe, comfortable feelings can contribute to strengthening self-confidence and a child's effort to try harder.

The experiences with positive, supportive teachers usually mark the times that kids tend to thrive in their learning and blossom in their personal development. Children who are in such a positive environment are usually motivated to please not only their teacher but also their parents and themselves.

It's no wonder that kids who feel they are in a negative classroom environment often lose interest in learning. When teachers seem to be less sensitive, insensitive, and less nurturing, children are usually less comfortable. If teachers yell a lot and discipline by fear, children will likely feel unsafe. Children in those environments may buckle under the strain, and might silence themselves for the entire school year. Our teaching and support as parents can help kids turn a negative classroom environment into a more positive experience.

POSITIVE APPROACHES TO WHAT KIDS PERCEIVE AS NEGATIVE TEACHER SITUATIONS

Why do teachers put so much pressure on us when we have so much other problems?

There is no question that some teachers do seem to be "out to get" certain students. Some really are sarcastic and do put down their students. Sometimes, when students think they hate a particular subject, the reality is that it's actually the teacher they don't like. They may not ever realize the subject is not the problem.

In many instances, a student's perception that a teacher feels negative toward him or her is not valid. When my daughter was in middle school, she thought one of her teachers didn't like her because he never called on her when her hand was raised. We talked with her about this and suggested it would be important for her to speak with her teacher privately before or after class, or after school, which she did.

We practiced with her so that she knew what she needed to say. Turning feelings into words, she said something like:

"It's not really comfortable for me to say this to you, but I was wondering if I did anything to make you upset with me. It seems like you are because every time my hand is raised, you don't call on me. I hope it's okay that I told you that."

This was the best thing she could have done, as the teacher responded in a very positive way. He thanked her for coming to him and letting him know what she was feeling. He was happy she told him, because he didn't realize he was passing over her and definitely did not mean to do that. From then on, he started calling on her, and my daughter's comfort and enjoyment level rose significantly. I realize it doesn't always work out that way. However, unless our daughter took a chance and told her teacher how she felt, he may never have known. And he may never have been given the chance to confirm that he really did not feel anything negative toward her. After speaking with him, she started feeling more positive in his classroom.

How do you discuss problems with teachers?

Teachers think I have a bad attitude. They all hate me! What should I do?

In elementary and middle school, kids can still be helped to view their classroom experience from the vantage point of what they can control. They can behave, do their work, not be disruptive in class, and do the best to learn what they can.

What kids perceive about how a teacher feels about them may or may not be true. We as parents can try to help validate those feelings to determine what might be the best approach to take with our kids and, potentially, with any teacher. For example, if your child thinks a teacher is negative about him or her, it's important to ask where those feelings are coming from. Does the teacher yell a lot? If so, whom is the yelling directed toward? Is your child singled out or does the teacher yell at just about everyone? Is there sarcasm? Does the teacher put kids down? Does the teacher direct it at your child or pretty much everyone? How does a teacher respond when students make a mistake?

Kids can be ultrasensitive to a teacher's insensitivity. That can make it extra hard to feel comfortable in class. Even if a teacher doesn't direct the yelling or sarcasm at them, they may sit in class worrying, "Will this be my day to be targeted?" rather than focusing on whatever lesson is being taught. So in either case, targeted or not, that may take away from their ability to learn as much as possible.

TURNING FEELINGS INTO WORDS

We can suggest to children that they approach their teacher and talk about their concerns. Most kids will probably feel scared to do that, but may be able to be encouraged to do it anyway as long as they know what to say. This is another place that it can help to reinforce the idea of how children can turn feelings into words. For example:

- If kids don't know an answer, they can tell a teacher:
  "I'm sorry, but I'm not sure of the answer."
- If kids feel they were blamed unfairly, they can say:
  "This is a little hard for me to say, but I just wanted you to know that I wasn't the one who did it."
- If kids are confused about the work, they can say:
  "I know you just explained this for the whole class period. I tried very hard to follow you, but I still don't get it. Could I come for extra help?"
- If kids are uncomfortable saying something to a teacher, they can start with: "This is hard for me to tell you . . ."
- If kids are upset because a teacher doesn't believe they really forgot their homework, they can say:
  "I realize there have been times when I didn't do my homework. But this time I really did. It's hard for me that you don't believe me. I just want you to know I spent a long time on it yesterday afternoon."
- If a child asks to have a seat change because other kids are making it difficult to concentrate, the teacher refuses, and it's still hard to concentrate, a child can approach the teacher again and say:
  "I know I already asked you this and you said there was nothing you could do. But those kids are still bothering me, and it would mean a lot if you could just change my seat so I could be farther away from them."

(In this case, if the teacher refuses to change the seat after a second request, it may be time for parents to contact the teacher directly.)

Two kids make fun of me for no reason. I told my mom. She said to tell the teacher in that class. The next day I told the teacher and the teacher said that there was nothing that the teacher could do. She won't even switch my seat. What should I do?

You can role-play with your children once you've discussed what issues and concerns they would like to air about school or a class. Remind your kids that even if they know the words, that doesn't mean it will be easy to say them. It may also help to offer the perspective that it's okay to be uncomfortable, it's even very normal to feel that way, but it's not okay to let being uncomfortable prevent them from saying something important to their teacher. They may just have to push the words out. This will help them build the skills everyone needs to stand up for oneself.

Some kids absolutely will not agree to speak with their teacher one-to-one. They're too scared, too uncomfortable, too unsure of how that teacher will respond. They might agree to talk with their teacher along with their parents. Or they might prefer parents to talk with the teacher alone. Whichever option your child is comfortable with, work through it with him or her. This can be of great help to your child.

APPROACHING A TEACHER

Regardless of what a particular teacher's nature is purported to be, it can help to give the teacher the benefit of the doubt when you or your child approach. It's not fair or smart to approach a teacher out of blame. For example, saying something like, "You were really mean to me in front of the class" or "I'm very upset that you're saying this kind of thing to my child!" is likely to get a teacher's back up and put the teacher on the defensive. So you may discuss with your child the anger and resentment he or she has felt in response to this teacher, but then move on to the words that can be used to calmly and respectfully address the situation.

Here are a few beginning approach ideas that might help you or your child start the conversation in a more positive way:

Child to teacher:

"This is hard for me to say. But I want to feel good in your class. The way you talk to me sometimes makes me feel that you might not like me.
"I wanted to say I'm sorry if I did anything to make you upset with me. I would like to feel good in your class and would like for us to get along."

Child to teacher:

"When you said _____ to me in class the other day, I had a hard time keeping back my tears. I figure you probably didn't mean to upset me, but that's how I felt and I thought you would want to know it.
"I kind of thought you were kidding around, and I know a lot of kids laughed. I did, too. I didn't know what else to do, because I really was very embarrassed. I hope it's okay that I'm saying this to you. But I didn't think it was very funny. It's hard for me to feel good when you say things like that."

By approaching a teacher in this way, your child leaves the conversation wide open for the teacher to take it in any direction he or she pleases. Your child will have stated clearly what the exact concern is, in a respectful, nonaccusatory way. The statements in both suggested approaches confirm that this child wants to feel more positive. Hopefully, the respectful tone will go a long way to make that teacher more receptive.

What do you do when your teacher don't believe you when you tell her you lost your homework?

If a child knows he or she has acted up in class, has been mean to other kids, has been disruptive in any way, the child can also approach the teacher and talk things out. If this is the case, a child might say something like:

"I know I haven't been acting so well in class. And I wanted to tell you I'm sorry. I understand why you would be upset with me. But I hope you will give me another chance. I want to get along better."

In that approach, the child was honest and apologetic. What is said reflects the fact that the child is taking ownership of what he or she did and recognizes there is a need to behave differently.

Here's how a parent might approach a teacher with the same concerns:

Parent to teacher:

"My son felt a bit uncomfortable saying this to you, so I appreciate your setting aside the time for us to be able to meet.

"I thought you'd want to know that he's been feeling uncomfortable in your class lately. He has the feeling that you don't like him and thinks that maybe you're angry at him.

"When I asked him what makes him feel that way, he said it's the way you talk with him. I realize that the way he's hearing you may not be how you feel. But just in case you are upset with him in any way, I thought it would be important to know. That way, we'll know what may be appropriate for him to work at changing. And if you're not, I know he'll be relieved to learn that . . . but I thought you'd want to know that he's hearing you that way."

This a straightforward attempt to let the teacher know how your child responded. You're also confirming that you know what went on but you're giving the teacher the benefit of not intentionally trying to be hurtful. Yet you clearly are saying this needs to stop. And it does. Will it? That remains to be seen.

Can we promise our kids that all they need to do is say these words and their teacher will definitely become kinder, more sensitive, and forgiving? No. We can only promise that a teacher may not know how their students feel unless they or their parents say so.

What do you do when a teacher doesn't like you?

If the teacher does not change his or her ways, ways that continue to feel negative for your child, you might choose to speak to the teacher one more time ("I realize we already spoke about this, but . . .") before going through the appropriate chain of command. You might next consider contacting your child's guidance counselor to discuss what steps would be best to take for you and your child.

Then you may want to go to the principal or assistant principal, and on up to the superintendent if need be.

While I'd like to believe that every teacher would care to listen and respond with sensitivity, I do know better. I say this respectfully, as I am a teacher myself. And I know that there are teachers who are sometimes the only people in a child's life who believe in them, who give them encouragement to believe in themselves, who nurture them and give them hope. But I also have heard too many agonizing stories about situations with teachers in which kids were not only turned off to a particular subject, learning in general, and school in general, but they were turned off to and gave up on themselves. That's absolutely not okay.

What do I do when a teacher gives up on teaching you?

It would seem unconscionable for a child or a parent not to be able to inform a teacher of these kinds of concerns. It would be very painful (and unacceptable) to me, as a parent, if a teacher made life more miserable for my child as a result of approaching that teacher in an honest and respectful way with the intent of coming to a better understanding.

Just as kids may still continue to tease after being asked to stop, kids cannot control what a teacher chooses to do in response to a plea for greater sensitivity or a new chance. Again, we can teach kids that while they can't control their teachers, they can control what they say and do in response to their teachers. That leaves them in control no matter what their teachers end up doing.

So if a teacher does not respond to a child's or parent's approaches, and the classroom experience remains negative, we can help kids take a different kind of charge of their learning experience. Kids can arrive on time; have their books, notebooks, pencils, and papers with them and ready; do their homework as assigned. They can be polite, be respectful, behave nicely to classmates. They can keep quiet in class except to answer the teacher's questions. They can learn to get along in a tough, undesirable situation and hopefully become stronger for it. And they can try to focus on putting forth a sincere effort to make the most out of learning what they can. If they do that, that will be doing a lot. The experience won't be wasted.

They will have learned far more than whatever subject was being taught.

KIDS NEED TO KNOW THAT TEACHERS ARE HUMAN, TOO

It would help to teach kids that teachers, like everyone else, are human. They may have good days and bad days. No matter how well they teach, some lessons may be better than others. They may be sad because an aunt is ill, frustrated because their own kids are having a rough time in school, and may or may not feel they fit in among teachers in the teachers' lounge.

If you remind kids that teachers are human, that will help them realize that normal, regular, "everyday"-type conversation can enhance their relationship with them. Your son or daughter can let a teacher know "I got a new puppy this weekend" or "My cow just had a calf" or "My grandma had to go to the hospital." He or she can ask a teacher, "Did you have a good weekend?"

This is not about becoming a teacher's pet, nor is it about invading privacy. And there's no guarantee that being a bit more personal and extra nice will make a difference in any teacher-student relationship. But, very often, a friendly smile and extra effort to show interest can go a long way. It can represent the beginning to more productive and positive associations.

SHOWING APPRECIATION

Just as it is important to help our children deal with difficult, negative feelings, we also need to help them appreciate teachers who are caring and put forth effort to make a positive difference in their lives. Kids can be taught that they don't have to wait for a holiday or the end of the school year to write their teacher a deep-felt note of thanks—for caring enough to listen to a problem that had nothing to do with school, for the extra help preparing for a test. Kids can write from their heart to thank teachers for believing in them, for giving them a new chance, and just for sharing how good it feels to be in their class.

It would be great for kids to know that those kinds of notes can be more precious to a teacher than they might imagine. This is a wonderful lesson, another gift we can give to our kids—what it can mean for them to express gratitude, and the ability to feel it in the first place. We can help our kids learn to appreciate others with that kind of communication. Instead of taking from others with an attitude that what they give is expected, is what they're supposed to be given by that particular person, we can teach kids not to take anything or anyone for granted. We can also teach them how to express their appreciation in many different ways.

DIFFERENT CLASSES, DIFFERENT FEELINGS

Beyond any feelings related to teachers, class placement and interaction among students can also contribute toward how kids feel about being in school.

> I hate it when I answer a question or say something and someone looks at me like I said the stupidest thing.

ADVANCED CLASSES

Kids in advanced classes may feel challenged, proud, and important. They're often "self-winding," very focused, and highly motivated. These are the kids who are usually considered the "smartest in the school." The pressure to achieve is often experienced by them in a very positive way.

> My dad is real smart and he thinks that I am just like him. Sometimes I think he expects too much. What can I do?

Some children stretch themselves academically to be able to qualify for an advanced class. Competition within the class can be strong and can often add to the pressure in both positive and negative ways. Some kids may take only advanced classes because their parents want them to do so or because most of their friends are in that class. They may struggle to stay at that level and not feel very comfortable. Beyond the pressure to get in, there can be pressure to keep up and stay in.

There are kids at this level who consistently earn higher grades.

Parents, teachers, and students themselves expect that this will be the case. If students fall short, that can jack up the pressure even more. If your child is placed in any advanced classes, how do you think he or she feels about being there? Do you think your child feels very pressured to achieve? Might your child be better off shining in a "regular" class, in a more relaxed environment, rather than struggling to keep up in the advanced class? Along with any expectations you might have for higher achievement from your child, do you also express appreciation?

"REGULAR" CLASSES

Students in regular classes are not pressure free. While the pressure may not be as obvious or widespread as it can be in the advanced classes, there still will be kids who work hard for their higher grades and have to deal with parental and teacher expectations. There will still be the "class brain," and comparison or competition with friends and other classmates.

There may be a feeling among kids in the regular classes that those in advanced classes are "better" or "smarter" than they are. This perception sometimes can diminish how kids value themselves and whether they define themselves as "good students."

If your child is in a regular class, it may help to discuss concerns about how kids label each other, perceptions of success, judgments, competition, and comparisons that might be made.

Our teachers often compare the brain "above average" class to us and we get angry and very insulted.

REMEDIAL CLASSES, SPECIAL EDUCATION

Many kids who are in special classes and resource rooms feel very thankful to be there. They feel comfortable, safe, and positive about the opportunity to learn in accordance with their special needs. Other kids may feel safe and comfortable when in these classrooms, but that changes for them when they walk into the halls. There they may be the brunt of teasing and other forms of denigration from kids who don't understand what special education actually means.

It's important for all kids, whether or not they're in special-needs classes, to understand how wonderful and important it is that these classes exist. All children need to become more sensitive to each other's differences and also must be reminded that friendship doesn't have to do with what class kids are placed in or what grades they earn.

> I always give the wrong answer to a question. I feel like everyone is thinking I am a jerk.

WHEN STUDENTS GIVE WRONG ANSWERS OR MAKE MISTAKES

No matter what class they are in, kids often feel humiliated when they attempt to answer a teacher's question and get it wrong. It would help for all children, regardless of their class placement, to have greater sensitivity for others. They need to know that it's not okay to laugh at someone who makes a mistake. Even put-down–type looks can be devastating enough to silence kids who tried, for the rest of the school year. Their respect can make a big difference to everyone else.

> A lot of the times I feel people judge me because I'm not that smart. Like for example if we need to choose groups, students only go with the class genius. And the last person left has to be in my group, and they put on a really snobby face that makes me feel left out.

GRADES

Children often mistakenly believe that their worth is measured by their report card. They frequently compare grades. Many feel "better grades, better person," "bad grade, bad or less adequate person." They think they will be considered special and important only if their grades are high. This assumption is often reinforced by parents and teachers who compare them to brothers and sisters or classmates and ask why their grades aren't as high. These comparisons may make kids feel that they can never measure up. They're often scared to bring grades home, and scared to approach their parents about concerns related to school.

If you know that one of the children in your family earns higher grades, it can help to anticipate that siblings might feel you make negative comparisons, even if you're careful not to do so.

REDEFINING SUCCESS

Comparisons related to achievement levels might be less devastating if we helped children understand that each person is capable of being a "good student". The mind-set so often is that to be a good student, one has to earn 100s or at least 90s. Too many children are defeated and even drop out of school because they don't feel they can be "successful" or don't feel they can measure up to those "good students" with their higher grades.

I feel like I can never achieve anything in school and what seems a good grade to me is laughable to others.

Several years ago, I listened with horror to a radio report about four students in one high school who committed suicide together. With regard to one of the girls, the commentator said, "She felt she had no future." I still get chills when I think about that. I suggest that we need to help students redefine the meaning of success. I say this respectfully, as we are clearly a grade-oriented society. Grades do count. The pressure seems to build each year for acceptances into undergraduate as well as graduate schools, and the job market is very competitive. But the fact remains, each child can only work at his or her own level and build from there.

It can help to talk with children about what they thinks it means to be a "good student." If you haven't already done so with your son or daughter, you can explain that all kids are capable of challenging themselves to raise their level of achievement. That means that no matter what their grades, they can study even harder, organize their notes even better, and spend more time getting help at school as well as from parents or others at home. They can sincerely work to raise their grades on the next test or project.

You can further share that if, having put in such sincere effort, a child raises his or her grade from a 70 to a 71 or 72, hopefully he or she can feel proud for that achievement as well as for the effort that was put in. The next time, perhaps the grade can be raised to a 73 or 74, and so on. There's no telling how high that grade can eventually be raised, even one point at a time.

Kids also need to be challenged to challenge themselves. They need only evaluate "What did I do last time?" to "What did I achieve this time?" Success has to do with what a child is able to accomplish for him- or herself. It's not about how that child compares to anyone else. We need to teach children that the only seat in a classroom they can fill is their own. The only achievement that will be meaningful for them is their own at their own level.

If parents say to their student who earned a 70, "What happened to the other 30 points?" or "Next time I expect you to get 100!", this may be totally unrealistic for that child to achieve. That child might sincerely have done his or her best. In that case, parents will likely remain disappointed, perhaps even punish and be negative about that child's schoolwork—and the child might never feel as if he or she can measure up. Consider how such expectations might impact kids who are never able to earn a 90 or 100. Does that mean they can never be considered a "good student"? They need to know they can.

I'm ~~cool~~ dumb.

I believe that many kids would be greatly relieved and perhaps even more motivated if they were encouraged to redefine what success means to them. For example, if they tried their very best, worked as hard as possible, took advantage of all the help and guidance available (i.e., from teachers and from parents or siblings), and put in serious study time, and these best efforts for that particular exam resulted in earning a 74, that 74 deserves to be considered their "A." Hardly anyone views achievement this way.

Bottom line, all kids deserve to understand that each child can be a good student by sincerely and actively trying to do the best they can in their schoolwork. We need to explain that this is a choice that kids can make. It can be important for parents to speak with their child's teacher about what level of achievement might be realistic to work toward as a goal. When children as well as parents have realistic perspectives about achievement levels and success, a child can feel that much more positive and less frustrated.

An Extra Note

Parents can gain insight from David, a ninth-grade student, who told me:

> "My parents always expect the best from me, and I expect it from myself. And I always get the best grades. But my parents never tell me they're proud."

Remember that no matter what a child's level of achievement, it's still important for parents to say, "I'm so proud of you." Even if you think your child knows how proud you are of his or her accomplishments, take the time to share that feeling. It can mean a lot.

PRESSURE TO ACHIEVE, PRESSURE TO EARN "GOOD" GRADES

There is a fine line of distinction between positive encouragement and negative pressure. Kids who feel they are being pressured negatively may not be able to concentrate fully on their work. They may be motivated to cheat because they're so afraid of not living up to parental expectations.

Kids may feel very frustrated when their parents don't ever seem to be satisfied. Rather than asking why a child didn't earn higher than a 70, it may be more positive to say something like:

> "Let's talk about how you studied for your test. How much time did you spend? How about getting your notebook so we can go over how you organized your notes. I may be able to make some suggestions to help you feel even better about preparing for your next test."

Before even getting into the above conversation, you might ask your child:

"How did you feel about your test results?"

Above all, the definition of "good" deserves to be evaluated for each individual child, separate from how a parent might have performed in school, separate from how sisters or brothers or anyone else are performing.

One child's C might represent working to capacity, while for another a C might fall short of what that child might be capable of doing. Kids as well as parents need to know that there deserves to be a different definition of success for each student. The expectations that teachers and parents may have can add a great deal of pressure to children's life, as well as make it hard for them to feel proud when they have accomplished something. Again, it can help to discuss realistic expectations with your child and your child's teachers.

My parents care too much about grades. I try but sometimes I don't do as well as I want to. How do I convince them I'm trying my best?

It might help for you to further consider:

· Would your child say you're pressuring him or her to achieve?
· How forgiving are you?
· Would your child be nervous or excited about bringing home a report card to share with you?
· Do you think your child is ever scared to let you know what he or she is achieving?
· Would you say your child feels positive or not so positive about schoolwork?
· Would your child say he or she is smart or not so smart?

DEALING WITH FAILING

What can I do about failing?

Kids who are failing often feel like failures. We can help them understand that if they're failing one or even several courses, that doesn't mean that they, personally, are failures. And just because they may have gotten what they feel is a bad grade, it doesn't mean they're a bad person. It also doesn't necessarily mean that they're stupid and not capable of passing or that they won't be able to be productive in their lives. It probably means that whatever they're doing to handle their work, however they're approaching their studying, is not working for them, and they need help. It could also mean that their family life is falling apart and it's very hard to concentrate on anything else. Or that they have a problem with alcohol or other drugs. There are so many possibilities.

Rather than focusing on taking away car keys, "grounding," or punishing a child in any other way because of the failing grades, it can be more helpful to make a more supportive approach. For example, you might say:

- "Well, I'm going to guess that wasn't the easiest thing you needed to tell me. I appreciate that probably took a lot of courage. More than anything, I hope I can help in some way.
- "What are your thoughts as to why you're having such a problem with math?"

Depending on your child's answer, you might continue with:

- "Okay, it seems like it would be important to find out from your teacher if there is a chance you could retake any of your tests or do any extra credit work."
- "Maybe we can find a tutor who could help you learn what you haven't been able to understand. Let's make an appointment to speak with your teacher first, so we can all figure out together what will help you the most."

How do you tell your parents you are failing every class?

- "I know a lot of times when kids are failing a subject, there may be other things going on in their life that are tough to handle. So besides dealing with how to understand math in a better way, I'm concerned about what else might be going on for you. I'm concerned that you're okay . . . I'm guessing that it's possible that there are some other things that are bothering you that it would help to talk about."

I'm failing everything. I hate this school.

When dealing with a failing grade, kids usually feel terrible. It's not surprising that they may "hate" school. It would be unfortunate to make children feel potentially even worse by telling them that "failing is unacceptable, they need to try harder", when they may have no idea how. It would be more helpful to work with them to develop the tools to more effectively approach their subject. With greater awareness and a more specific understanding of what they can do to try again, kids will have a better chance to attain more positive results.

If people give up on kids who fail, is it any wonder why the kids would give up on themselves and drop out? One student's comment on failure was, "The only time I really fail is when I give up." It would be great if more kids shared that view.

WHEN KIDS MUST REPEAT A GRADE

Why do people make fun of me when I stayed back?

When kids are "left back," other kids might refer to them as "losers." They might even think of themselves that way. The fact that they are now going to class with a majority of kids who are younger may make them feel uncomfortable and out of place. A child might have less in common with these younger classmates and may worry if anyone is going to give him or her a chance. Kids who repeat a grade might also feel ashamed and embarrassed among their original classmates. They may worry about keeping old friendships, especially if former classmates have just moved on to a different school building.

Sometimes it's not academic performance but extensive absences due to illness or the need to recover from surgery that might cause a child to have to repeat a grade. In those situations, kids seem to be more forgiving and less judgmental. While social adjustments might be difficult no matter what the reason, kids who have to repeat a grade might even feel relieved about doing so if they realize it's not a measure of their self-worth. They should know that if they repeat a grade or not, they're still valuable, still important, and still equal to everyone else. Repeating a grade also has nothing to do with a child's ability to still be a good friend.

It would help if all kids could be taught to appreciate the positive opportunity that repeating a grade can provide for students who need to do this. Staying back for a year provides the chance for students to gain a stronger foundation of knowledge so that they will be more confident, and prepared to more effectively handle the work at the next grade level. Hopefully, kids will be more supportive of classmates who must repeat a grade if they realize the good that can result from doing so. Instead of denigrating kids who are left back, it would be so much more helpful if kids could just ask, "How are you doing?" and follow with, "Hey, we miss you in class!"

WHEN KIDS "SKIP" A GRADE

Kids who skip a grade also can have strong emotions regarding the challenges they feel about fitting in socially. Children who move ahead may be physically and emotionally less mature than their older classmates, even though their scholastic ability may be exceptional. They may wonder whether they will be accepted, wonder if they'll make new friends, and worry if they will be able to hold on to friendships with former classmates. Depending on their age at "skipping," they may also be among the only students who are too young to go through rites of passage that classmates are experiencing, like getting a driver's license.

It's important to anticipate that kids who skip a grade might experience heightened performance pressure, as well. They're not only advanced, but they're considered "super-advanced." They may feel they must prove to everyone that the move was warranted. They may also be concerned about being labeled "a brain."

How can I get people to quit teasing me about being smart?

Whether they're repeating a grade or skipping a grade, it would be helpful to talk about these possible concerns and remind students that every change is an adjustment, and every adjustment can only take its own time. They can also be reminded to ask for help.

HOMEWORK

I wish I didn't have a lot of homework.

"Don't they realize we have other classes, too!?" I can't even count the number of times that my friends and I said this about the volumes of homework we had to do growing up.

Kids have a variety of feelings about homework. While younger elementary-school kids may feel proud to finally have "big kids"–type homework assignments, most kids think homework is a pain, a necessary evil, and something they wish they didn't have to bother doing. Sometimes it doesn't get done because a child might not have any idea how to do what's required of them. Since students may find it difficult to admit that to a classroom teacher, the end result is that it's hurried through, not providing the kind of practice lesson it was intended to give. Or it may not be completed—unless, of course, a child copies from a friend. That's another issue entirely.

No matter how many times teachers may have explained how, children may still not know how to approach their work with any degree of organization. It's not enough to tell kids, "You need to be responsible." Except for knowing that their homework needs to get done, kids may not know how to put their notes in order, how to approach their work, or how to effectively balance their time. A specific step-by-step approach can make it easier for kids to organize homework. For example, your child can:

- write down daily assignments on a special homework assignment pad
- next to each assignment, write down approximate time needed for completion ("a lot" or "a little" may be fine enough for younger kids until they learn how to figure time requirements)
- write down future assignments in a daily planner
- next to each assignment, put a special mark for date due, a special mark for test date
- write down starting date to read a book for a book report and minimum number of pages that need to be read each day

- write down starting date necessary for a project to be completed in time without rushing (i.e., start outlining, go to library)
- cross off assignments as they are finished
- make a new assignment list for each day

In my other school I got As and Bs. Now I get lower grades. How should I help myself?

You can also talk with your child about establishing priorities and balancing time. If kids are able to be specific and disciplined about what needs to be accomplished each day, they'll be able to have greater flexibility to spend time with friends, play sports, watch television, work on the computer, or do anything else. The ability to know when book reports and papers need to be started will help to eliminate the last-minute frenzy and potentially make the experience of actually doing the assignments more rewarding.

It may help to consider these questions:

- How many times has your child forgotten to write down the homework assignment?
- How many times has your child had to copy homework on the bus or in the lunchroom because it wasn't done, or he or she forgot to bring it from home?
- How many times have you had to bring your child to the home of a friend to "copy the notes" or "get the list"?
- How would you describe your child's work patterns?
- Does your child have one area where homework is done?
- Are papers and books strewn all around your home with no special manner of organization?
- Is the area where your child works well lit? Comfortable?
- Is there enough storage space to keep books and papers neat and organized?

Think about what areas would be helpful to work on with your child. He or she may feel much more confident and positive about approaching homework if stronger organizational skills can be developed. Kids usually love file folders. Your child might feel terrific about learning how to file papers and actually being able to locate them when needed. It's all a growing process.

OWNERSHIP—KIDS VS. PARENTS? WHO'S DOING THE WORK?

Kids who rely on their parents to nag or make sure their homework has been started on time are potentially being robbed of the chance to develop their own sense of responsibility. Children will have less of a chance to practice estimating how much time they need to accomplish certain school tasks if parents continue to say, "Have you started your book yet? Isn't your book report due next Friday?" They need to be helped to reach the point where they own their own commitment to their assignments.

Kids will have to pay more attention to what is due and when, if they're encouraged to take charge of their own assignments. They'll be able to develop greater self-reliance and feel more confident if they take ownership of their homework assignments. Kids who weren't as enthusiastic about school might even find they will begin to feel more positive the more organized and in control they feel. The idea is to help kids take control over what they can put into their work, in order to gain the most from it.

If you have been in the habit of constantly reminding your child about starting book reports, studying for tests, or doing nightly homework, you might consider saying something like:

> "I've been thinking . . . and I realize that all the times I've reminded you to start your book report or to make sure you leave enough time to get your homework done, I haven't been doing you any favors. I need to make some changes.
>
> "I'm not saying that I won't offer guidance. Of course, I'll always try to be there for you in that way. I'm not saying that I'm planning to back off completely. I'll be around to see how things are going and offer help when you need it.
>
> "But I'm going to stop reminding you every night about your homework. Since I've always reminded you, I may just start by reminding a bit less. Then less and less until you are completely in charge of remembering your homework for yourself.

"You deserve to be able to count on yourself to be in charge of what you have to do. I have some ideas that might help. . . ."

Then you can go on to have a conversation about prioritizing and balancing time, and can share the ideas about organizing homework with your child. This may need to be a weaning process. It will probably take a bit of time for both you and your child to get used to the transition, but the outcome will be worth it for you and especially for your child and his or her confidence.

MOTIVATION

I wish I had more internal drive for schoolwork.

While some kids aren't motivated in their schoolwork because they really don't care, the majority do. Reasons for a child's lack of motivation can run a gamut of possibilities. Some kids may be so caught up with their social relationships that they leave very little time to be able to do their schoolwork. Some kids care, they wish to achieve, but they don't achieve at the level that perhaps they could. That's their protection. If they really tried and then didn't achieve, that might be too painful. It's easier for them to hold back, not try as hard, and still have the leeway to be able to say, "Well, if I tried, I could do better."

Other kids don't know how to approach their work. It's possible that they would be more motivated if they knew how to be more organized, how to study, or how to take notes better. Some kids truly don't believe they are smart enough to bother with trying. Still others may think it's just not "cool" to seem like you're interested in schoolwork. There are so many factors that could potentially influence a child's motivation.

EARRINGS, HIGHER ALLOWANCE, EXTRA PRIVILEGES, FEAR

Sometimes, kids are enticed to do well in school with promises of increased allowance, jewelry, new clothes, and other material things from parents or grandparents. In these situations, it's not surprising that some kids tend to work harder, sincerely try for the goals that their parents have set for them, and often succeed in qualifying for their rewards. But, if they go through life always expecting to have a trinket as a reward for a job well done, then aren't we robbing them of what it can feel like to really just accomplish something on their own and feel terrific about it? I think so.

Instead of trying to motivate with presents, other parents use their kid's fears: fear of being "grounded," fear of parental wrath or disapproval, fear of losing telephone, stereo, or television privileges, or fear of being physically beaten if they don't get good grades. It's no wonder some kids think they need to cheat in order to survive.

I am afraid I will get bad grades and my parents will get angry at me.

Some parents might argue, "Well, fear works! My son's grades are higher than they ever were." Students themselves might even agree that if it weren't for that "outside" threat, they wouldn't take their work as seriously. However, ongoing fear-induced stress over academic performance can eventually take its toll. Students have told me how pressured they feel and how hard it is to even concentrate on exams knowing that they must get a certain grade "or else."

OTHER REASONS WHY KIDS MIGHT NOT WORK UP TO CAPACITY

Kids may work below their capacity for any number of other reasons. In addition to the possibility that kids are bored, or truly don't care, perhaps they're afraid to achieve because friends aren't getting higher grades and they don't want to be labeled a "brain" in comparison. Perhaps they're trying to get needed attention in any way they can. They might be bitter over not being in the advanced classes again this year, and have made the decision not to work as hard. Maybe their closest friends are in the regular classes so they're purposely not doing as well in order to be moved down to be with them. Maybe they don't want to transfer to the private school their parents want them to attend, and are also purposely not putting as much effort into their schoolwork in the hopes that they won't be accepted. Maybe they have learning disabilities that haven't been identified yet. Maybe they don't like their teacher. Maybe they simply aren't ready to perform up to their capacity. Maybe they don't know how to organize their work or ask for help. Maybe they're a little lazy. These are just some of the reasons children might not do as well in school as they could.

My parents want me to go to a private school, but I don't want to go. My friends say I should fail the test, what should I do?

I hate school! But I love computers.

Since each child will have his or her own reason for not being motivated—or for achieving below capacity—it's important to talk with your son or daughter about what feelings might be influencing his or her attitudes toward schoolwork if they are less than enthusiastic. It would help to make it clear that you're approaching your child mainly because you care and wish to offer support and guidance—not out of blame or with punishment in mind.

IF YOU THINK YOUR CHILD COULD BE DOING BETTER ACADEMICALLY

If you think your child really could be doing better academically and doesn't seem to want that for him- or herself, you might choose to say:

> "I've been walking around trying to figure out what to say to you. There's a part of me that wants to shake you. There's a part of me that feels that if you really decided to do your work, who knows what you'd achieve.
>
> "I don't know if it's that you really don't care. A lot of kids probably don't. I don't know if that's really where you're at. I'm wondering if there's something going on at school. Or maybe you don't think you can do it, or maybe you're comparing. . . .
>
> "I don't know what I can say to you to help you want it for yourself. I love you and want to help you in any way I can. But I know I can't want to achieve *for* you. Will you at least think about this?"

To determine what possible deterrents might be influencing your child's level of motivation, think of his or her circumstances. How do your child's achievement levels compare to those of brothers or sisters? Could your child think you or other relatives are making comparisons? Have expectations been realistic? Think of social issues, home issues, school issues. What could possibly be influencing your child? It can also be helpful to talk with your child's teacher to get additional feedback.

Then you can substitute those concerns into the suggested script or you can come up with your own dialogue to start your conversation.

GOING FORWARD

Each child has the capacity to go forward in his or her learning. While we can't be motivated *for* our kids, we can help them understand that being motivated is another choice they can make. We can also help them realize this is an attainable goal, regardless of what their achievement level has been in the past. Regardless of how they have related to teachers, they can make a decision to go forward differently, and they can ask for help in doing so. They need to know they don't have to work at this alone.

Note: If kids start to put forth extra effort, it would probably feel wonderful to them if you let them know how much that effort is appreciated. They need to know they can take only one step at a time. It helps when praise is realistic, but even baby steps can be major. Don't make the mistake of just waiting for the very obvious changes. Praise the process.

TAKING TESTS

Some students don't mind tests. Others panic, no matter how high their grades may be in any particular class. The pressure of being tested can make it very hard for children to concentrate. We can help ease the pressure by talking with kids about their "test feelings."

Not all test feelings are ones that kids will keep hidden. If they're panicked, they'll probably say so. If they're nervous and intimidated by how much they have to remember, they'll probably say that, too. What they may not say is how pressured they are in response to parental expectations. They may not express how concerned they are about living up to what teachers expect of them. And they may not express how pressured they feel simply because they're "supposed" to be the class "brain" and "everyone" just expects them to do well.

It can help to acknowledge that it's very natural to feel nervous about a test. You might even talk about your own feelings and share one of your own childhood test-taking experiences that might make your child smile (anything to help ease the tension!).

If kids are not sure about how to approach their work or how to study for a particular test, it's important that they make an appointment with their teacher before or after school or during a free period so that they can get the help they deserve. Many kids feel very uncomfortable asking a teacher for such help. They're often afraid to be judged as inadequate, worry that the teacher will think they weren't paying attention, or fear that the teacher will lower their grade. We need to help our kids understand that most teachers are very positive about the fact that a student asks for help. Doing so is usually taken as a statement of interest. It means that the child cared enough to make the extra effort.

If your child is uncomfortable, the idea of "turning feelings into words" can help him or her figure out what words to say. For example:

"This is hard for me to ask you, but I'm not sure how to study for the test. Can you help me?"

WHEN KIDS WANT TO CHEAT
OFF YOUR CHILD'S HOMEWORK OR TESTS

As much as teachers have classroom rules about cheating, this is also very much a peer-pressure issue. Many kids have told me how confused they have been about what to do when asked by another student if he or she can cheat off their paper. Even though kids know it's wrong, they usually don't want to take a chance on ruining their friendship with that person by saying "no." In some cases, it's that they would like to have that person become their friend.

We need to help kids realize that they can make the decision to stop giving the answers. That's a choice they rightfully can make. If the person ends up getting angry and doesn't want to be friends, perhaps that person was in fact "using" them and was never a true friend.

The perspective that can be reinforced by you is that if kids have to compromise their own values and their work ethic just to get someone to be a friend, then what kind of friendship base would that be? They don't deserve to allow themselves to be used. They don't deserve to compromise themselves for either holding on to or creating the chance to be friends with someone. If someone is a true friend, that person will respect your child's right to choose what to do in any situation.

LOCKER-ROOM FEELINGS

In the locker room at wrestling I am embarrassed. How can I help that?

Depending on whether your child is more or less developed than other kids, he or she may be more or less comfortable when changing in the locker room. This is also true for summer camp and spending the night at a friend's home ("sleepovers").

In these situations, kids may worry about being teased, and worry whether their stage of development will affect friendships. Just in case your son or daughter is uncomfortable, it can help to mention that lots of kids might feel funny about changing clothes in front of others. Kids often feel better when they know they're not alone. They might also feel better knowing that in this situation, as well, there are choices. You can tell your children that they can choose to change in the bathroom instead of the locker changing area. They can be creative about the order in which they remove their clothes. For example, by leaving a long shirt on and changing their pants before changing their shirt, they can remain pretty much covered on bottom. On top, they may need to just face the lockers while they're changing to give them more privacy. And they can become very quick change artists!

It would help for all parents to remind their children about respecting differences in the locker room or anywhere else. Periodically, it's important to encourage kids to be sensitive to the feelings of others, reinforcing the fact that all the children are trying to feel good about their own stage of development, their own shape and size. It's no child's fault what stage the body is at. That's up to a kid's body. So it would be great if everyone just "chilled" and left everyone else alone.

Note: While I'm in the locker room, I might as well keep going into the gymnasium. Kids who are not as athletic as others in their gym class often have a difficult time feeling good about themselves or the class. This is the kind of experience that kids often dread every time it's scheduled, which is usually a few times a week.

Many kids would greatly appreciate if the respect that is encouraged for the locker room could extend into the gym. They might feel freer to try, less pressured to perform, and might even look forward to their class if kids didn't tease about their athletic abilities. If this is an area of concern, besides talking with your child at home, it can help to speak with the physical education teacher.

WHEN KIDS MOVE TO A NEW SCHOOL

If kids are moving to a new school in a new town, it's natural for them to feel excited, happy, nervous, and unsure—all at once. Even when kids are simply moving to another school in the same town, they may have similar feelings.

Although talking about these feelings with your child may not eliminate them, confirming that they're normal will probably be appreciated. The scary feelings usually stem from the unknown. Kids worry about being accepted, making friends, if the work will be harder, not knowing how to find their classrooms, having enough time to go to their lockers between classes. They may also worry about dealing with older kids, and being able to handle any pressure to do things that might be uncomfortable (like smoking in the bathrooms).

> I am new in this school, and I don't know what to do because people might not accept me. Also, this school is a lot harder and people might tell other people I get low test scores. And I stutter, so it's hard for me to talk to other people. I always feel conscious of myself.

Kids who have been considered popular in their other town might have a very rough time walking around the halls knowing nobody, and being recognized by no one, at this new school. Kids who were not socially involved in their hometown, and may not have been accepted, might worry if anyone will give them a chance among the new students in their new school.

It can be crucial to anticipate these kinds of feelings and talk about them with your child before school starts. That will give you the chance to offer perspectives about how any change is an adjustment that will take time, how kids may judge, and how it may be uncomfortable at first to be in such a new environment. You can talk about how to start friendships (refer back to chapter 6), and encourage your child to join at least one school club or organization soon after starting to attend the school. You can also remind your child not to take other students' uninterest too personally. Sometimes kids who might be very interested in people who are new might also feel jealous, worried that the new student is cuter, has a better personality, and/or will take away girlfriends or boyfriends of theirs. It may take a while for kids to get past those feelings.

There are many factors that could influence how welcoming some kids will be to a new student. As long as your child is nice, stays true to who he or she is, tries to actively become involved, and is patient, things eventually should become more comfortable and turn out fine. Children just need to know that the beginning may not be easy. That doesn't mean things won't work out. It just means it may take some time. If our kids are aware this could be the case, they hopefully won't be thrown about not feeling instantly comfortable.

If your child is moving to a new school in the same town, and there are kids to meet from other schools in your district, it would also help to talk about the freedom to meet new friends, confusions about how to hold on to old friendships and deal with potential jealousies among old friends, and how to handle lunch-table dilemmas (like "Do I sit with my new friends?" "What will my old friends feel?" "What if my old friends don't want me to come back to their lunch table?").

It would help to encourage all kids to go out of their way to welcome others who have just moved from another town, and to realize they can be nice without feeling pressured to be that person's friend. The same goes for meeting new kids from other schools within the same district. It just feels better when kids are nice, and are sensitive to what others might feel if they're moving to a new place, especially if they don't know anyone else and everyone else seems to know each other.

It's especially important to remind kids to "be yourself," to trust that they have personal resources and that they'll be okay in their new school. It's all an adjustment process; it's going to take time. Trying to find that first friend may require some patience, but the fact that kids can take charge of looking beats waiting around!

SOME FINAL THOUGHTS (Before the Bell Rings!)

No matter what their report card average, all kids are entitled to a classroom experience that feels good, builds confidence, nurtures acceptance, and fosters respect for differences in others. All kids are entitled to be respected for who they are, rather than being made to feel less valuable because they don't seem to measure up to who parents and teachers expect them to be. They deserve to be encouraged, to feel a sense of pride in their achievement, to feel achievement is attainable for them.

No children deserve to feel less valuable because they or their parents or anyone else is defining their worth and potential for success in terms of their letter or number grades.

While we cannot be motivated for our kids, and we cannot live their school life or any aspect of their life for them, our awareness of what they may feel and how those feelings can be influenced by others can go a long way in helping them believe in themselves—as well as feel more positive about school.

What do you do
when someone close

Croaks?

My brother died a few years ago
and we used to go to the park together
with my mom and dad. How can I cope
with having my brother dead and me going
to the park alone without him?

My brother has tried to comit suicide
3 times in the past month I feel
like a failure as a sister, how can I
realize I try my best? I alway try
my best, but it doesn't seem good enough!

My great grandpa died about
2 years ago. My great grandma
is still alive but I don't
have the relationship that
I had with her when I
was young. I still love
her alot but its hard for
me to show it. How can I
tell her I still love her?

11

ILLNESS, DEATH, SUICIDE

I couldn't resist starting with this card. I also figure that if we ever lose our sense of humor, we might as well give up now. Kids often have a most special way with words. The problem with regard to these difficult topics of illness, death, and suicide is that so many of the words they wish they could say are kept hidden in their hearts.

This chapter will identify many of the feelings kids hold back related to illness and death. You'll probably find, as I did, that many of the sharing cards are painful statements of how hard it is for kids to let you in on their sadness or talk about the loved one who died, even with the people who are closest in their lives. Here, too, as with other areas of concern, it is clear that there is no age or time cutoff for how long kids might carry around feelings they wish they could express.

How hard it is for me to deal with the loss of my father, even though he has been gone for a few years.

This is not an easy topic area for many adults, let alone children. My hope is that the information I offer, based on what children, parents, and teachers have shared with me, will help you be more sensitive to what your child wants to express and needs to know in order to better understand, discuss, and handle these difficult life experiences.

WHEN A LOVED ONE IS SERIOUSLY ILL

Children become very frightened when someone they love is ill. They often think the worst, which is that the person will die. Since kids may not tell their parents how worried they are, it's important for us to anticipate that possibility.

Depending on how family life has been disrupted, how much information your child already has, and how close a relationship he or she has with the person who is ill, you can determine what else your child might need to know.

For example:

· If a loved one has to undergo chemotherapy that will cause loss of hair, it would help to explain this to your child before it happens.
· If the person who is ill will probably lose a lot of weight, it may be less of a shock for your child to see him or her if you talk about this ahead of time.
· If the person who is ill will need long recuperation at home, all family members, younger and older, could gather and discuss how this might change family life and what each person can do to help.
· If the person who is ill requires surgery, it can help to explain why the surgery is needed, what it involves, how it will help the person get better, and what the recovery will involve.

VISITING

Children usually feel very uncomfortable with hospital visits or visits to a nursing home. They might even feel scared to be there, uncomfortable about knowing what to say to the person who is ill, and worry that they'll be upset when they see their loved one. The more you help your child be prepared for what can be expected, the better.

My grandmother is in a wheelchair and she stays in a nursing home. I really don't know her that well and I'm not

sure I want to. Whenever my father visits her I think of some
excuse not to go. What should I do?

Think about what the experience might be like for you and your
son or daughter. That will help you know what specifics will be
important to share with your child. Will there be tubes? An intra-
venous hookup? Hospital smells? Will the person be coherent, alert,
sleeping, dozing?

My own kids couldn't stand the smell at the nursing home where
they cared for my grandfather. At the time, one child was in early elementary school and the other was in nursery school. They reluctantly
came with me to visit him. It wasn't that they didn't want to see him,
they just hated the nursing home smells. I did the best I could to help
put those smells in perspective. My kids actually walked through the
halls of the nursing home holding their noses, but when they arrived
at my grandfather's room, they seemed to forget about the smells.
They usually ran in to hold his hands, and were drawn in by the joy
their visit seemed to bring him.

My grandfather ("Little Poppy") really was so thrilled to see my
kids. I don't think they'll ever forget our special ritual of bringing him
a dish of his favorite ice cream. Although he has been gone for almost
twenty years, I'll bet my kids still remember the flavors he loved so
much and how his eyes sparkled when he saw them. Actually, I left a
message for my daughter as I was writing this section earlier this
evening. She just returned my call and told me, without hesita-
tion, "Strawberry and chocolate from Baskin-Robbins." He died the
evening of my daughter's seventh birthday. She recently turned
twenty-seven. She wasn't very old at the time of our visits with him,
but the experience is something that touched her in a way that will
probably never be forgotten.

If we think about what our kids have been exposed to, that can
help us better anticipate what they wish they could share with us.
Even when kids are young, it's possible that experiences with illness
and death could have impacted them more than we might imagine.

KEEPING KIDS INFORMED, TEACHING KIDS LIFE LESSONS

If they're kept informed about a loved one's illness, our children will likely feel more secure and have greater trust that we as parents won't hold back when changes occur. Involving kids with an honest sense of what's going on will also give them the chance to learn some important lessons about the realities of life.

As we all know, sometimes life is very hard. When dealing with a close friend or relative's serious illness, that can be upsetting, sad, scary, and very strained. That's all part of life. Kids deserve to learn how to deal with this, too. We'd be shortchanging their development if we shared only the fun, joyous times.

Dealing with serious illness is a chance for kids to learn more about how to cope, and how strengthening it can be for the family to bond together and give each other support in a time of need. They can learn by your example as well as through specific discussions how much it can mean to express difficult feelings during experiences like this, and that it's okay to cry.

Some parents think their kids can't handle the truth because of what it might mean. But kids can usually sense the strain within their home, sense when their parents are upset. If parents are distressed, scared about the severity of the ill person's condition, that will probably come through to the kids.

What worries me is mainly my mom, because she is very sick.

As I've already stated, children are more than likely fearing the worst, anyway. Especially if a parent is the one who is sick, kids will be extremely upset about the possibility that their parent could die. Most kids cannot imagine life without their parent. If these worries are valid, it is crucial to provide a chance to get these feelings out, offer support, and help kids realize it will be possible to go on.

If the person who is sick is actually terminal, it would be unfortunate to allow kids to sense this and have to deal with this on their own. If the illness is not life-threatening, kids deserve to know that, too.

TALKING WITH YOUR CHILD ABOUT ILLNESS

Here again, turning feelings into words will help your child (and you) be able to express uncomfortable feelings and ask hard questions. While it's great to say to your children, "Ask me anything you want," it would be smart to anticipate that they will most likely have questions they won't know how or won't know if it's okay to express.

You may want to consider helping your child open his or her conversation by suggesting the following:

If they're sad, they can start with:

"I'm really sad to say this to you . . ."

If they're worried about making you sadder by bringing up the subject of how ill their loved one is, they can start with:

"I hope it's okay to talk about Grandma. I was afraid of making you sadder. But I'm scared. I'd really like to talk about how she is. I'm scared. . . ."

These are actual examples you might offer to your child as guides for expressing what they might want and need to say. It's a good idea to choose examples that might zero in on what your child might be worried about, that will let your child know that you know, and hopefully pave the way for more open and helpful sharing.

TALKING WITH THE PERSON WHO IS ILL

My Grandma is dying, and all she talks about is death and her hospital experience. What should I do?

When kids are in the presence of someone who is ill, they often don't know what to say. They may be nervous and unsure of how honest they can be about the ill person's condition. They may talk about everything else that really isn't very important and avoid centering in on the illness, which is the only thing they're really thinking about.

Children need to be informed if the person who is ill actually knows the extent of his or her illness. That will be a good guide to help them know what might be appropriate to say. If, for example, the person is aware of being seriously ill, it might be appreciated if your child openly states how sad he or she is about the illness. If the person knows he or she is terminally ill, your child might even tell that person how much he or she will be missed later on. While it can be painful to acknowledge the truth about someone's serious condition, your child might feel relieved to do so. It can help to tell kids that it also can be a relief to the person who is ill to know that he or she no longer has to pretend that everything will be fine. Your child and the person who is ill might find it very comforting and strengthening to be able to cry together. It's possible that your child's honesty will open the door for sharing that would never otherwise be expressed.

This is yet another lesson to teach kids about accepting what you cannot change and making the most of what you can. While kids may not have the power to change how ill their loved one is, they can express how much they care for that person. They can attempt to make the most of the remaining time they have with that person. Many kids also find peace and solace through keeping that person in their prayers.

OTHER WAYS TO COMMUNICATE WITH SOMEONE WHO IS ILL

If the ill person is too weak or sick to be able to have visitors or your child is too young, too uncomfortable, or lives too far away to visit, there are other ways to show concern. Your child might:

- Draw a picture
- Send a picture of himself or herself to the person who is ill
- Write a letter
- Write a poem or a story
- Send a card
- Send a talking message on an audiocassette tape
- Make a music tape with all the special type of music that the person who is ill likes
- Talk with the person who is ill on the telephone

It would be terribly sad for a child to choose not to communicate with someone he or she loves just because that person is ill and then decide, too late, that they really wanted to do so. Kids may not get another chance. They need to be encouraged to share while they still can.

IF YOUR CHILD IS THE ONE WHO IS ILL

"When will I get better?" "Will my friends still be my friends?"

If children are ill, they may worry about several different things in addition to when they'll recover. They may worry if they'll be absent from school for any significant amount of time, whether they'll be able to keep up with or make up their schoolwork, and if their friendships will remain the same.

The more your child is kept informed of the progress of his or her illness, the better. Being honest about the condition can help eliminate any anxiety. If there is something serious to worry about, the worry deserves to be reality based. If your son or daughter is ill, it is important to clearly explain the anticipated recovery time, any social or school-oriented concern that is relevant, and how life might be affected as a result of the illness.

Even when fears they have relate to themselves and their own situation, children might hesitate to express them. Your child might feel very relieved if you initiate discussion about concerns that might possibly relate to his or her illness. You might wish to start the conversation with something like the following:

- "A lot of kids would probably be very scared. I know you haven't said anything, but just in case you might feel the same way . . ."
- "A lot of kids would probably be worried that they'll have a really hard time catching up with schoolwork."
- "A lot of kids who end up staying out of school for a while because of illness might worry that their friendships won't still be the same when they finally go back."

REALISTIC HOPE

If a loved one is ill, children deserve to be told the truth about his or her chances for recovery. If a child is old enough to ask, "Is Grandma going to die?" he or she is old enough to get an answer. Simple, age-appropriate, but honest explanations would probably be appreciated and help kids feel more secure, even if the truth might hurt.

False hope will not help strengthen your child's ability to cope. By not knowing the true status of a loved one's prognosis, a child might miss the opportunity for closure, or for writing that final "You will always mean so much to me," "I will never forget what we shared," or "I'm going to miss you so much" kind of note.

Adults often think that kids can't take the hurt, so they decide for them that such information is too much to handle and must be with-held. I wonder how many adults hold back from their kids because of their own denial, their own fear of breaking down in front of their kids, their own inability to cope. Sometimes life is very difficult, painful, and sad. It may not seem fair, especially if someone close to you is dying. I don't know of any way of getting around that reality. But if we can help kids talk about their feelings and offer support and guidance to help them put what they're experiencing in positive per-spective, that will be contributing to a more solid foundation for han-dling all that life will have in store for them. We should do our best to give our children that knowledge and support in handling a difficult situation. It's likely that they will never forget it.

TEACHING KIDS TO MAKE THE MOST
OF THE TIME THEY HAVE WITH OLDER RELATIVES

My uncle is very old and will die in a few years I know, but I can't spend time with him because he lives so far away. What should I do?

The ideas for communicating with someone who is ill can also be wonderful for elderly (or not so elderly) relatives and friends with whom your child wishes to keep in active touch. Even if the child who wrote the card above won't physically be able to be with her uncle, she can share so much of herself long-distance. The miles between her and her uncle do not have to prevent her from getting closer to him.

The child who wrote the following card needs to erase the question mark, replace it with a period, and say to her great-grandmother exactly what she's feeling. She doesn't realize that she already has the words, already knows what to say. She actually said what she needs to express in the words she used to ask her question.

My great-grandpa died about two years ago. My great-grandma is still alive but I don't have the relationship that I had with her when I was young. I still love her a lot but it's hard for me to show it. How can I tell her I still love her?

For example, she could say just what she feels, in writing or aloud:

"Grandma, I know we haven't spent as much time as we did when I was young. We were so close then. It seems like we haven't been together as much. But I want you to know that I love you very much. It's just hard for me to show it."

Kids often ask how to prepare for a loved one's death. The key is to concentrate on making the most of the time that is still left to share with those special people. Living in the present is the message. Appreciating the moment is what we have to help our children do in these situations—focusing on sharing what's left of life, rather than wasting time dwelling on how sad it will be when they're physically no longer there. In addition, we must help our kids work at being able to express feelings that may be difficult. Doing so will not only help to enrich the time spent with loved ones, but will increase the amount of support a child will be able to have when dealing with grief related to their passing.

How do you prepare for a parent or grandparent's death when you know it will hurt so much you want to die yourself?

A grandmother once asked me how she could respond to her seven-year-old grandchild who always talked about how afraid she was that her grandmother was going to die. My suggestion was that she explain that if her grandchild only talked about her dying, she would miss the time she had with her while she is still here. This, too, is an attitude change. It's all how we view things. Kids can gain much from learning this early, but they need our help to move into a different mind-set. Our example can help them tremendously as well.

Children can also gain from learning that they have a degree of control to do the best they can to make the most out of life each day, for themselves and the people they love. For example, if they are careful crossing the street, have a safety-minded attitude toward protecting themselves from strangers, are mindful of eating healthful and balanced meals, stay away from dangerous drugs, let parents know if something doesn't seem right about their body or if they don't feel well, and take their need for regular medical checkups seriously, they'll be doing what they can to have a chance to live a longer, healthier life. We can help our children learn that if they communicate openly with and share as much "quality time" as possible with the people they love, they will be doing what they can to make the most of the time they have together. That's all they can hope to do.

I think that since my grandpa died he has always been with me.

Some kids have told me they were scared to get too close with a grandparent or other relative who was dying. They were afraid that becoming closer would make it even harder to deal with that person's death. It would help to anticipate the possibility that kids might feel this way in order to help put those feelings in perspective and, hopefully, help to turn them around.

When we are helping our children understand the reality of death, we are also teaching them to value life, to appreciate and be grateful for it, and not take anyone for granted. We are helping them realize that because time is limited for all of us, and because death is so final, more than anything else, preparing for the death of loved ones involves sharing life with them as fully as possible while they're physically here.

In that case, when someone whom they love does die, though they may be grief stricken, at least in their heart, they will know that they made the most of the time they had.

WHEN DEATH IS SUDDEN

With illness, whether long or short term, there is some period of time to attempt to prepare emotionally for the impending loss of a loved one. When death is sudden, with no warning and no time to say good-bye, children as well as adults can be left in a state of disbelief and shock. That can make the grieving process even more difficult.

Because life experiences such as death cannot always be anticipated exactly when they happen, it's even more important to teach kids to value the moment and share their love and lives with the people who count the most to them.

HELPING YOUR CHILD DEAL WITH DEATH

HELPING KIDS KNOW WHAT WORDS THEY CAN SAY

Many kids have told me they don't know what to say or how to act when someone dies. The sharing cards included in this section confirm how difficult it can be for kids to talk about death, even with the closest people in their lives.

Here again, we can help by offering kids words and specific sentences to say when they don't know what to say. Here are some examples of basic sentences your child can consider as guides to expressing feelings in a variety of situations. Your own examples can be structured around what you suspect your child is experiencing and feeling but not telling.

> **One of my parents (my mother) passed away and I have trouble talking to the other sometimes. I don't know how to deal with it because my father doesn't understand how aggravated I get.**

Child to parent, if a parent has died:

"Dad, sometimes I have trouble talking with you about Mom. I'm not sure what to say. . . . Can we please talk?"

Child to a parent about the death of a grandparent:

"Mom, I just want you to know how sad I am about Grandma. I'd really love to talk with you about her. But I don't know how. And I'm afraid if I say anything I'll make you sadder. I'd really love if we could talk about her."

Child to other children about the death of a brother or sister:

My brother died a while ago but I only mentioned it to my best friend. How can I express it more since I don't like talking about it?

"I know I haven't talked about my brother who died. I was thinking that maybe you don't know if it's okay to talk about him and I want you to know that it really is okay. It's not so easy to miss him so much, but I really would feel good if we talked about him."

In this situation, it can help to anticipate the difficulty kids have in knowing how or whether or not to talk about their brother or sister who has died. They may be comforted by being told that not only is it okay but it's good to let closest friends know.

If friends who count the most are aware of his or her brother's death, they'll at least be more understanding and, hopefully, supportive at those times that are particularly difficult. By letting best friends know, this child won't have to pretend that "nothing's wrong."

To help kids who have lost a brother or sister express more:

"I know I told you that my brother died two years ago. There are lots of times that I wanted to tell you more about him, but it's very hard for me to talk about him." (The child can add: "I'd like to try . . .")

Just acknowledging those kinds of feelings to a friend is a beginning. If your child could have written this card, and you know it's been very difficult for him or her to talk about a brother or sister who has died, you might make it a point to let your child know you realize this. It can help for you to be even more aware of moments when the memories might be particularly poignant, and address the situation then, such as what a child shared on the following card:

My brother died a few years ago and we used to go to the park together with my mom and dad. How can I cope with having my brother dead and me going to the park alone without him?

When passing the park, or actually going to the park, this child's parents might say:

"I keep thinking of all the times we were all here together. It's so hard to be here without _____."

That will likely be right on target, identifying aloud what that child is secretly thinking and feeling. While it may not decrease the hurt or how much that brother is missed, at the very least the child won't be so alone with those feelings. And the fact that parents brought this up is giving that child permission to talk with them about his or her brother.

Kids often think they're not allowed to even mention the person who died. The more memories are shared, pictures are displayed around your home, and discussion includes reference to the child who died, the more kids will realize that this is not a forbidden topic.

While it may be hard to draw a child's feelings out on a hurtful subject such as a sibling's death, this is a process that can grow less difficult over time.

More ways to express feelings about the death of a grandparent (exactly what kids are feeling can be expressed in sentences using their own words. This can help them pattern other sharing):

My grandpa died recently and I feel really bad about it and we were very close, but I don't feel comfortable talking about it and sometimes I think about him and start crying. What should I do?

"I'm so sad about Grandpa. I can't stop thinking about him. But it's so hard for me to talk about him. Sometimes I think about him and start crying . . . and I don't know what I should do. Can you help me?"

We can also encourage more open expression by our example. We can share with our kids our own feelings of sadness, our own memories about a loved one who died. That can help to reinforce that it is still important and can continue to mean so much to talk about that person. And that it is still normal to cry.

Child to an aunt or uncle after the loss of a cousin:

My cousin died one month ago and we were close. I don't know what to say to my aunt and uncle. I really feel upset. But I don't want to bring it up. We went everywhere together.

Hopefully, family members will anticipate how difficult it would be for a child whose cousin died to talk about their cousin—especially with their aunt or uncle. Kids need to know that they don't have to say more than:

"I'm so sad about _____. I'll miss her so much. We went everywhere together. I don't even know what to say to you. I didn't want to make you sadder by bringing it up."

This is the kind of expression that a child may be more comfortable writing to an aunt or uncle in a note.

What do you say to someone whose parent or relative just died?

Child to friends who are dealing with loss of a loved one:

One of my best friends' uncle just died and they were really close. I don't know how to talk to her about it.

"I just wanted to tell you how sad I am about your uncle. I know you were really close with him. I'm so sorry. . . . If you want to talk, or if you just want an extra hug, I'm here for you."

Child to a parent about the death of that parent's friend:

"Mom, I'm so sad about _____. She was one of your best friends, and I can't even imagine what you must be feeling. I've been afraid to talk to you about her because I didn't know if it would be okay to bring it up. I didn't want to make you sadder. But I love you, and I just wanted to tell you I'm so sorry."

If a child prefers not to say this aloud, this can be written and left in a note on his or her mom's pillow.

Child to friend whose parent died a few years ago:

I have a friend whose father died a few years ago. How can I let her know that I am here for her to talk to if she needs me?

Here again, all this child needs to do is erase the question mark, put a period at the end, and that will capture exactly what he or she wants to say:

"I wasn't sure how to say this to you. I know it's been a few years since your father died. But I wanted to let you know that I am here for you to talk to if you ever need me."

Kids need to learn they don't have to search for words they already have within them. They just have to have the courage to open their mouths and speak them, or express them in writing.

Kids also need to be taught that it can mean so much to let someone know they care. In response to learning about anyone's loss, kids can say to that person:

- "I'm so sorry about your _____."
- "I'm so sad about _____."
- "How can I help?"
- "I really want you to know I'm here for you."
- "I'll keep you in my prayers."

There is this boy who I see all summer and sometimes in the winter. His brother recently died this winter and I don't know how to act when I see him again this summer!

The child who worries about "how to act" needs to know that just acknowledging that he or she remembers that boy's brother's death can mean so much to him. Most kids have such trouble bringing up the subject. The fact that someone else cares enough to bring it up can be a relief, a comfort in and of itself. No acting is required; just being thoughtful will go a long way.

FINALITY OF DEATH

Kids need to know that it may take time for them to stop looking out the window for an uncle who passed away when relatives arrive for Thanksgiving. It may take time to get used to the idea that they can no longer pick up the phone to tell a grandparent who has passed away about the part they got in the school play.

I wish I can have my grandpa back.

All of those adjustments are part of the process of getting used to the fact that someone is actually physically gone from your life. If you are dealing with a loss in your family, your child might be comforted by your own comments about how odd it is not to be able to pick up the phone and call to speak with that loved one as you always were able to do. It may not lessen the feelings of loss, but it can help kids to know that they're not alone in what they're feeling.

DEALING WITH GRIEF

My grandfather lived with me and then died—I felt like dying. What do I do about my feelings?

Children need to understand that everyone will express and deal with grief in his or her own way, even if they are in the same family. It can help to explain that some people are very vocal while others are more private in their grief. Some might scream or cry and not try to hide their emotions from anyone; others may seem very controlled in front of friends and family but may cry for hours when they're by themselves. Still others may not cry at all. No matter how a person expresses emotions, children need to know that's not a measure of their love.

Grief is very personal. There's no "correct" way to grieve. Kids often think that if they don't cry, relatives will think they didn't love that person as much. Some kids, themselves, question their own feelings because of how confused they are about not crying—especially when it seems like everyone else is.

Shortly after a loved one dies, kids may be surprised to find that people are even joking and laughing at the memories they shared with him or her. They may not realize that talking openly about that person not only is okay but can be very comforting and important. People who are grieving are happy to remember the special times they shared with the deceased.

My dad almost died once. What do you do if someone dear to you dies? I'm scared.

Some kids think they need to hold up and be strong for everyone else around them. It may take a great deal of effort to try not to allow themselves to "break down" and let their feelings out.

When you lose something you love and live for and that person said they would never leave but they do. I can't face not having that person and seeing my best friend's grave. You promised you wouldn't leave. How can I get as close to another friend? I'm tired of being so strong. I want to just break down and cry but I'm scared.

The pain kids are feeling doesn't deserve to be compounded by judging or trying to stifle their emotions.

It may also help to explain that following a death of a close friend or family member, it may take a while for the loss to begin to sink in and become more real. Some kids in the family may be ready to go back to school earlier than others. Again, this is private and personal. Each person needs to honor his or her needs and respect the needs of others in order to handle this difficult time of mourning. Just because someone wants to go back to school or work doesn't have anything to do with how much he or she loved the person who died. Children need to be told that each person will experience grief in his or her own way and own time.

WHAT TO DO WITH THE FEELINGS

Kids often wonder what to do with their feelings. They don't have to "do" anything except allow themselves to feel. It would be good if they could express their feelings to an adult they trust.

> **My cousin died in November. I can't believe it. I cannot deal with it. It seems impossible. I had so many special memories with her. I almost feel guilty about it, like I didn't do enough with her. How can I deal with this?**

I wish I could just hold the child who wrote this card and say, "Don't do this to yourself. You've got enough pain to deal with without making it hurt worse by feeling guilty." If he or she has special memories, the time that was shared with this cousin was probably well spent. It might help to explain to a child you suspect might feel this way that what's most important is not how much time we spend with someone. There could always be more time. It's more about what is done with the time that we have with that person.

If only this child could talk about these feelings with his or her parents or other relatives. Especially when younger people die, the shock alone can be very difficult to handle. Then add dealing with the loss. It's all a process that takes time. For each person, it's going to be a bit different. If feelings are kept hidden, the process of "dealing with it" can be much more difficult.

The reality is that the child who wrote the following card may always feel hurt when he or she sees friends playing with their father. That doesn't mean that something is wrong with this child, that he or she didn't grieve "properly." It mainly means that it can hurt terribly to lose a parent.

> **My father died when I was very, very young, and when somebody mentions anything about it, it hurts. When I see my**

friend's father playing with her, I really feel bad. What should I do to stop from feeling this way?

When kids are face-to-face with how life can be if a parent is still alive, that can be hard to take. Even though this child's father died when he or she was "very, very young," hearing someone mention "anything about it," or seeing other kids with their father, will probably continue to hurt.

Rather than trying to stop these natural feelings, it may help to suggest a paradigm shift. In this case, my thoughts are that while feeling hurt might not change for this child, how this child views the hurt can. It's this child's decision what he or she chooses to do with those feelings. (I'm not saying such a shift is easy, just that it's feasible—even realistic—because it's a choice that a child can make.)

First of all, if a child feels hurt when thinking of a parent who has passed away, that can be taken as a statement on how special that relationship was, how much that parent is missed, and what the parent must have given of himself or herself to that child. Rather than dwelling on this as the terrible loss that it is, kids might feel more positive, and even smile, if they view those pangs that hurt so much as "memory hugs." This can be viewed as a statement of the fact that their parent is still very much alive within them, and a reminder that all that they shared with their parent is something that their mother's or father's death can't take away from them. They're lucky to have loved that parent so much to feel such hurt.

Gross rationalization? Maybe. But while I wouldn't wish such a loss on any child, it need not be considered a negative that kids feel hurt because they miss their parent who died. It just means that they love them and miss them. While some kids really do say they hate their parents and mean it, for most kids it would be surprising if they felt differently than the child who wrote the card.

So instead of expecting to be able to change what is so natural to feel, kids can realize it's okay to feel that way. And they can decide to respond to these feelings in a more positive, embracing way.

I have just lost a very good friend. I am having a very rough time getting over it. How can I get over this?

I don't know that any of us ever completely "gets over" the loss of someone we love. But we can reach a point where we are ready to go on with our daily lives and not be held back by our grief. Gradually, day by day, we can ease back into our old schedules. I've never had the experience of losing a very good friend, and I can't even begin to imagine what that must feel like. Here again, the deep-felt pain is a most positive statement on how special this person was in the life of the child who wrote this card.

If "just lost" means very recently, this child needs to know to be kind to himself or herself and not try to push the process of healing.

CEREMONIES, SERVICES, FUNERALS

Children need to understand any ritual or traditional practices that will follow a person's death, such as services, ceremonies, wakes, visiting at a designated home to pay respects, and any others that may apply.

My great-grandfather died. I don't know how to act at the funeral.

Kids who ask if they can attend a funeral may feel very upset if their parents say they're too young to go. More than likely, if they're old enough to ask, they may well be old enough to go.

I share with you my son's first experience at a funeral in the hopes that it will help put what can be gained in positive perspective:

Several years ago, when my son's closest friend's grandmother died, my son asked to attend the funeral in order to "be there" for his friend. My husband and I thought it was very special that he felt this way and gave him, as well as our daughter, permission to go with us.

Since our children had never before experienced a funeral service and had never gone to a cemetery for a burial, we felt it was very important to explain exactly what they might expect. Besides letting them know what the service might be like, we specifically described the cemetery experience. We also felt it important to give them options in case they felt very upset. For example, they knew that if they got too sad, they could stand closer with us, walk to the side, or get back into the car.

In this particular ceremony at the cemetery, the casket was lowered into the ground while everyone in attendance watched. Dirt was then shoveled over it. As the last shovelful of dirt was pitched to make the casket disappear, our son started to cry hysterically on my shoulder. He turned to me and said, "She's gone!"

I don't know if any book we could have read together about death or any conversation in the abstract could have brought home the message about the finality of death as did that moment. My son didn't "break" or crumble. He eventually stopped crying. And after a few moments, he said, "I want to spend more time with Grandma." He was twelve at the time.

Sometimes when a person dies and you don't cry at their funeral a lot of people look at you and think you are weird because they think that you don't care.

While some kids want to attend funerals, others would rather not. Sometimes it's the parent who wants the child to go, and the child who doesn't feel he or she can or wants to face it. Each parent will need to make a judgment call, based on knowing his or her child, as to whether the situation may be too difficult for that child to handle.

If your child's feelings are strong about wanting to attend a funeral with your family, it may be important to his or her emotional well-being to make an extra effort to give appropriate explanations, offer support, and help your child to be a part of the experience. If you feel your child's attendance is inappropriate, he or she would probably feel a little better if you at least explained why.

If your child does not want to go to a funeral, he or she may feel guilty, thinking that decision will be associated with how much love was felt for the person who died. To lessen the possibility of your child making such an association (or thinking anyone else is), it might help to let your child know this decision is very personal and has nothing to do with love.

If kids want to go and are not given permission, there may always be a void from not having that chance to say a final good-bye. My high school boyfriend's father died a few years after I got married (to someone else). My mother-in-law was a friend of his mother at the time. When my ex-boyfriend's father died, my mother-in-law didn't think to tell me about the funeral. To this day, and actually, at this very moment, my stomach reacts with such tightness just thinking about how much it hurt not having the chance to be there. Thirty-plus years later, I still haven't forgotten. It still upsets me.

DEATH CAN BE A BLESSING

The finality of death is usually very difficult, no matter when it comes. But if it follows a lengthy or even short-term serious illness involving much pain and suffering, then it can be consoling to children if you explain that death can be considered a blessing—that the loved one who was so ill is now at rest and is no longer suffering.

IF A PET DIES

Loss of a pet can be devastating. Our son grieved for his dog for at least a year. Owen was like his child. It was a painful and terribly difficult time period for him. I remember being incredulous when I heard that Owen was killed. I couldn't imagine our son without his dog that he loved so much. It took a long while for our son to reach the point where the pain of that loss started to ease, little by little.

How do I get over my dog dying?

Dealing with the death of a pet is significant in and of itself. The experience can also help prepare children to be better able to cope when a person whom they love dies. The same words for people can help kids express feelings about the death of a pet:

- "I'm so sad about your calf."
- "I was so sorry to hear that your cat got run over. I know how much you loved her. I'm sorry I didn't call you before, but I didn't know what to say to you when I heard it happened."
- "I am so very upset about your dog. I can't imagine what you're feeling right now. Please let me know if I can help. Do you feel my hug through the phone?"

SUICIDE

I'm scared my best friend is going to kill herself. What can I do?

When Jeff's brother told him on the phone, "I was thinking of hanging myself," Jeff responded with, "I can't live without you. How could you do this to me?" It was the farthest thing from Jeff's mind that his brother actually meant it. Had Jeff thought he meant it, he might have asked, "Why are you thinking this?" and "What can I do to help you?" When Jeff called him back the next night, his brother said, "Oh, don't worry about it. I didn't mean it." That was the last chance he had to talk with him. Two days later, his brother was found hanging in his residence hall at college.

Children need to be made aware that lots of people talk about wanting to kill themselves. Probably more than they might think. Many, like Jeff's brother, mean it and follow through with a successful attempt. Many mean it but don't follow through with the intention of being successful. It may just end up that way because they're not found in time to save them. But, for example, what they're doing by slitting their wrists not quite deep enough to kill themselves, or taking not quite enough pills to kill themselves, is saying "I need help! Someone, please help me!"

I'm in seventh grade and I get into a lot of fights with my parents. In fifth grade I tried to kill myself twice by cutting my wrists. I don't know what to do. Sometimes I feel like doing it again.

Others don't mean it but say it, anyway. They may truly be troubled, but they don't actually intend to make a suicide attempt. Still others may be bothered at the moment by some passing disturbance, and just use "I'm going to kill myself!" as an expression of frustration.

Jeff told me that he hopes many kids and families will be able to learn from his brother's death that no one should think suicide can't happen to their family or to someone they know. No one should be lulled into complacency because they think it could happen only to "other people." No one is exempt.

All kids need to be taught that suicide could happen to anyone, in any family, no matter what the person's age or background. The cards I've included in this section are but a sampling of the many like them that I have collected over the years. They're testimony to the need to help kids value themselves more and be more prepared to cope with difficult life circumstances.

I always think about killing myself. What should I do?

The cards also represent a serious statement about how troubled so many kids really are, and how children are likely not to know what to say or do when they hear someone talk about suicide. Even if only one child wasn't sure of what to do, that would be too many.

KIDS NEED TO KNOW TO TELL AN ADULT

Upon hearing a friend say he or she is thinking of suicide, your child might wish to say something like:

- "I think it would be a great idea to talk with that guy counselor who was new to our school last year. I heard that he's really cool, and I know a few kids who were able to deal with things better after they talked with him. Come on, why don't I walk you down there."

We can help by teaching kids that every single time they hear someone talk about committing suicide, they need to take it seriously. Beyond anything they might choose to say to a friend (or anyone else), that means thinking in terms of taking action by telling an adult.

If a child hears a friend talk about suicide, he or she can offer support, try to help put whatever is troubling that friend in perspective, urge that friend to get help, and even offer to keep the friend company when he or she is going for help. Kids who hear suicide mentioned by a friend also need to speak about their concern for that friend with an adult, such as their own parent, or another adult in a helping category (grandparent, aunt or uncle, teacher, coach, school guidance counselor, school social worker, school psychologist, priest, rabbi, family doctor, as well as suicide hot lines, etc.).

If a sister or brother talks about suicide, siblings can do the same thing. However, besides letting their sister or brother know how much they're loved, and besides offering support or urging the sibling to get help, they still need to speak with an adult. Hopefully, children can approach their parents. But if they feel they can't, they need to approach another adult. If one adult doesn't seem like he or she is being supportive or helpful, then kids need to know to go to another and, if need be, another until they find someone willing and able to help.

We must also explain to kids that it doesn't matter who the person is who talks about suicide, they still need to take action. Whether it's the captain of the football team, the head cheerleader, the lead in the school play, the valedictorian, the person who is considered the most popular kid in the school, a person who always seems like he or she is in a good mood—no matter who says it, an early-warning alarm needs to go off in their brain.

If it turns out the person wasn't serious, great. If it turns out that he or she is truly troubled, hopefully, by saying something to an adult, that person will be able to be helped.

If Someone Says, "Do You Promise You Won't Tell?"

Kids need to be alerted to the possibility that someone might say to them, "Do you promise you won't tell anybody?" If that's the case, it would probably take a very strong, mature child to be able to say something like:

> "No, I can't promise you that. If what you're going to tell me is very serious, I may feel it's important to talk with someone who can help. And I wouldn't want to break your trust. But I promise I won't talk with someone without talking with you first. Or maybe we could talk together with someone. When I know what you're planning to tell me, we can take it from there."

If a child actually said that, it's possible the friend or sibling wouldn't tell him or her anything further. It may be that your child might be better off promising not to tell, and then determine what to do after being told. When it comes to something as serious as suicide, if someone even hints of being in trouble and is not getting help, your child needs to know to break his or her promise not to tell an adult.

This is usually an uncomfortable situation for kids. But, as I said in chapter 8, p. 198, children are better off with an angry friend than a dead friend. Kids need to know there's a fine line between betrayal and attempting to save a life.

WHAT SUPPORT CAN MEAN

It might help to explain to your child in more specific terms exactly what "support" can mean. Examples of support are the attempts to make every effort to talk with or be with that person as often as possible (keep up the contact); to let the person know they're valued; to actually express to them, "Hi, I just called to see how you're doing" or "Hi, just checking in . . . I was thinking about you" or "Hi . . . just wanted you to know how much you mean to me."

All this kind of extra attention and concern can help to confirm the message to the person considering suicide that "you mean a lot to me," that somebody truly wants him or her to stay alive, that the person is valued and valuable.

KIDS MUST KNOW THEY CAN'T
CONTROL SOMEONE ELSE'S SUICIDE

Hopefully, some form of counseling or guidance will help the person who talked about suicide to work through what is so disturbing and be able to go forward in a more positive way.

Kids deserve to feel good about knowing they did everything they could to help a friend or a sibling who was considering harming him- or herself. However, even if kids do everything, including going to an adult for help, we need to make sure they understand that it's possible that friend or sibling might commit suicide, anyway. That doesn't mean they should not try to help. It means that they do not have control over their friend's or sibling's (or anyone's) suicide decision.

We can explain that it would probably be very difficult to watch over someone every single minute of every day. Unless they're actually physically restrained and under twenty-four-hour surveillance, if people are seriously intent on killing themselves, they will probably find a way.

My brother has tried to commit suicide three times in the past month I feel like a failure as a sister. How can I realize I try my best? I always try my best, but it doesn't seem good enough!

The child who wrote that card needs to know that it cannot be her fault if her brother ends up committing suicide. If he does, it would not be because she wasn't a better sister. She needs to know she's not a failure. She needs to be helped to appreciate what she has been trying to do to help make a difference. For example, she can talk with her brother, spend time with him, tell him how much she loves him, talk with her parents or other adults to make sure they know he needs help (and how worried she is about him). But she cannot be responsible for his life. Lots of kids don't know this.

I've spoken with kids who wanted to break up with their girlfriend or boyfriend but were afraid if they did—given all the other things going wrong in that person's life at the time—that would cause their boyfriend or girlfriend to commit suicide. Here again, we need to explain that it's too much of a burden for kids to think that they can control someone else's decision about whether to stay alive. (If your child has similar concerns, it might help to suggest that even if someone breaks up a boyfriend or girlfriend relationship, it doesn't have to mean he or she needs to be completely out of that person's life. As a close friend, your child can still be there for that person.)

It would be tragic for kids to be encumbered with feelings of guilt or blame for the rest of their lives because they believe there was something else they could have or should have done to stop a friend or sibling from committing suicide.

You might find it will help to reinforce this point further by making another distinction as to what kids can or cannot control. For example, they can control the decision to let an adult know that someone is talking about committing suicide. They can do everything they can to try to encourage that person to value himself or herself

and value staying alive. But they cannot control what that person ultimately decides to do.

TALKING ABOUT TOUGH FEELINGS

Adults do need to say to kids, "I'm here for you. Please trust you can
come to me if you need help, if you're in trouble." And kids do need to
know a variety of resource people—including hot-line numbers for suicide, alcohol and other drugs, domestic violence, rape, and anything
else of serious concern. But as I've stated many times before, if they're
too scared or uncomfortable, if they don't have the inner strength, and
if they don't know what words to say, they may not ask for help.

Throughout this book, I've been suggesting different ways to turn
feelings into words. I'm guessing that there may be many parents and
other adults who might still think these words are "obvious." How
could kids not know how or not be able to say, "Please help me?" Too
many just don't. The more reinforcement, the more practice, the
better.

**I have many problems and I want to talk to somebody, but I
either don't know what to say or I can't trust anyone—what
should I do?**

It's important to remind kids periodically that if they're scared,
that's exactly what they can say: "I'm scared to say this to you. . . ."
Other opening lines to ask for help include:

- "I've never talked with anyone about this before. This is really
  hard for me. But I'm having a rough time and I need help. Can you
  help me?"
- "I didn't know how to say this to you. But I've been doing some scary
  things and I'm afraid I might hurt myself. I need help."

Kids who are worried about a friend can just change the words
slightly to read:

- "This is really hard for me to say this to you. But I'm worried that my
  friend is having a rough time and needs help. I'm afraid she might

hurt herself. She's been talking about suicide. Can you help? I don't know what to do."

The words are very simple, but they continue to be difficult to express, even for high-school and college students. This area of concern is too serious to chance taking anything for granted. Don't wait for a difficult circumstance to help kids know what to say in order to get help.

EARLY WARNING SIGNS

Besides a previous suicide attempt and talking about suicide, the following are among some of the possible warning signs for someone who might be at risk for committing suicide:

- Talking about death, concentrating on the topic (actually saying, "I'm going to kill myself" or "I want to kill myself")
- Talking about death in more specific terms, such as, "I'm thinking of hanging myself" or "I'm thinking of cutting my wrists." (It can be a more serious signal if the person has already thought out a specific method.)
- Drinking alcohol or using other drugs
- Less care about appearance (starting to look sloppy)
- Change of eating and sleeping patterns
- Becoming more withdrawn, more to oneself, less involved with friends or family
- Giving away an important possession, like a CD collection or a favorite leather jacket

These changes may not definitely mean someone is seriously thinking about suicide. Sometimes there aren't any signs. However, if there is even a remote possibility that you're picking up a warning signal, be that much more attentive to these kinds of signs or anything else that might indicate clearer likelihood of trouble.

Sometimes people who are troubled don't tell the whole story to any one person. For example, parents might get 5 percent, a sibling might get 40 percent, and a friend might get a different 40 percent.

Even if you have only one clue, it might help to check with other people who are close to that person.

Sometimes, when there's a question if a child's personality has gone through changes, parents and others may be unsure if their perceptions are real. If other people have a different concern, or confirm a similar concern, it all might add up to confirmation that helps to identify that this child is in fact at serious risk and needs help.

Consider what's going on in your child's life at home and at school. What about friendships? Achievement in school? Is there great strain in your home? Are you dealing with divorce or separation? Could your child feel isolated or neglected? Did someone just break up with him or her? Do you have enough money for food? Has your child made a serious mistake or gotten into serious trouble?

Life sucks.

Try to find out what could be bothering your child. Talk with your child's teacher to double-check on what's happening in the classroom, socially and academically. You can also approach your child directly and ask, "Are you okay? You seem really stressed lately" or "I get the feeling you might be depressed. You don't seem like yourself lately."

You can also come right out and ask, "Are you thinking about suicide?" "I know things haven't been good for you. Are you low enough to hurt yourself?"

If your son or daughter says, "I'm fine. There's no problem!" and you still sense that there is (kids may or may not be truthful when confronted), then you might say something like:

- "I know I already asked you this. I want to believe that things are fine, but the way you've been acting makes me still question if that's true."
- "I know some kids are very afraid of letting their parents know they're having a rough time. They're afraid of telling them things like the fact that they're pregnant or are using serious drugs. I'm really worried about you and I want to help, if you're having trouble."
- "Please, if there's something wrong and you're not okay, don't worry

about hurting me or getting me angry or upset. I want to be there for you. . . . Please let me help or help you find help."

I feel *dead*.

KIDS MAY NOT ACKNOWLEDGE WHAT'S GOING ON

I don't know if any approach can guarantee that kids will acknowledge that they're considering suicide, even if they are. That's a choice that each child can only make for himself or herself. Those words I suggested can be said aloud or in writing. If there continues to be denial of any problem and you're still very concerned, you can share these feelings with teachers, coaches, and counselors at your child's school and ask that the school personnel remain attentive and on guard.

Keep your doors for communication open, continue to offer your support, and continue to tell your child how much you love him or her. You can also keep your child in your prayers. You can make further approaches to your child about your specific concern. The fact that you are concerned and attentive to your child's situation can help immensely, even if the child doesn't admit it.

PERSPECTIVES AND PREVENTION IDEAS THAT MAY HELP

One of the best ways to prevent suicide is to try to prevent the conditions that could lead to it and promote the conditions that would help strengthen self-acceptance and how kids value themselves.

We can teach our children the following perspectives and "life lessons" that can help prevent suicide (the list is not in any special order):

- How to express difficult inner feelings
- That everyone, regardless of differences, is important, special, equal, valuable, and deserves to be respected
- To put differences in healthy perspective (i.e., what sex a person is, race, nationality, religion, if someone has a disability, size, achievement, athletic ability, looks, sexual orientation, etc.)

- That their value is not dependent on or measured by things like how many friends they have, grades, sports ability, if they have a boyfriend or girlfriend, if their parents or family members seem to love them
- No matter how someone might put them down, that doesn't make what they say true. Someone else doesn't have the power to define who they are or how valuable they are—unless they give them that power.
- That they are valuable no matter what. That no one and nothing that they do can take away from their personal worth, unless they choose to allow that to happen—not making a mistake, failing grades, drinking alcohol or using other drugs, truancy, early pregnancy, stealing, gambling, going to jail, or anything else.
- That everyone makes mistakes, and everyone has the ability to learn from them and go forward in a more positive way. That if someone makes a bad mistake, it doesn't mean he or she is a bad person.
- How to make friends, handle social situations, and how to deal with changing relationships
- How to cope with disappointments, frustrations, pressure, day-to-day ups and downs. That life is not always fair, happy, or exciting; down times are normal and expected.
- To develop a sense of responsibility, compassion and appreciation for family
- How to make effective decisions by examining choices, evaluating what choices might mean, identifying risks, and evaluating consequences
- Accurate factual information related to sex, alcohol, and other drugs; perspectives to help them believe for themselves that the risks are real.
- How to cope with family strains, illness, death, or other traumas
- Perspectives about the definition of success
- To be realistic about expectations
- To appreciate and respect the beauty of nature
- To establish a balance between work and play in their life; to include exercise and eat healthy meals

- To cherish and try to make the most of the time they share with those they love
- That there's a limit to time. Live in the moment, learn from the past, and set goals and dreams for the future. Take deep breaths. Be present.
- How much it can mean to make a difference in the lives of others
- If they feel unloved, it doesn't mean they're not lovable. It means that the people who by all rights deserve to give them that love aren't capable or don't choose to.
- That people are special because they are. People don't have to do anything to become special, they just are. They're born already special.
- If they don't feel very special or valuable, it doesn't mean they're not. It only means that it may be hard for them to see the specialness in themselves (because of all the measures, judgments, etc.).
- If they don't feel they could ever get out of the deep hole it feels like they're in, and life seems so hard and painful, it doesn't mean it's going to stay that way. It just means that probably it's hard to believe that positive change can be possible. And it may mean they don't know where or how to begin to try to climb back up. ("This too shall pass" may be hard to believe, but most things, in time, become "history.")
- They don't have to deal with tough stuff alone. There are people who care very deeply, but they must let those people know when they're in need. They may not be able to guess.
- It's not a sign of weakness to go for help, but a sign of tremendous strength.

Even if our children hear just a fraction of these positive messages and incorporate only a selection of these coping mechanisms, they will be much better off.

I wish I could tell my parents that I love them and how I feel

I always fight with my dad. We're so much alike we clash. I can't do anything right in his eyes, or that's the message I get. We're not very close and it's hard to talk to him so I'm hesitant to say anything to him about our fighting, because I don't want to make him mad. Hearing you helped me at least start thinking about what to say. Thanks!

My parents had a child before me and he's smart, and whenever I do something wrong they say well your brother never did that. I told them that it hurts me but sometimes they still do it, It makes me so upset Even when my grandpa calls he always asks about him and not me. What should I do?

I want to get closer with my mother. I want to tell her that I love her, but I just can't. I know she loves me alot, but we don't relate very well. I try to talk to her, to share with her my problems, and feelings, and she tries to listen, but she never really hears me.

IN CLOSING

The ability to understand, relate to, and grow closer with our children is a process of unfolding that can continue throughout our lifetime together with them. It's exciting to realize that no matter how well we might think we know our children, there's always more to learn. We can always relate better, be more sensitive to their needs, and become an even stronger source of support.

The more you understand your child's world, the greater will your capacity be to "be there" in a way that you and your child may not have thought possible. If you reach out to your child and he or she isn't responding as you would wish, at least you know you have the capacity to keep reaching and hoping that someday you'll strike the right nerve.

Relating in a more positive way with our children involves taking chances, risking vulnerability, and testing trust. It is a process of actively working to let your child know the real you and encouraging your child to do the same. It's sharing tears as well as laughter, disappointments as well as successes, fears as well as dreams.

There are so many different feelings, experiences, pressures, and choices that any child growing up today must be prepared to face. And there will always be new feelings, new issues, new experiences, new challenges, as well as the ups and downs that go with them. I hope that what I've shared with you in *Get a Clue!* will make a difference in your ability to help your child effectively handle anything that comes his or her way.

Through it all, if you can talk honestly with each other, and can trust the love between you, then you've got the strength and the resources to deal with any situation, any change, and any misunderstanding you'll face together.

Parenting is all an adventure, anyway. It's a journey that will likely take many twists and turns. Just remember to hold on to your sense of humor. If you know that your heart is in the right place, give yourself extra hugs for your love and your caring. I've learned you can't fake caring with kids. Deep down, your child is likely to know what you've given of yourself, even if he or she never tells you.

As far as what all of this will mean in the big picture, my husband always said, "The jury is out until our kids are at least thirty-five!"

About the Author

ELLEN ROSENBERG is the author of *Growing Up Feeling Good* and a lecturer who has given her interactive presentations to more than a million students, teachers, and parents in forty-six states. She holds a master's degree in education and is certified as a sex educator. The mother of two grown children, she lives with her husband in Long Beach, New York.